WAR AND WESTERN CIVILIZATION
1832—1932

WAR AND WESTERN CIVILIZATION
1832–1932
A Study of War as a Political Instrument and the Expression of Mass Democracy

by

Major-General John Frederick Charles Fuller

What is the good of experience if you do not reflect?"
Frederick the Great.

Select Bibliographies Reprint Series

 BOOKS FOR LIBRARIES PRESS
FREEPORT, NEW YORK

First Published 1932
Reprinted 1969

STANDARD BOOK NUMBER:
8369-5123-9

LIBRARY OF CONGRESS CATALOG CARD NUMBER:
72-102238

PRINTED IN THE UNITED STATES OF AMERICA

TO
THE MEMORY OF
MY FATHER
1832–1927

PREFACE

To those who read between the lines,
There's food indeed—for those who read.

BEFORE he begins this book I will ask the reader to turn
to the Appendix and glance through it. Then I will ask
him to put himself this question : " Is it worth while ?"
And then another : " Is *what* worth while ? " To me,
the answer to this second question is, *modern* democracy—
that is " demagogy " ; not the will of the people but
their emotions which have provided the driving force of
the last hundred years and the " drug " which has
hallucinated them with war. Is it necessary to love
peace so ardently that in order to settle every political
problem of importance we must tear each other to pieces
like hyenas in rut ? If so, then we are animals, and this
appears to me to be the fundamental and hidden disease
of Western civilization. Yet, cannot we open our eyes
and become as gods, and take of the tree of life in place of
the tree of death ? For be it remembered, though energy
can destroy it can also create.

The next point I will ask the reader to consider is this :
Since 1832 the world has been transformed in one
direction. This transformation has been stupendous,
bewildering, magical ; yet it has been almost entirely
material. This age has not been pre-eminent in art or in
religion ; science has probed into the outer world and
has revealed to us a new universe ; but still the inner
world remains all but unexplored. Science has analysed
and weighed the stars ; yet the human soul remains a
mystery, a hidden and seemingly unfathomable secret.
All this has taken place in the span of one long life. This
book opens at the time when my father was born ; when

7

his father was born, the Bastille was still standing, and Napoleon, a poverty-stricken sub-lieutenant of artillery, was cutting down his frugal meals in order that he might buy candles to light his studies of great books on war. In one hundred years, or at most one hundred and forty-four, we have this stupendous change in one direction. Is not it equally possible for us to effect as stupendous a change in another ? Is not this the problem of the hundred years which now faces us ? And is not one of the clues which will assist us as we advance into this shrouded labyrinth to be found in the words of Frederick the Great : " What is the good of experience if you do not reflect ? "

Here then is the object of this book : To reflect on the experiences of the last hundred years in order that we may fashion a little candle which will light our way through the next hundred ; a flickering flame which will cast a glimmer here and there on the bindings of the great books on war which this century will see published ; a glimmer which will make it possible for us to read their titles, and by reading them enable future generations, who lift them from their shelves, to open them and to read within : " This war was avoided through the wisdom of our ancestors." That, studious reader, is a noble text.

To be bound by tradition, to live in a groove and trickle down the gutter of life is to blaspheme against the Spirit of the Age, that spirit which we call " Progress " ; that intangible all-compelling force which drives the peoples on into the unknown of future history. To grasp the skirts of this spirit is to become wise and understanding ; but to grasp them demands courage and truthfulness. Let me say with modesty that these twin virtues have been my guiding stars. That this book should be without blemish is absurd to expect ; no man can examine the last hundred years without making mistakes. It is not accuracy which in itself is virtuous but the courage and the truthfulness expended in its seeking.

This age, in my mind, is an age of spiritual decay, an age of saurian materialism. I stand before Magic, yet I see little of God. There is an essential ugliness in it which must give way to beauty ; a yawning chasm of selfishness which must be filled up by right-mindedness. Praise I frequently withhold ; for praise is a mighty stimulant, and over much of it kills like strychnine. Democracies are founded upon praise, the praise of colossal numbers, gigantic size, immense genius, bullet-proof heroes, ecstatic heroines and all the glittering servitors of the magician's trade ; for it fascinates the herd to discover in others qualities it does not itself possess. Until these phantoms vanish, until this black magic is smitten low, all I see in the crystal of the future is this : the engine of Western civilization, speeding along the lines of narrow thoughts, roaring towards the Abyss.

J. F. C. F.

September 9, 1932.

CONTENTS

MAPS

INTRODUCTION
THE FOUNDATIONS OF NATIONALISM,
1815-1831

INTRODUCTION

Napoleon the Liberator. The Holy Alliance. Reaction and Revolution. The Conqueror of the Nineteenth Century. Influence of Democracy on War. Napoleon as Tactician. Tactical Reaction and Decay

NAPOLEON THE LIBERATOR

In 1770, or thereabouts, Guibert, Jacques Antoine Hippolyte, aristocrat and soldier, made the following remarkable prophecy :

" There will come a man who perhaps till then was hidden in a crowd and in obscurity—a man who had never made a name by words or letters, but who thought much in silence ; a man who perhaps did not know his talents, who only becomes aware of them when exercising them, and who has studied very little. That man will seize those ideas, his opportunity and his fortune, and say to the great man of theories what the practical architect said who addressed the Athenians, ' What my rival has proposed to you I shall execute '." [1]

This man was Napoleon Bonaparte, of whom Carlyle says : " There was an eye to see in this man, a soul to dare and do. He rose naturally to be the King. All men saw that he *was* such." [2] This strange soldier, emerging from outer darkness, erupting the world with his volcanic glory, and lastly being transfigured into a god, between that day at Toulon, that day of " la batterie des hommes sans peur " in 1793, and the fateful field of Jena thirteen years later, was the incarnation of the Revolution, for on his standards was emblazoned " Liberty." Then, from 1806 onwards to the gathering of the nations, first at Leipzig and lastly at Waterloo, following the giddy path of his spiritual ancestor, Alexander of Macedon, he sought to establish a World Empire, and through the oppression resulting he drove the meaning of " Liberty " from the heads of the philosophers into the hearts of the people, and it intoxicated them. This is the pivotal fact of the nineteenth century.

In 1805, at Austerlitz, Austria was trampled under foot ; in 1806, at Jena, Prussia was trampled under foot, the wraith of the Holy Roman Empire vanishing to be replaced by the amorphous Confederation of the Rhine. In 1807, Spain was overrun ; but the following year the tide began to turn ; General Dupont and 17,000 French soldiers surrendered to the Spaniards at Baylen. At this small city where, in 1212, Alphonso VIII slew two-hundred thousand Moors with a loss of twenty-five men, Napoleon's star reached the limits of its ascendency ; henceforth it was destined to sink, for the spirit of Spanish nationality was aroused.

It swept over Austria, once again to be pulverized at Wagram in 1809. It swept into Italy, into Prussia, and Germany awoke to the cry of " Mit Gott für König und Vaterland." Onwards it sped over the steppes and swamps of Russia to the smouldering gates of Moscow. Then it swept back, roaring into life at Leipzig where, on October 18, 1813, the Battle of the Nations raged around the Johanniskirche and in its surgings shook off the yoke of despotism. There modern Europe was born a congeries of emerging nations which through agony had transmuted the ecstatic cosmopolitanism of the Revolution into the self-consciousness of individual peoples—a strange transmutation, and one little dreamt of by Marat, by Danton, by Robespierre.

Then came the first Treaty of Paris to bless and curse an exhausted continent ; so thoughts slipped back to 1792. Next, the Congress of Vienna, an assembly of elder statesmen . . . much dining, talking and drawing-room whisperings . . . traditional principles, or lack of principles . . . parabolic diplomacy, hyperbole, and heated words. Sterile seeds cast on a newly ploughed world, and an outlook as if there had never been a revolution or a war. Thus it came about that Europe " was treated as real estate to be parcelled out by the executors of

Napoleon's empire among sovereigns by divine right, regardless of the wishes of the populations, which figured in the protocols merely as numbers to be balanced and bartered one against the other." [3]

England bled white by war was nevertheless reborn in this conflict. When the Revolution began she had practically no empire. Now, largely thanks to Lake and Wellesley, she had a vast one. Between 1792 and 1815 her imports and exports had doubled, though the purchasing power of money was halved, and in spite of her national debt having swollen to £800,000,000, her annual revenue from taxation had risen from £19,000,000 to £72,000,000. Instead of soldiers, capitalists had flocked to her, the greatest being Nathan Rothschild, and in London, that city which had heard no tramp of hostile armies, these supreme " shopkeepers " wanted peace— peace at any price—and their wants were met at Vienna.

Old Blücher said : " Oh ! ye politicians are poor judges of men : the good Vienna Congress is like a fair in a small town, whither everyone drives his cattle, either for sale or exchange. We have brought here a first-rate bull, and have got in exchange only a miserable bullock." [4]

This was an exaggeration, for most of them took their fine bulls away.

Prussia, though girt about with tariff walls and fissured by economic entrenchments which disunited her, expanded, while Austria, under Metternich's " Govern and change nothing," wanting only the *status quo*, sank into petrification. In 1814 Prussia's population was 5,000,000, in 1815 it was 10,500,000. Truer than Blücher's words was it that the Congress resulted in nothing but restorations " which had already been effected by arms " [5] outside calling into being a Germanic Confederation of 38 sovereign Powers to fill the gap created by the dissolution of the old Empire in 1806. It was a *Staatenbund* and not a *Bundesstaat*, that is to say a federation of States and not a federated State, which prepared the ground for the events of 1866 and 1870.

Russia gained Finland, Bessarabia and the greater part

of Poland which was incorporated as a separate kingdom under the dominion of the Czar, the rest of this country being divided between Prussia and Austria. Austria gained Dalmatia and retained her hold over Venetia and Lombardy; Switzerland was given a constitution; Sweden obtained Norway, and Holland was confirmed in the possession of Belgium, Luxemburg, Limburg and Liége.

As her share of the spoils Great Britain received Malta, a declaration that the slave trade would cease, and Castlereagh, her representative, was about to insist on the Powers solemnly guaranteeing the territorial settlements by promising to make collective war on whoever should disturb them, when Napoleon escaped from Elba. Hurry and scurry, and nine days after the Final Act of the Congress was signed the liberator of modern Europe was defeated at Waterloo. Then followed the Second Treaty of Paris, signed on November 20, 1815, by which France was compelled to pay an indemnity of £40,000,000, and submit to occupation by 150,000 allied troops for a period of not more than five years. At the time German statesmen were furious, they demanded that France should be disarmed and that Alsace and Lorraine should be annexed. Wellington objected and carried the day. France was already hemmed in by a circle of newly constituted Powers, and he was wise, as Fyffe says, " in leaving to France the whole of its territory of 1815," and so avoiding the infliction of " the most galling of all tokens of defeat upon a spirited and still most powerful nation." [6]

THE HOLY ALLIANCE

The Congress of Vienna and the two Treaties of Paris were largely the work of reactionaries, and consequently reaction was immediate. The first act of Louis XVIII on his restoration, in 1814, was to abolish the tricolour and substitute for it the white flag of the Bourbons. Military ceremonials replaced military exercises, the details of which were culled from old almanacks, court-tailors'

records and the " memories of decayed gallants." At
once the Church under cover of royalty crept back into
power. In Spain the clergy demanded the restoration of
the Inquisition, and Ferdinand restored it in July, 1814 ;
in France the Church called for the abolition of divorce,
and divorce was abolished in 1816. In Austria the
Emperor Francis was set on neither going backwards nor
forwards ; he was the " personification of resistance to
progress," whilst his Minister—Prince Metternich—
considered that the unification of Germany was an
" infamous object." In England both Whig and Tory,
oblivious of the onrush of the industrial revolution and
" convinced that the country gentlemen were the proper
and legitimate rulers of England,"(7) demanded protection for their agricultural interests and close trade within
the Empire, forgetting that such trading had been the
underlying cause of the revolt of her American colonies.

Reaction, however, had no fulcrum to work upon, so
one had to be created. The Holy Roman Empire had
carried with it the idea of a central European constitution ; so had the Concert of Europe born in Count
Kaunitz's circular letter of July 1791. In the name of the
Emperor Leopold he had urged upon the Powers to make
common cause for the preservation of the " public peace,
the tranquillity of States, the inviolability of possessions,
and the faith of treaties,"(8) and this is what the Congress
of Vienna did not achieve. For twenty years Napoleon
had given Europe a common interest ; fear of him had
established a common life and a common struggle. By
means unseen and in no way appreciated his idea of a
World Empire had been infused into the blood of his
conquerors. At St. Helena he had said to Las Cases, that
" he had aimed at concentrating the great European
peoples, divided hitherto by a multiplicity of artificial
boundaries, into homogeneous nations, out of which he
would have formed a confederation bound together ' by a
unity of codes, principles, opinions, feelings and interests.'
At the head of this league, under the ægis of his Empire,
he had dreamed of establishing a central assembly . . .

to watch over the common weal of 'the great European family.' The dream had been dissipated by his ruin; but he prophesied that it would yet be realized, sooner or later, ' by force of circumstances .' "[9]

Nevertheless, though unseen, this idea was felt, it tingled in the finger-tips of Europe, then these fingers fashioned something which was monstrous to behold, not a graven image but a veritable abortion. On September 26, 1815, two months before the second Treaty of Paris was signed, Alexander of Russia, a religious fanatic, persuaded the Emperor of Austria and the King of Prussia to sign with him, " In the name of the Most Holy and Indivisible Trinity," a treaty named " The Holy Alliance." Metternich called it " loud-sounding nothing," and Castlereagh " a piece of sublime mysticism and nonsense." It was both, and to it may be traced turmoil and revolution from then onwards to 1849. The " blessings which it has pleased Divine Providence to shower down " on the conquering States were to be rendered permanent, while the spirit of awakened nationalism was to be suppressed. The principles of rule were to be those of " Holy Religion . . . Justice, Christian Charity and Peace." Princes were to look upon themselves as delegates of Providence, and the peoples were to be brought to realize this and exercise " the duties which the Divine Saviour has taught to mankind." Later on the Kings of Naples and Sardinia, Louis XVIII and Ferdinand of Spain subscribed to this treaty. In England the Prince Regent refused to do so, and the only two potentates who received no invitation were the Pope and the Sultan of Turkey! In the West the answer to this sublime nonsense was the establishment of the " Monroe Doctrine " on December 2, 1823.

REACTION AND REVOLUTION

The Holy Alliance and all it stood for, narrowness, stupidity and reaction, poured as it was into the still open wounds of a mangled continent, burnt in like a corroding acid. We hear much of the *Pax Europa* which blessed the world for forty years ; but it was a peace of nightmares and delirium. No sooner was Napoleon bound like Andromeda to his island rock than England was bombarding Algiers. This is but an incident ; but it is a remarkable fact that, though Europe had been bled white, between 1815 and 1830 European nations went on merrily fighting with Mahomedans. Spain was in a desperate state, and, though war was anathematized, on July 23, 1816, an edict was issued to seize all beggars overnight and enroll them in the army ; but the beggars suddenly vanished and so frustrated a measure by which it had been calculated that her miserable forces would gain 60,000 warriors. [10]

In 1820 her South American Colonies revolted, regiment after regiment was sent from Spain to perish by bullet and fever, until on December 9, 1824, her rule was finally overthrown in Peru on the field of Ayacuchio. As Fyffe writes : " Whether a continent [South America] claimed its independence, or a German schoolboy wore a forbidden ribbon in his cap, the chiefs of the Holy Alliance . . . assumed the frown of offended Providence." [11]

Next, Spain herself surged with revolution, and to assist Ferdinand, Alexander sold him a fleet of ships, which when they arived at Cadiz were found to be rotten. Next Portugal was inflicted with insurrection ; then, in 1821, revolution in Greece nearly brought Russia and Austria to war. On April 7, 1823, France, in the name of the Holy Alliance, invaded Spain. The next year Louis XVIII died, and was succeeded by Charles X, bloated with clericalism and reaction. In 1825 a sacrilege law was passed, which legalized as punishment the amputation of the hand. In 1826 Russia went to war with Persia ; in 1827, France with Algeria, because her consul had been struck on the face with a fly-flap. This same year, under the Protocol of St. Petersburg, England, Russia and France agreed to put an end to the conflict between Greece and Turkey, and the result was the naval battle of Navarino, fought on October 20.

The next year Russia invaded Bulgaria, and the year following General Diebitsch laid siege to Silistria and marched on Adrianople. Meanwhile civil war had broken out in Portugal : Then came the year of reckoning—1830. In July Charles X was driven off the throne of France ; in August Belgium revolted against Holland ; in November Poland was in open war against Russia and Diebitsch marched on Warsaw. Hanover and Hesse-Cassel boiled over in turmoil ; disturbances rent Austria, Hungary and Switzerland, whilst many risings took place in Italy. In the spring of 1831 the Poles were defeated at Ostrolenka and the Constitution of Poland was abolished. Simultaneously the Papal States revolted to be crushed by Austria, and Mehemet Ali of Egypt invaded Syria, laying siege to the fortress of St. Jean d'Acre and occupying Damascus.

Such, in brief, was the almost universal urge of nationalism against reaction. The years 1816-1831 were some of the most bloody in European history, yet not a single great battle was fought.

THE CONQUEROR OF THE NINETEENTH CENTURY

While fear held the statesmen back greed pushed the industrialists forwards. In England manufacture was rapidly replacing agriculture as the staple industry, and the Napoleonic wars stimulated this replacement ; for whilst Europe was being hammered this way and that upon the anvil of the French Emperor's ambition, England became the workshop and repair shop of the shattered continent. Then the war ended, and people could no longer afford to buy. Prices fell, the markets were flooded with manufactured articles and colonial produce ; thousands of men were thrown out of work by the sudden stoppage in the production of warlike stores ; so it came about that universal distress accompanied by much rioting swept over Europe. In 1819 prices declined by a half in six months ; in 1820, " 'How savoury a thing roast veal is ! ' said one Hamburg beggar to another.

' Where did you eat it ? ' said his friend, admiringly. ' I
never ate it at all, but I smelt it as I passed a great man's
house while the dog was being fed.' " Thus did the clash
between the classes begin. A savoury smell was destined
to develop into a nauseating stench.

Yet there were some who could see things as they were
and would be, and among this small band of seers was
Lord Cochrane, later on tenth Earl of Dundonald, one
of the most remarkable men in British history.

On June 2, 1818, he said in the House of Commons :

" I will appeal to the knowledge of those members engaged in
commerce, and ask them whether the acts of the legislative body
have not been of a description, during the late war, that would,
if not for the timely intervention of the use of machinery, have
sent this nation to total ruin ? The country is burthened to a
degree which, but for this intervention, it would have been
impossible for the people to bear." [12]

He saw clearly that the whole of the eighteenth
century had been an age of increasing industrial development, a development which must accelerate as the years
advanced. Until about 1730 British manufacture depended
on foreign inventions. Ten years later smelting with coal,
or coke, instead of charcoal, was adopted. In 1740 the
annual output of iron in Great Britain was about 17,000
tons ; in 1800 it was 150,000 tons, and later on, in 1840,
1,400,000 tons. In the second half of the eighteenth
century machines began to make machines. And this is
the true birth of the industrial revolution. In 1769,
the year Napoleon was born and Wellington his
conqueror, James Watt produced the first practical
steam-engine ; and in the year Napoleon was finally
defeated, namely 1815, the first steamer made the
passage from London to Glasgow ; and three years later
the *Rising Star*, built under the direction of the Earl of
Dundonald and his brother, was the first steam vessel
to cross the Atlantic. [13]

Nor was land transport behindhand ; in 1769, Cugnot,
in France, invented a rudimentary steam carriage, and,

in 1802, Trevethick produced a more serviceable one in England. Napoleon considered their military use; meanwhile came Trevethick's first locomotive in 1801, and, in 1825, the first true railway was constructed by George Stephenson between Stockton and Darlington. Here were forces Cyclopean, as yet one-eyed, which were about to change the face of the world, and, in the changing of it, raise war from the cockpit of gladiatorial armies to the grand amphitheatre of contending nations.

INFLUENCE OF DEMOCRACY ON WAR

The influence of the spirit of nationality, that is of democracy, on war was profound, as also were the influences of science and industrial development. The first emotionalized war and, consequently, brutalized it; and the second delivered into the hands of the masses more and more deadly means of destruction.

Walt Whitman has written, " I utter the word democratic, I utter the word *en masse.*" He is right. And have not Maurras, Leon Daudet and Bainville called democracy *l'anthropophage*—the eater of men ? When, a few years ago, we heard echoing through the avenues, streets and alley-ways of such great cities as London, Paris and Washington the cries of a war fought " to make the world safe for democracy," and of a war fought " to make the world fit for heroes to live in," those who could see (and there were few) saw that we were faced by two forms of war, that of the nineteenth and that of the eighteenth century. Both may be absurd ; yet let it be remembered that democracy has little or nothing to do with heroism. To make the world safe for democracy is to turn it into a charnel house, and this, as I will show, the wars of the nineteenth and twentieth centuries succeeded in doing.

In the eighteenth century wars were largely the occupation of kings, courtiers and gentlemen. Armies lived on their depots, they interfered as little as possible with the people, and as soldiers were paid out of the king's privy purse they were too costly to be thrown away lightly on massed attacks. The change came about with the French Revolution, *sans culottism* replaced *courtiership*, and as armies became more and more the instruments of the people, not only did they grow in size but in ferocity. National armies fight nations, royal armies fight their like, the first obey a mob—always demented, the second a king—generally sane.

" The day of Cabinet wars is over. It is no longer the weakness of a single man, at the head of affairs, or of a dominant party, that is decisive, but only the exhaustion of the belligerent nations. . . . Wars have become solely the concern of the nations engaged. . . . A clashing of interests leads to war, but the passion of the nations decide, independently of these, up to what point the war shall be carried. . . . National egotism is inseparable from our ideas of national greatness. This egotism will always appeal to arms when other means fail. . . . The mutual mistrust between nations even makes all proposals of disarmament exceedingly suspicious." [14]

So writes General von der Goltz, and very similarly writes Mr. Fullerton. He says :

" . . . the clamour of the populace . . . armed by the humanitarianism of our special form of Christian civilization, possesses, in the devices of universal suffrage and parliamentary government, sure instruments for the immediate and frequently selfish utilization of the wealth of the community, and for the satisfaction of party interests and class appetites in injudicious and often anti-national ways." [15]

All this evolved out of the French Revolution, which also gave to the world conscription—herd warfare, and the herd coupling with finance and commerce has begotten new realms of war. For when once the whole nation fights, then is the whole national credit available for the purposes of war. Lastly comes the Press and breathes into this monstrous organization the breath of lying fury.

Under Frederick the Great it took two years and cost a hundred pounds to train a soldier ; under Napoleon it

took two months and a handful of francs. Guibert, who
lived in between these two epochs, once again dipped his
pen into prophetic ink. He wrote : " The standing
armies, while a burden on the people, are inadequate for
the achievement of great and decisive results in war, and
meanwhile the masses of the people, untrained in arms,
degenerate. . . . The hegemony over Europe will fall
to that nation which . . . becomes possessed of manly
virtues and creates a national army." [16]

In Guibert's days officers were recruited " from the
perfumed selections made in the boudoirs of the Pompa-
dours and the Dubarrys," [17] and even towards the end of
the eighteenth century European sentiment " held the
soldier as a useless unproductive drone," [18] Sir Walter
Elliot remarking—" The profession [the Navy in this
case] has its utility, but I should be sorry to see any friend
of mine belong to it." [19]

All this was gradually changed by the spirit of the
French Revolution. A new order of living and of killing
emerged out of the cry of " Vive la nation ! Vive les
sansculottes !" The occult powers behind the destiny
of the efflorescent world were wealth and public opinion
—economics and emotionalism. " The only premonitory
indication of war, in our democratic epoch," writes
M. René Pinon, " is the temper of public opinion.
When a nation's pulse beats at the fever cadence, when
its blood is boiling and the whole organism shivers and
trembles, the danger is near. At such psychological
moments in the life of a people, arguments based on
Constitutional Law have no longer any hold, and Governments become powerless to arrest the impulses of the
nation. The epoch of the old " politiques des Cabinets "
has gone by, and the best diplomatist to-day is he who is
able to penetrate the deep-lying intentions of the people
and to divine their spontaneous impulses." [20]

These impulses in their present day form date from
1789-1792, from the day of the storming of the Bastille
and the *Garde Nationale*, a force of some 2,000,000 to
3,000,000 citizens, out of which emerged Napoleon's

conscript army. An army living on the countries it invaded, an army which welcomed talent and which reduced fighting to bludgeon work. Nevertheless, how different was war then from what it is to-day. At Jena we find the Prussian army nearly perishing of cold close by huge stacks of felled wood and not daring to touch them, whilst after Auerstädt the troops went for two days without provisions because to requisition from the peasants would have been a " system of robbery . . . unknown in the Prussian army, and repugnant to its spirit."

As late as 1813 we find Sir Humphrey Davy and Michael Faraday visiting France, Switzerland, Italy and the Tyrol. In Paris they are entertained by French scientists—Ampère, Clement and Desormes, yet it never occurred to any of these men that because their countries were at war there was a lack of patriotism in such a visit. In 1914-18 scientists anathematized each other roundly, the enemy's language was banned from the schools, and even his music was placed under interdict.

In 1832 Marshal Gérard and 60,000 French troops marched on Antwerp, the citadel of which was held by the Dutch under General Chassé. In order to spare the citizens the horrors of war, Chassé agreed to direct the fire of his guns on the open plains only if Gérard would agree to approach in no other direction. This plan was decided upon. " Rarely, if ever, was a siege conducted with so much chivalry and courtesy. . . . The stipulations regarding the neutrality of the city and the restrictions of the line of fire of both parties are noteworthy, and so well were they carried out that not a single non-combatant beyond the lines was harmed in person or property."[21] Exactly one hundred years later, what do we see ? The crowded city of Shanghai is bombarded and then bombed from the air !

NAPOLEON AS TACTICIAN

Lastly, I will turn from the discussion of the nature of war to that of war as an art ; for unless the Napoleonic method of fighting is in part understood much which follows in this book will be incomprehensible. His weapon was the flintlock musket, with an effective range of about 100 yards and a maximum range of 300. It could be fired twice a minute, and each man carried with him into battle 60 rounds of ammunition. His field gun was the twelve-pounder with a round-shot range of 1,500 yards and a case-shot range of 500. His other weapons, bayonet, sword and lance were much as they are to-day.

His fundamental principle of attack was to take his opponent in flank or rear, and to prepare this manœuvre he first attacked his enemy in front in order to draw in his reserves and so fix him. He was not pre-eminently a great tactician, but his amazing strategy, the rapidity of his marches, the masses of men he used, and above all the unity of command which he exercised, normally forced him to assume the aggressive rôle. In his early campaigns shortage of artillery compelled him, as General Duhesme says, to hurl his battalions against his enemy " like a battering ram." Again he did so at Waterloo, but this time he did not understand how to meet Wellington's tactics. He believed in the attack, but he did not believe in it blindly, and, consequently, he believed in numerical superiority, yet again with his eyes wide open, for he says : " An army of 10,000 men that can move twenty miles a day is superior for war to one of 20,000 whose average speed does not exceed ten miles a day."

It is curious that, believing as he did in quickness of movement, he never appears to have paid much attention to quickness of fire. For instance, in 1800, on the day before crossing the St. Bernard, we find Berthier ordering that all conscripts should fire a few shots " that they may know which eye to aim with and how to load their muskets." [22]   And not until 1811 do we hear of Napoleon approving target practice for recruits, and then only if inferior powder is fired. [23]

His use of cavalry in reconnaissance and pursuit was frequently superb, but it is in his employment of artillery that he stands second to none, except the great Frederick himself.

The reason why the field gun *should* have been recognized as the superior weapon of war, and artillery tactics as the most important of problems of study, lay in the simple fact that case-shot outranged the musket ball by 200 yards, and a round-shot fired in ricochet was a deadly weapon at 1,000 yards. That this was not seen was due to two causes : the first is constitutional in all armies, owing to the conservative mentality of the soldier. Field guns had become only reasonably mobile during the middle of the eighteenth century, and this was too recent a date for soldiers towards the end of this century to notice. The second has generally been overlooked, namely, the cost of the artillery arm. Wars and civil wars ruin States, and ruined States cannot afford cannon.

Frederick the Great opened his career as a general by believing in shock tactics, but he soon learnt that artillery fire was the deciding factor and that guns should be massed in order to attain their fullest effect. As his enemy, the Austrians, frequently took up positions on the reverse side of a slope, he increased his howitzers to one-third of his artillery, so that by curved fire he could dislodge him. Though these tactics were forgotten, after his death they were rediscovered by the Prussians towards the end of the Napoleonic Wars. On August 10, 1813, Frederick William III issued the following instructions : " Should the enemy be on the reverse side of heights or otherwise protected, it will be advantageous to unite the howitzers, as a large number of shells thrown upon one spot produce a fearful effect, which for the most part it would be impossible to withstand." [24]

Napoleon, though an artillery officer by training, learnt Frederick's lesson somewhat slowly. Even as late as the battles of Eylau (1807), Friedland (1807) and Aspern (1809) his infantry dashed themselves to pieces against the enemy guns. After Aspern he massed his artillery on the point to be attacked, and at Wagram (1809) and Borodino (1812) he blew great holes through the enemy's lines and columns. " In every case where the services of the artillery, owing to the want of this weapon, failed, Napoleon was obliged to have recourse to a series of successive efforts, which cost him infinite forces and time." [25] At Waterloo (1815) the want of howitzers, or their misuse, resulted in his inability to dislodge Wellington from his covered position, and cost him the battle. Frederick in his place would probably have routed the " Iron Duke " in a couple of hours.

In spite of his misuse of howitzers Napoleon was a very great gunner, and this will be realised from the following quotations :

" He who can rapidly bring on to the field a mass of artillery at the crisis of the battle and at a decisive point is certain to carry it." The reason for this is that the artillery fight depends for success on the *simultaneous* employment of force, whilst the infantry fight depends on *successive* employment. A serried line of infantry cannot attack skirmishers, and, as it advances, suffers great loss from their fire, consequently it is exhausted by the time it approaches the enemy's serried line ; whilst artillery can keep out of range of musket fire and still carry out its attack by bombardment.

Further, Napoleon said : " The better the infantry, the more one must husband it and support it with good batteries." [26]. . . . " Missile weapons are now become the principal ones : it is by fire and not by shock that battles are decided to-day " [27] . . . . . . " The power of the infantry lies in its fire. In seige warfare, as in the open field, it is the gun which plays the chief part ; it has effected a complete revolution . . . . . . it is with artillery that war is made." [28]

TACTICAL REACTION AND DECAY.

Once Napoleon was safely ensconced in St. Helena, military reaction was as complete as political reaction.

In 1831 a new French *Field Regulations* was issued and it follows the lines of the *Regulations* of 1791, and those of 1862 were on the same lines as those of 1831. [29]

Some French authorities preferred the line to the column. Napoleon had laid down a general order of two lines without counting skirmishers. Marshal Bugeaud, of Algerian fame, agreed, because the line " allows infantry to make use of its fire, which is its main strength."[30] Jomini, however, disagreed, and supported battalion columns and lines of three ranks, for, as he said : " What European army (except the English) could be trusted in line only two deep.'[31] The third rank was for the bayonet charge, or to resist calvary. Napoleon considered it of no value, [32] yet it was retained in the French army until 1859, " and even then old soldiers shook their heads at its abandonment." [33]

In the Prussian service the reaction was towards close-order drill. The three ranks were retained, but the third rank was used as skirmishers. In 1847 a new drill book was issued, battalion columns gave way to company columns, and the third rank was replaced by whole companies of skirmishers.

In England reaction was still more pronounced ; there was a general cry for retrenchment, but none for military reform. In 1815, when the United Service Club was constituted, it was " held up to Parliament as a national danger, likely to foster the military spirit and the professional pride of officers to the peril of the State," [34] and the Royal Military College at Sandhurst was attacked because the education it imparted would inculcate " that military spirit which every good Englishman abhorred."[35]

Tactics remained as they were in 1809, and except that the *Rules and Regulations* of 1824 officially recognized light infantry, few other changes were made. Even in 1874 Sir Garnet Wolseley could still write : " The fighting tactics of Frederick the Great, improved by the Duke of Wellington to suit the arms of his day, are still alone to be found in our Field Exercise Book." [36]

c

Into such a miserable condition had the army fallen that when the Duke of York died in 1827 " He was buried at Windsor with civil ceremony, for there were not troops enough in England to pay due honour to a Field Marshal." [37]   Yet progress had not altogether halted, for in this same year iron bedsteads were issued to English soldiers [38]

PART I

PERIOD OF NATIONAL INCUBATION,
1832-1852

CHAPTER I

THE CHANGING WORLD, 1832-1847

Steam-Power and Military Values. Steam-Power and Human Values. Internal
and External Changes. Jomini and Clausewitz.

STEAM-POWER AND MILITARY VALUES

In 1832, eleven years after the " Corsican Ogre " had
found a resting place in the valley above Jamestown, the
peoples of Europe were more exhausted than they had
been in 1815 ; for to the attrition of war had been added
the attrition of disappointment. Hopes had been blighted,
and the flamboyant ideals of the Revolution had been
driven underground to simmer and to fret. Nationalism
had been rigorously suppressed, reaction was in the
saddle ; the art of war had been utterly changed, yet
once again military traditionalism was donning its old
harness. Nevertheless, one factor advanced irresistably,
a slow, inflowing tide which was destined to submerge
the old world and refertilize it. This factor was steam-
power, which, like a little cloud, had appeared on the
horizon of an agriculturally constituted order of society,
and was now daily swelling in size, and darkening this
horizon with much future thunder.

Here was the Master fated to dominate the hundred
years under review ; which no reaction could halt,
which no reform could enchain. A one-eyed force, as I
have called it, which was destined like Polyphemus to
lose his eye and become the blind tyrant of peace and
war—energy, stupendous, roaring, sightless, energy—the
consumer of human flesh.

It would be out of place here to examine the civil side
of this question, but as I shall later on have occasion to
show how slowly the soldier learnt to realize what science
and industry meant to him, it is only fair to point out

that his obtuseness was no greater than that of his civilian brothers. For example, excepting the short line between Stockton and Darlington, in 1832 the only railway in England was the one joining Liverpool to Manchester. When a few years before this date the construction of this line was proposed, a meeting of Manchester ministers denounced the project as being " contrary to the law of God." Lord Derby drove the surveyors off his land, and Stephenson had to hire a prize-fighter to carry his theodolite to prevent it from being smashed to pieces. Pamphlets were written and newspapers hired to revile his work. It was declared that the railway would prevent cows grazing, hens laying, and would cause ladies to give premature birth to children at " the sight of these things going forward at the rate of four and a half miles an hour."

For many years steam-power did not influence the Army as it did the Navy, though the sailor, like the civilian, did not want to be influenced. In 1832 there were actually nine small steamships on the Navy List ; but the Admiralty was not interested in steam-power outside laying down a regulation that " on no account are ratings to be allowed to place their clothes in the boiler when it is under steam." Should a flue get choked, then the method advocated for clearing it was " to fire a musket up the funnel ! "[1] In 1828, when the Colonial Office asked the Admiralty for a steamer to convey mails from Malta to the Ionian Islands, the following reply was received : Their lordships " felt it their bounden duty to discourage to the utmost of their ability the employment of steam vessels, as they considered that the introduction of steam was calculated to strike a fatal blow to the naval supremacy of the Empire."[2] From Dundonald we learn that the same outlook prevailed in 1834.[3] " Give me," he often said, " a fast small steamer, with a heavy long-range gun in the bow, and another in the hold to fall back upon, and I would not hesitate to attack the largest ship afloat. . . . As large a gun as possible in a vessel as small and swift as possible, and as many of them as you can put upon the sea."(⁴) Such was the outlook of this remarkable man, born half a century before his time.

In spite of reaction, England was the only country which was even partially industrialized during the thirties. In Prussia advance was painfully slow. In 1837 her total machinery was under 10,000 horse-power, and in 1846 not more than 22,000. In France, in this last-mentioned year, more than half the French pig-iron was still smelted by charcoal, and there was very little steam-power in the country. Nevertheless, such steam-power as did exist in Europe began to make it possible for military inventions to be manufactured at an increasingly economical price. Many of these inventions were centuries old in conception, but on account of the rudimentary conditions of engineering it had been either impossible to make them, or too costly to do so. Thus, for instance, rifles had been known in the fifteenth century; and in 1742, in his book *New Principles of Gunnery*, Benjamin Robins had pointed out that ". . . .whatever State shall thoroughly comprehend the nature and advantage of rifled barrel pieces, and having facilitated and completed their construction, shall introduce into their armies their general use, with a dexterity in the management of them, will by this means acquire a superiority which will almost equal anything that has been done at any time by the particular excellence of any one kind of arms, and will perhaps fall but little short of the wonderful effect which historians relate to have been formerly produced by the first invention of firearms."(⁵) The trouble here was not only one of manufacture, but of producing a powder which would not foul the barrel, and this was impossible until an advance in chemistry had been made.

In 1805 the Rev. Alexander John Forsyth devised the percussion system, and offered it to the Army but with no results. In 1814 copper percussion caps were first manufactured, but they were not adapted for the "Brown Bess" until 1842. In 1824 Captain Norton invented the cylindro-conoidal bullet, but the British Government failed to adopt this form of projectile until 1851. Both these inventions, indirectly due to steam-power, had eventually an enormous influence on tactics. The percussion cap rendered the musket serviceable in wet weather, reducing miss-fires in each thousand rounds from 411 to 4.5, hits being raised from 270 to 385 in a thousand shots ; whilst the cylindro-conoidal bullet caused the rifle to become the most deadly weapon of the century

On the Continent, between the years 1838-1840, the French raised *Chasseurs à pied* in Algeria arming them with the rifle, and in 1841, the breech-loading Dreyse needle-gun was introduced into certain Prussian regiments.

STEAM-POWER AND HUMAN VALUES

As steam-power gave birth to machinery, productive and destructive, so did machinery give birth to a new social order. Already during the final decades of the eighteenth century had the machine and the engine begun to unravel the weft from the warp of agricultural society, and separating the human threads it piled them into two great heaps—the manual workers on the one side, and their employers and investors in manual work on the other. To the masters the ideals of the French Revolution were abhorrent, consequently these ideals soon found a nesting-place in the hearts of their men, whose conditions during the first half of the nineteenth century were worse than those of the Russian workers under the Five-Year Plan to-day.

In this early period of industrialization the governing idea of the manufacturers was that machinery displaced brains in the workers, and that hands were but a species of tools. As long as wealth could be accumulated the contentment and happiness of their men meant nothing to them. " It may well be doubted," writes Colonel Maude . . . " whether the French feudal laws at their worst, inflicted greater misery on the people than the untrammelled action of the *laissez faire* school . . . brought upon our unfortunate working classes in the dark days before the Factory Acts."[6]

By 1832 widespread misery had become universal in England. In 1842 women and children were still working in the coal-pits of South Staffordshire, and of deaths among the miners 57 per cent. were due to accidents. " In one part of Manchester the wants of upwards of 7,000 people " were " supplied by thirty-three necessaries only."[7]

If such were the conditions under which the workers lived, those under which the soldiers lived were even worse. The Army was unpopular, officers had to take to plain clothes so as not to be seen in the streets in uniform ; duelling was not prohibited until 1843 ; professional education was all but non-existent, and age counted for far more than efficiency. For instance, in 1826, in one regiment there was an ensign on full pay aged 61 ; as late as 1852 there were thirteen generals of 70 years' service and upwards, thirty-seven of 60 to 70, one hundred and sixty-three of 50 to 60, seventy-two of 40 to 50 and seven under 40 years' service. Whilst in the Navy, in 1831, on the Admirals list there was one above 90, seven between 80 and 90, twenty-five between 70 and 80, seven between 70 and 65, and one, the youngest, aged 65. Also on the active list—six commanders between 81 and 76, and eleven lieutenants between 81 and 63.[8]

As regards other ranks, their existence was that of a penal community, enlistment being for life. The following are some of the conditions as given by Fortescue[9] : " The only urinals for barrack rooms were wooden tubs, the stench of which was appalling. Moreover the same tubs, when emptied, were the only vessels furnished to the soldier to wash in. . . . The barrack-rooms were shared by the wives of soldiers married ' on the strength,' the proportion of wives allowed in barracks being six to every hundred men. It was in these rooms that the soldier brought his newly-wedded partner for the honeymoon, and it was in these that his children were born, all in the presence of half a dozen comrades.". . . Sanitation was practically non-existent. . . two tallow dips were allowed to every room of twelve men. . . . Discipline was based on punishment ; at Fort Charles, Jamaica, " three hundred men had within two years received among them fifty-four thousand lashes.". . . (In 1832, a Regimental Court Martial could order three hundred lashes, and a District Court Martial five hundred.) . . . The diet was un-alterable—" beef-broth and boiled beef " ; there were only two meals a day—breakfast at 7.30 a.m. and dinner at 12.30 p.m. . . . Bad food drove the soldier to drink. " To the clerks at the Treasury rations represented not the means of keeping soldiers alive, but simply a charge of pounds, shillings and pence against the national purse." The canteen system was pernicious in the extreme, there were no recreations, and drinking in the evenings was due to sheer exhaustion. . . . On the West Coast of Africa the annual death-rate ranged from 75 to 80 per cent. In 1825 there were 441 deaths out of 571 troops, and the next year 342 out of 471.

With such conditions as these in both civil and military life, the much boasted years of peace are apt to lose their glamour. Those unfortunates who could not emigrate—and 337,000 did so in 1840-1842 ; 221,000 in 1842-1845 ; 130,000 in 1846, and on an average 248,000 a year between 1847 and 1852—turned to the only hope offered to them—the as yet narrow path of Socialism. In 1834, under the auspices of Robert Owen, the " Grand National Consolidated Trades' Union " was launched, and in 1842 Karl Marx, one of the most remarkable men of the century, began to edit the *Rheinische Zeitung.* These two men were to found a new form of war which reached its climax in the Russian Revolution of 1917 and has not yet run its course.

Opposed to Socialism, yet akin to it, was the rising spirit of Humanitarianism. Whilst the one caught hold of the principle of equality the other caught hold of that

of fraternity.   Both were sympots of the religious
revival which the prolonged wars had stimulated, and
it is no coincidence that the word " Socialism " became
current about the same time that Newman began the
Oxford Movement in 1833.   Whilst Socialism aimed at
bettering the condition of the workers Humanitarianism
aimed at bettering the condition of the Negroes.   In
1807 the slave trade was abolished by act of Parliament,
and in 1834 the slaves were emancipated in the West
Indies.   These fervent one-eyed people " could spare no
sympathy for men of their own colour.   They did not
rally, as might have been expected, to the help of the
Tory Lord Ashley when, in 1833, he sought to regulate
the employment of English children in factories " ; [10]
neither did they in the least interest themselves in the
welfare of the soldier who lived in conditions far worse
than most of the West Indian slaves.   Yet what happened
was this : The doctrines of Marx, by playing upon the
intellect of man, led to the most devastating of
revolutions, while the doctrines of Wilberforce, by playing
upon the emotions of man, went a long way towards
stimulating the Abolitionist Movement in the United
States of America and so led indirectly to the greatest
civil war in history.   These are strange origins, but life
is a perpetual conflict, and war trickles from many
hidden springs.

INTERNAL AND EXTERNAL CHANGES

Thus Peace jerked along its rutty road.   The wheels
of the European coach wobbled from side to side, and
at any moment one might come off and land the
Continent in another series of revolutions.   Something
had to be done, and it was done in a heated and,
consequently, half-blind way.

In Great Britain social conditions were as bad as they
had ever been.   Reform was in the air—literally so, for
though the would-be reformers talked much of reformation, they never really considered what the word meant.

Bentham had declared that the end of all government was utility, a materialistic conception which he nevertheless bracketed with the good of the governed—an ethical conception. Bentham wanted every man to have a vote; Macaulay in his turn would have given it to shopkeepers only. The Bill which resulted was the culminating point of a period extending over nearly a hundred and fifty years. In Great Britain it was in fact the climax of the eighteenth century order and philosophies, and it was largely hastened by the comparative freedom gained by the Press after 1815.

In October 1831, the Reform Bill was carried in the Commons and thrown out by the Lords. Then, in June 1832, it was carried through both Houses and received Royal assent. " The Revolution of 1688 was completed by the Revolution of 1832. By the first change power was transferred from the king to the landed class; by the second the landed class was forced to extend its privileges to the commercial and industrial middle classes. The first change was largely political; the second could not have been accomplished unless social and industrial revolution had preceded and occasioned the political. After 1688 the representatives of the parties contending for power had consisted for the most part of the landed interest; after 1832 the Whig landowners made common cause with the commercial interests, and admitted a whole new class to a share of political representation."(11)

The ultimate effects resulting from this political change were deep and occult. The immediate ones were insignificant, because it generally takes a long time for political reform to mend social and industrial fractures. Between 1838 and 1842 foreign trade was stagnant and the people were hustled into the workhouses, by them called " Bastilles "—an ominous word. *Oliver Twist* represents this period. Then, in 1842-43, came the Factory Acts which led to a definite and immediate social amelioration, and which were actually preceded by military reforms; for, in 1840, £3,500 was

voted for the education of soldiers' children, and, in
1841, regimental libraries were sanctioned though
scarcely encouraged.

Humanitarianism could not, however, restore trade,
and as trade was at a standstill poverty was all-prevalent ;
consequently a demand was made to abolish protective
duty on corn. The manufacturers seeing that cheap
corn would mean cheap wages supported this movement.
It was no concern of theirs whether British agriculture
was ruined as long as they could increase their profits,
and destroy the political power of the landed class.
They saw gold glittering before them, and were so
blinded by its sheen that they could not see that a
country deprived of its agricultural foundations must of
necessity be protected by a strong and costly navy to
police the trade routes. As corn cheapened war-ships
grew more costly.

Meanwhile, on the continent, the Germanic States
were moving in a somewhat similar economic direction.
Between 1828 and 1836 the German Zollverien, or
Customs-Union, was founded, and ultimately it embraced
practically the whole of non-Austrian Germany. Further
still, by laying the foundations of a united German
nation, the members of this Zollverien soon began to
consider the necessity of creating a powerful German
army to protect its interests. This idea, as yet amorphous,
received a stimulus in 1840, when France began to
agitate for the recovery of her old Rhine frontier. The
German answer to this move, one which has been the
pivot of French foreign policy since the days of Richelieu,
was *Die Wacht am Rhein* which was written at this time.

In Spain chaos prevailed, and in 1834 the Carlist wars
began. In France conditions were critical. In 1832 an
insurrection broke out in Paris, and disputes between
masters and workmen were of daily occurrence. The
discipline of the French army was bad, and in 1835 an
attempt was made on the life of Louis Philippe who had
succeeded Charles X after the 1830 upheaval.

In 1832 the relationship between England and France

became strained. The French invasion of Belgium had a
perturbing influence, and when once again Mehemet Ali
revolted against the Sultan, utterly defeating his troops
at Konieh, on December 21, 1832, France backed Egypt
whilst Great Britain sided with Turkey. Then came the
Peace of Kutaya, in April 1833, and in the following year
France turned her attention seriously to the conquest of
Algeria. This left England's hands free, and whilst
Russia was fixing her eyes on Asia, the British Government engineered the Opium War in China which gave
England Hong Kong in 1842 and threw open to the
foreigner the ports of Canton, Amoy, Foochow, Ningpo
and Shanghai. This most iniquitous piece of banditry
laid the foundations of the present Civil War in China.
Also Great Britain turned her attention seriously to
India. This led to a series of wars : the disastrous First
Afghan War of 1839-1842 ; the Sind War, the Gwalior
War ; the first Sikh War, and the Second Sikh War (all
fought during the forties) and the Second Burmese War
of 1852 ; all more or less land-grabbing operations which
led direct to the Indian Mutiny in 1857.

From the point of view of the art of war there is
little to be learnt from the engagements fought. Generally speaking the enemy was badly organized, led and
equipped, whilst the Army in India was in its normal
state of oriental dry-rot. For example, when at the
opening of the first Afghan War the Army marched
against Shah Shuja, " one brigadier had sixty camels to
convey the various articles which he deemed necessary
for himself alone."[12]

JOMINI AND CLAUSEWITZ

Though military ineptitude was at its height, it was
largely during the thirties that a new philosophy of war
was established, and this philosophy was destined to
influence the whole nature of fighting from 1866 onwards.
In 1832, Clausewitz having died the year before, his widow
published his famous unfinished work *On War,* and in

1837 Jomini published his *Summary of the Art of War*, which, though one of his lesser works, was probably his most influential. Clausewitz did not like formalism in war, Jomini did. To Clausewitz " war is the province of chance," to Jomini it was far more the province of calculations. The first was a generation before his time, for the success of his doctrines depended on the establishment of a national military system. The second, basing his arguments on a professional army, in spite of the fact that it might be a conscript one, carried more influence with the soldier up to the date of the American Civil War. This being so, I will deal with Clausewitz ; his work, in any case, is far and away the more important.

As there is not space here for a critical essay on his doctrines, it will be best, I think, to summarize his main arguments by quotations. First ; to him

" War is only a continuation of State policy by other means." . . . " War is not merely a political act, but also a real political instrument, a continuation of political commerce." . . . " War is only a part of political intercourse, therefore by no means an independent thing in itself." . . . " Is not war merely another kind of writing and language for political thought ? " . . . " If War belongs to policy, it will naturally take its character from thence. If policy is grand and powerful, so will also be the war."

Secondly ; as to the nature of war :

" War is nothing but a duel on an extensive scale." . . . " Let us not hear of Generals who conquer without bloodshed." " War is an act of violence pushed to its utmost bounds." . . . " Our aim is directed upon the destruction of the enemy's power." . . . " Destruction of the enemy's military forces is in reality the object of all combats." . . . " The more is war in earnest, the more is it a venting of animosity and hostility."

This leads, thirdly, to the offensive :

There is only one form of war : " To wit, the attack of the enemy." . . . " The combat is the single activity in war. . . . "

Which demands, fourthly, numerical superiority :

" The best strategy is always to be strong." . . .   " A war " should be " waged with the whole weight of the national power." . . .   " A people's war in civilized Europe is a phenomenon of the nineteenth century."

And, fifthly, moral and intellectual superiority :

" Courage is the highest of virtues." . . .   " The chief qualities are the talents of the Commander ; the military virtue of the Army ; its National feeling." . . .   " There is nothing in War which is of greater importance than obedience."

Sixthly ; as regards tactics :

" The destructive principle of fire in the Wars of the present time is plainly beyond measure the most effective." . . .   " The defensive form of War is in itself stronger than the offensive . . . but has a negative object." . . .   " The attack is the positive intention, the defence the negative." . . .   " Only great and general battles can produce great results."

Lastly ; organization :

" War is divided into preparation and action. . . .   " Everything is very simple in War, but the simplest thing is difficult." . . .   " War belongs not to the province of Arts and Sciences, but to the province of social life."

Such, in brief, is the doctrine of Clausewitz, a kind of " Spartanism " which turns the State into a military machine (just as industry was then turning it into an economic machine) in place of merely providing it with a protective servant. In his eyes the main object of the State was to manufacture war-power instead of merely insuring itself against war. What Clausewitz really did was to democratize war, and when the spirit of his doctrines was coupled with that of Darwin's *The Origin of Species* (1859), they produced the Prussian Military System ; and when with that of Karl Marx's *Das Kapital* (1867), they produced the Russian Revolutionary System. All three writers based their theories upon " *mass* struggle "—in war, in life and in economics.

His doctrines had no influence whatever on English military thought. In 1846 Wellington pathetically said : " I am bordering upon seventy-seven years of age passed in honour. . . . I hope that the Almighty may protect me from being the witness of the tragedy which I cannot persuade my contemporaries to take measures to avert." [14]

The next year the " Congress of the Communist Union " was held in London under Marx and Engels, and from this date the *Marseillaise* passed to the bourgeoisie, for an even more formidable battle-song, the *Internationale*, was about to vibrate from the throats of the workers.

> " Debout ! les damnés de la terre !
> Debout ! les forçats de la faim !
>
> .   .   .   .   .
>
> Le raison tonne en son cratère,
> C'est l'éruption de la fin.
> Du passé faisons table rase,
> Foule esclave, debout, debout !
> Le monde va changer de base :
> Nous ne sommes rien, soyons tout ! "

A new war period was approaching . . . the peoples were stirring like an awakening man. . . . Mars no longer fumbled uncertainly for his sword—this time he meant to draw it.

D

CHAPTER II

NATIONALISM TAKES FORM, 1848-1852

Revolution in France. Revolution in Italy and Austria. Revolution in
Germany. The Rise of Louis Napoleon. The War Clouds Gather.

REVOLUTION IN FRANCE

THE wave of revolution which swept over Europe in 1848
was of a totally different nature from the one which had
done so in 1789. The French Revolution, decisive and
epoch making as it had been, was a local affair, for it
caused no popular rising outside of France. The
revolution of 1830 was more general, and this may be
seen from the fact that the expulsion of Charles X was
followed by many national rebellions. But, in 1848, the
downfall of Louis Philippe convulsed the whole of central
Europe, menacing every government except that of the
Swiss. Since 1789 the seeds of nationalism had taken
root, and watered as they had been by reaction, poverty
and despair, the universal problem was no longer one of
merely substituting popular for aristocratic rule but of
establishing nations which could decide their own destin-
ies. It was no longer a question of a change in the form
of government but of a change in the national structure.
It was not so much the work of men like Rousseau and
Voltaire as the work of Fulton and Stephenson which
rendered sympathy and similarity of action spontaneous ;
for during the forties steamships and railways had begun
to link peoples together socially and economically, and
not merely intellectually as had done the theories of the
philosophers.

In England and Russia only the backwash was felt, for
the revolution of 1848 was pre-eminently a central
European upheaval. In England reforms had in part

insulated the country against rebellion; in Russia barbarism was still so prevalent that the people were in place insulated by their ignorance against revolt. And though the Emperor Nicholas I, who had succeeded his brother Alexander I in 1825, was a liberal-minded man, in 1840 anatomical and physiological books were forbidden to include anything which might hurt the instinct of decency, and, in 1848, newspapers were not allowed to commend inventions " until they had been investigated according to the rules of science,"[1]—whatever these rules may have been.

In January, 1848, a popular rising occurred in Palermo, a flash in the pan. Then, suddenly, on February 22, the barrel of European order exploded in France, and two days later the mob sacked the Tuileries. Whereupon Louis Philippe and his queen slipped out of a back door and eventually arrived in England disguised as Mr. and Mrs. Smith.

Seldom has a revolution been less bloody to start with. The " right to work " was established as the leading principle of reform, and to attain it the National Guard was suppressed and the workmen armed. This divided the country, or rather Paris which is more French than France itself, into two camps—those who had and those who had not. A clash was inevitable, and it took place in June when General Cavaignac, who had been appointed dictator to save the Republic, led the west-end of the city against the industrial east-end under Pujol, and slaughtered it with his cannon. Then the revolution subsided, mainly because, as Fyffe says : " The combatants fought not for a political principle or form of government, but for the preservation or the overthrow of society based on the institution of private property."[2] Further, he writes : " France had given to Central Eroupe the signal for the Revolution of 1848, and it was in France, where the conflict was not one for national independence but for political and social interests, that the Revolution most rapidly ran its course and first exhausted its powers."[3] Nevertheless, France was badly shaken, and

it was at this time that the Duke of Wellington wrote :
" France needs a Napoleon ! I cannot yet see him. . . .
Where is he ? " [4] Strange as it may seem, he was under
his own command enrolled as a special constable.

In England there was general excitement, much thunder but little lightning. Poverty was universal, [5] but
nationalism was already a fact and no longer a theory.
The Tower of London and the Bank of England were
placed in a state of defence, the military were called out
under the command of Wellington, and 170,000 special
constables, among whom was the future Emperor of
France, were enrolled. Then the Chartists' demonstra-
tions proved themselves to be Chinese attacks, and, in
1849, the corn-laws were repealed, and Great Britain
slid definitely into free trade.

REVOLUTION IN ITALY AND AUSTRIA

In the discord of the " March Days " is seen a unity in
dim form, a unity casting off reaction, and a unity which
proclaimed not only change but a future. At heart all
Italy was under Charles Albert of Piedmont when he
revolted against Austria, and all Germany was at heart
with Frederick William of Prussia when he, as we shall see,
entered Holstein. Venetia and Holstein were the two
pivots of a new war epoch. To one belong the conflicts
of 1848 and 1849, and the war of 1859 : to the other the
Danish wars of 1848 and 1864, and the wars of 1866 and of
1870, after which warfare ceases to be a profession and
becomes the central institution of European nations.
Thus did the West develop into a powder factory, to
blow up in 1914.

To turn now to the events of these strenuous days.
Italy was in a state of utter rottenness ; Lucca under a
madman, Modena ruled by a petty tyrant, and Parma in
the hands of the widow of Napoleon—dominated by a
succession of lovers. But the spirit of Mazzini was
abroad. This strange man, in his lonely prison at Savona
in presence of " those symbols of the infinite, the sky and

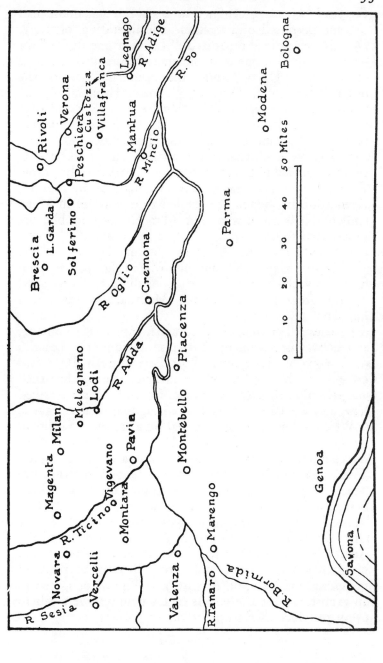

ITALIAN WARS OF 1848-1859.

the sea " with a greenfinch as his sole companion, had become possessed of a mission—the liberation of Italy. On his release he organized " La Giovene Italia," or Young Italy Movement, upon whose banner was inscribed on one side " Unity " and " Independence," and on the other " Liberty," " Equality " and " Humanity "—its national and international aims. Between 1824 and 1847 it was Mazzini more than any other man who broke the period of " pacific beatitude " in Tuscany.

In March revolution broke out in Vienna ; whereupon Metternich fled to England to walk the parade of Brighton. Then followed a general upheaval throughout the Empire. Revolution in Vienna at once led to revolution in Milan and then in Venice, where, on March 22, a Republic was proclaimed to the shouts of " Viva San Marco." Whereupon Radetzky, the Austrian commander, moved on Verona and Mantua placing his army in the Quadrilateral flanked by the rivers Mincio and Ádige, and protected by the fortresses of Verona, Mantua, Peschiera and Legnano.

Charles Albert King of Piedmont, now decided on war, and he was urged on by that formidable patriot Camillo di Cavour in his paper *Risorgimento*. All Italy was behind the King ; but whilst in Rome people breathed war, the Pontiff breathed peace, for nationalism terrified him, and what he wanted was a League of Italian States.

Whilst a Tuscan army watched Mantua and a Sardinian lay siege to Peschiera, Charles Albert and the bulk of his forces moved northwards to cut Verona from the Tyrol. Then, on April 29, the Pope denounced the war which deprived the king of the support of the Southern States, and, on May 6, Charles Albert was defeated at Santa Lucia and compelled to fall back on the Mincio. On July 25 he was again defeated at Custozza and the Austrians entered Milan. But Radetzky, fearing the intervention of France and Great Britain, in place of marching on Turin, on August 9, at Vigevano, agreed to an armistice ; yet the effects of his triumph were felt in every province in Europe. [6]

This armistice was, however, but a lull in the storm; for the Austrian military tyranny in Lombardy was so brutal that, on March 19, 1849, Charles Albert once again took the field, and five days later, having been decisively beaten at Novara, he abdicated his crown in favour of his son Victor Emmanuel, and shortly afterwards died a broken-hearted man. Yet Cavour remained, and was to prove himself worthy to take his place among that small brotherhood of the elect—the men of destiny.

Meanwhile Hungary burst into flames; then the Czechs in Bohemia who, ever since 1820, had been bent on reviving their language followed suit. Next the Serbs in southern Hungary took up arms, and so also did the Croats in Croatia, where Colonel Jellacic the Ban, or Governor, at once deposed all the Hungarian officials. On September 11, 1848, he crossed the Drave and marched on Pesth, whereupon the Palatine took command of the Hungarian army and, on October 3, the Emperor declared the Hungarian Parliament dissolved. This led to a recurrence of revolution in Vienna which for the time being saved the Hungarians.

Prince Felix Schwartzenberg then became head of the new Austrian Government which forthwith deposed the Emperor Ferdinand and offered the crown to his nephew Francis Joseph—a boy of eighteen. Hungary, refusing to acknowledge him, summoned the entire Magyar peoples to arms. This resulted in General Windischgrätz, in command of the main Austrian army, occupying Pesth, on January 5, 1849; but in place of putting an end to the war he was driven out of Hungary and, on April 19, this country declared its independence. Instead of marching on Vienna the Hungarians laid siege to Buda, whereupon the Austrian Government called to Russia to assist her, and the Czar, still under the baneful influence of the expiring Holy Alliance, sent 80,000 troops to her support. These, on August 9, fell upon the Hungarians at Temesvar and routed them; then followed a reign of terror in which Hungary sank into silence and despair.

In the Empire revolution had been quashed. Italy

was back in chains and so was Hungary. Once again the Empire stood where it had in 1847. Outwardly it was the same, but to the discerning it was but the shell of a blown egg. Meanwhile in the north revolution took another turn.

REVOLUTION IN GERMANY

Though the German workmen, following the lead of the French, clamoured for a greater share in the profits of their masters, and free thought and democracy were rampant in Leipzig, the revolution in Germany was not a social or an economic movement but a national upheaval. For whilst in Austria a variety of races were held together by one crown, and, consequently, the national instinct was impelled towards separation, the peoples of Germany were one race divided under many govermnents, there-fore, the urge was towards unity. This urge had been vastly stimulated by Hegel, whose idealistic philosophy led back to reality, and also by a host of young poets such as Herwegh, Dingelstedt, Freilgrath and Prutz. Further still, railways had begun to consolidate the land.

While Kossuth was stirring up Hungary Bavaria lay divided between the Ultramontanes and the " Lola-montanes," that is between the followers of the Jesuits and those of Lola Montez, the King's mistress. And the quarrel ended in the famous Irish adventuress having to pack up bag and baggage and depart. Prussia, however, was united ; and on March 18 Frederick William put forward a scheme whereby a Parliament for all Germany was to be created and a Constitutional Government established in each German State. Three days later he placed himself at the head of the German nation.

Meanwhile the Duchies of Schleswig and Holstein, which were no more a part of Denmark than Hanover was of England, revolted against the Danish Crown, and on March 24 the Holsteiners formed a Provisional Govern-ment at Kiel. Whereupon the Prussian Government recognized the autonomy of the Duchies, and the Diet of Frankfort, expressing the will of Germany, demanded that Schleswig and Holstein should enter the Federation. Frederick William thereupon sent an army under General Wrangel into Holstein to drive the Danes out. Russia, Sweden and Austria resenting this action, Frederick William ordered the troops to be withdrawn. Wrangel refused and the invasion continued until Austria and Prussia were on the verge of war. As the only alternative to meeting Austria (backed by Russia) was an alliance with " the devil's nephew " Louis Napoloen, who was already dreaming of a Rhine frontier for France, Frederick William gave way and the Danish troops reoccupied the Duchies.

The real trouble between Austria and Germany was not so much Schleswig Holstein as the former's fear of a united Germany. Austria was supported by Bavaria ; but Brunswick, Baden, Nassau, Mecklenburg and various other States sided with Prussia. The crisis came in March 1849, when Frederick William was chosen Emperor. Though at the time Austria was overburdened with troubles, Frederick William was too democratically-minded " to pick up a crown out of the gutter " and refused to assume the title. He invited the States to send representatives to Berlin to examine the condition of Germany. Meanwhile came Novara and Temesvar, and Austria, once again in her old saddle, sent troops to Hesse to put down a disturbance, whereupon a Prussian army occupied Cassel and a war appeared imminent. Prussia was, however, wholly unprepared for war, and on November 29, 1850, Austria brought such pressure to bear on her that she forced her to sign a humiliating convention at Olmütz. " First to humiliate Prussia, then to destroy her " was Schwartzenberg's summary of his German policy. Prussia, having abandoned every-thing she had striven for, stood degraded in the eyes of Europe, and in 1852 the German national fleet was sold by auction. Yet from the cracked shell which now repre-sented Germany was to hatch out within a dozen years a fire-eating eagle.

THE RISE OF LOUIS NAPOLEON

In France, after the " June Days " of 1848, Cavaignac reigned as dictator, but failing to establish a strong and stable government, on December 20 he was defeated by Louis Napoleon in the Presidential elections, obtaining but 1,448,107 votes to his opponent's 5,434,226. Here was the man who, less than a year back, Wellington could see nowhere.

This twentieth day of December, 1848, was in the history of Europe as portentous as the eighteenth of June 1815. Then, Napoleon I was defeated at Waterloo, and a long period of peace was established. Now, his nephew was elected President of France and almost at once this peace was to be broken ; the spirit of the Little Corporal entering the body of the mystic who knew, as Thiers says, " like the snail, how to draw in his horns as soon as he met with an obstacle " and how once again to extend them when the obstacle was passed. The two men, otherwise so different, had, however, this in common—both were utterly unscrupulous.

The French, said Thiers, made two mistakes about this man : " The first when they took him for a fool, the second when they took him for a man of genius." He was neither ; but instead—one of the earliest examples of the opportunist politician so beloved by democracies, who would be looked upon to-day as an able and popular statesman.

He had a great belief in himself and his destiny. When in London he had said to Taglioni, the dancer : " They [the people of France] will come to me without any effort of my own " ; and to Lady Douglas he once replied : " Though fortune has twice betrayed me, yet my destiny will none the less surely be fulfilled. I wait."[7] He did ; not really believing in democracy yet understanding better than any of his contemporaries the weaknesses of the people, upon which he played as on the keys of a musical instrument. He knew their reverence for the intoxicating glory of his uncle, so he proferred them this potent draught. He realized that the people must have a religion, so he allied himself with the Church. Further, he knew that they must have a hero ; they were disgusted with such men as Louis XVIII, Charles X and Louis Philippe ; so he wound himself into the panegyrics of Thiers' *Histoire du Consulat et de l'Empire*, and popularized Béranger's lyrics—advertising himself in the Press, by pictures and by songs.

In June he was elected by four Departments, and though the Assembly ratified his election he sent in his resignation saying : " If the people impose duties on me, I shall know how to fulfil them." This was to whet their appetite ; and it did not fail to do so, for, on September 26, he was re-elected by the same Departments, and, on October 11, the law banishing the Bonapartes was abrogated. Thus it happened that he became President and took the oath " to remain faithful to the democratic Republic," and, " to regard as enemies of the nation all those who may attempt by illegal means to change the form of the established govermnent."

On March 31, 1849, his military career began. On the 23rd, as we have seen, Charles Albert had been defeated at Novara. This roused Louis Napoléon's apprehension, so, in order to anticipate Austria's restoration of the Papal power, he sent General Oudinot, son of the Marshal, and a body of French troops to Rome. Here, after an initial repulse by Garibaldi, Oudinot laid siege to the city, entered it on July 3, whereupon the Pope restored the Inquisition.

Having thus strengthened the religious factor, the next step was to weaken the home political factor. In 1846 the principle of universal suffrage had been proclaimed in France. In May, 1850, the Assembly blindly reduced the number of electors from nine to six millions, and so rendered itself highly unpopular. Here was Louis Napoleon's chance ; he had, a year or two back, stood as a vindicator of universal suffrage, and yet he now supported the Assembly ; for by doing so he knew that he was preparing its ruin. When a friend said to him : " But you will perish with it," he replied : " On the contrary, when the Assembly is hanging over the precipice I shall cut the rope."[8]

His Presidency was due to expire on May 8, 1852, so having discredited the Assembly he now set to work. He flattered the clergy, promised prosperity to the bourgeoisie, wealth to the workers, and distributed cigars and sausages to the soldiers. In the eyes of the people he rose from simple *citoyen* to *notre prince*. To prepare for his contemplated *coup d'état* he filled the government offices with his creatures—General St. Arnaud became minister of war, Maupas was given the prefecture of police, and Magnan command of the troops in Paris. Having carefully prepared everything, he brought about the overthrow of the Government on December 2, 1851, and a year later he was elected by popular vote Emperor of the French under the title of Napoleon III.

THE WAR CLOUDS GATHER

Raised to power on the bayonets of a corrupted army, his destiny demanded that he be supported by war. Shortly before he had become Emperor he had said : " Certain persons say that the Empire is war. I say that the Empire is peace, and when France is satisfied the world is tranquil."[9] " Satisfaction " meant hegemony ; for he was obsessed by the " Napoleonic idea," which in " The Cambridge Modern History " is interpreted as follows :

" The ' Napoleonic ' conceptions of foreign policy may be summed up in a phrase, ' a European Confederation.' No more peace without honour, as under Louis Philippe ; no more universal war, as under the Republic ; but the ' loyal offer of alliance with France, to every government willing to continue with her in the defence of those interests which are common to all ? ' "[10]

But what were these interests ? Exoterically—liberty and national autonomy ; esoterically—French security,

the outward expression of the inward search after glory.
As Bismarck said : " He was vaguely aware that he
wanted war."

In 1851 the Great Exhibition was held in England.
It " seemed the emblem and harbinger of a new epoch in
the history of mankind, in which war should cease, and
the rivalry of the nations should at length find its true
scope in the advancement of the arts of peace."[11]
Then Mr. Fyffe writes :

> " Never had the ideal of industrious peace been more im-
> pressively set before mankind than in the years which succeeded
> the convulsion of 1848. Yet the epoch on which Europe was
> then about to enter proved to be pre-eminently an epoch of
> war. In the next quarter of a century there was not one of
> the Great Powers which was not engaged in an armed struggle
> with its rivals. Nor were the wars of this period in any sense
> the result of accident, or disconnected with the stream of
> political tendencies which make the history of the age. With
> one exception [the war in the Crimea] they left in their train
> great changes for which the time was ripe, changes which for
> more than a generation had been the recognized objects of
> national desire, but which persuasion and revolution had equally
> failed to bring into effect." [12]

War was to solve what peace desired but could not
establish ; war was to compel change, because peace
could only argue over consequences. It is not easy to
hammer a dozen pieces of iron into one lump, but it is
easy to fuse them together by fire, and what fire is in
the physical world war is in the political. So it happened
that once again Europe was to be plunged into the
crucible by blind forces and by blind men.

If a new war-epoch was about to open, as indeed it
was, what would be its nature ? What form would it
take, and what would be its deciding factor ? Did the
soldiers ask themselves these questions ? No ; once
again were they going to stumble into war blindfolded.
In 1851 a rifled musket of the Minié pattern was first
introduced into the British Army and tried out in the

Kaffir War of 1852, during which it was discovered that " at a range of from twelve to thirteen hundred yards small bodies of Kaffirs could be dispersed." [13] Its weight with bayonet was 10½ lbs., its bore ·702 inch and it was sighted from 100 to 1,000 yards. What did this mean ? It meant that the danger zone, the reach of the bullet, had been increased from 200 yards to at least 800 yards, and that, consequently, the whole of tactics had been changed, because soldiers would now have to fight their way forward single-handed over 800 yards of ground ; for smooth-bore case-shot, being out-ranged, could no longer support them.

Since 1851 no two European armies have met on the battlefield on equal terms. From now onwards in the hands of brave and disciplined men weapon-power was to dominate war as it had not done since the days of Gustavus Adolphus. Brave men there were, as the loss, on October 25, 1852, of the *Birkenhead* showed ; men worthy of the new rifle ; but the generals were as they had been depicted by Charles Napier fifty years before this date : " Under a long feather and cocked hat, trembling, though supported by stiff Hessian boots, gold-headed cane and long sword, I see the wizened face of a general grinning over the parapet of a fine frill, and telling extraordinary lies, while his claret, if he can afford claret, is going down the throats of his wondering or quizzing aides-de-camp." [14] These old men carried the old Brown Bess spirit into the new rifle tactics.

PART II

PERIOD OF NATIONAL CONSOLIDATION
1853—1871

CHAPTER III

THE WAR PERIOD OPENS, 1853—1860

Origins of the Crimean War. Condition of the British Army. War in the Crimea. Tactical Inventions. The Mutiny in India. Cavour and the Liberation of Italy. The Franco-Italian War of 1859. Progress in the Art of War.

ORIGINS OF THE CRIMEAN WAR

THE war in the Crimea was, in a sense, a political "throw-back"; it should have taken place in the eleventh century and not in the nineteenth, and the mere fact that it did take place in the middle of the nineteenth shows how electric and obscure the European atmosphere had become.

The elevation of Louis Napoleon as Emperor of the French had upset the balance of power. Nicholas looked upon him as an adventurer, and but grudgingly acknowledged his accession. Louis Napoleon not only felt this insult but recognized that his one hope of founding a dynasty was to wage a successful war, for choice against Russia, to cripple her and to grow strong on her lost blood. Nicholas's object was to control the Black Sea and its outlet; he believed Turkey to be in a dying condition and, ever since 1844, he had been bent on her partition.

As is generally the case in politics, neither side would openly state what it wanted, so a pretext had to be invented, and the one Louis Napoleon settled upon was the same which in the eleventh century had given rise to the Crusades, namely, the protection of the Holy Places in Palestine. He saw in this the means not only of launching a war against Russia but of conciliating Roman Catholic sentiment in France; for during this period a similar religious revival was taking place in

France as was represented in England by the Tractarian Movement. Greek and Latin monks had for centuries quarrelled over the guardianship of the Holy Places, when, in 1740, Louis XV had obtained from the Sultan, Mahmud I, Capitulations under which the members of "Christian and hostile nations" visiting the Ottoman Empire "were placed under the protection of the French flag." These Capitulations had fallen into abeyance; nevertheless, in order to stir up Russia, Louis Napoleon demanded their revival. Nicholas objected and, feeling that Austria would not oppose him on account of the assistance he had rendered her in 1849, that England was at the moment under the sway of a pacifist Government, and that Prussia was in the hands of a religious maniac who could not but welcome a crusade against the infidel, early in 1853 he sent Prince Menshikov with an ultimatum to Constantinople demanding (1) A recognition of the *status quo* as regards the Holy Places, and (2) the right to protect all orthodox Christians in the Ottoman Empire. On May 22, Menshikov, failing to obtain satisfaction, withdrew from Constantinople, and exactly a month later a Russian army under Prince Gorchakov crossed the Pruth, occupied the Danubian provinces and advanced into Moldavia and Wallachia.

The Turks, feeling certain of the support of the Western Powers, presented an ultimatum to Russia, which was rejected; whereupon, on November 30, the Russians destroyed a Turkish squadron at Sinope. This resulted, on January 3, 1854, in the British and French fleets entering the Black Sea. In February the Russian ambassador left London, and on March 27 Great Britain and France, and later on Sardinia, declared war.

CONDITION OF THE BRITISH ARMY

In 1852 the British budgetary expenditure stood at £52,000,000, of which an insignificant part was spent on military preparations. The army was in no state for any active service undertaking, small or large. For example, in an article under the heading of " Army Reform " published in *Blackwood's Magazine* about this time may be read the following effusion by General Sir John Fox Burgoyne :

" This great popular movement for an educational test for the army is uncalled for, delusive and mischievous. . . . At the public school will be found one set of boys who apply to their studies, and make the greater progress in them ; another set take to cricket, boating, fives, swimming, etc. Now, of the two, I should prefer the latter, as much more likely to make good officers ; but they are to be absolutely rejected, and for ever, unless they can come up to the mark in other matters, which are of no absolute use to them in their profession. . . . To extend these examinations to the higher ranks, even to that of captain, as the principal test of promotion, would be to keep men in school-boy trammels up to the age of between 30 and 40. It would be intolerable, and would destroy emulation in the real qualities for a good officer and soldier." [1]

I quote this not only to show the outlook of an eminent soldier at the date of the Crimean War but because a similar outlook has largely controlled promotion in the British Army until to-day. In 1930 I knew of a Major-General, aged 53, being adversely reported on for not playing field games.

However, in spite of Sir John Burgoyne and others, in 1853 the first field exercises since Waterloo were held at Chobham and in the following year 10,000 acres of training ground were bought in the Aldershot area. It was time that officers should be brought to realize that war was a serious undertaking. General Sir John Adye tells us that on his way out to the Crimea the ship he was in passed, near the entrance of the Dardanelles, a transport carrying British cavalry. " The officers in the transport," he writes, " made signs of their wish to communicate, so we lowered a bottle tied to a long string, which they picked up as it floated past, and we then pulled it back. We expected their inquiries might be as to the position of the Russians and the progress of the war, but their message was : ' Can you tell us who won the Two Thousand Guineas ? We have several bets, and are very anxious ! ' " (2)

WAR IN THE CRIMEA

Nicholas's calculations had been erroneous in the extreme. Not only had Great Britain joined France, but Austria had determined to march an army of 50,000 men into the Danubian States, which threat caused the Russian forces to fall back in August and recross the Pruth.

This done, it became the problem of the Allied Powers where to strike at Russia, and, though the difficulties were in no way examined, it was decided to occupy Sebastopol, destroy that growing fortress and so cripple Russian naval power in the Mediterranean. This decided upon, on September 7 the allied armies embarked at Varna, where they had already assembled, and began to cross the Black Sea.

The point selected for disembarkation was at Old Fort, thirty-five miles north of Sebastopol ; from here the allies marched south and were opposed by Menshikov on the river Alma. St. Arnaud, the French commander, already a dying man, put forward a vague plan of attack with little or no reference to the Russian dispositions of which he was ignorant, and Lord Raglan, commanding the British Army, was so afraid of friction arising that all unity of action was lost in attempts to maintain concord. On September 20 a battle was fought which compelled Menshikov to retire, but as no pursuit was attempted he did so at his ease.

At this juncture, somewhat late in the day, it was discovered that Old Fort was a most unsuitable base of operations ; it was, therefore, decided to march round the eastern flank of Sebastopol and establish another base at Balaklava and Kamiesh. Meanwhile Menshikov, having provided for the defences of the fortress, marched

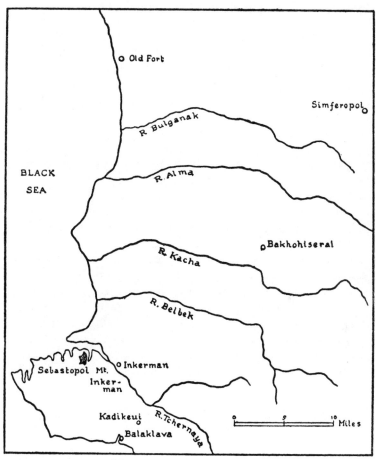

WAR IN THE CRIMEA, 1854-1856.

out to Simferopol, and such was the inefficiency of the security services in both armies, that, on September 25, each without knowing it crossed the other, the head of the British forces actually striking the tail of the Russians.

The base of operations having been changed, the next operation was to lay siege to Sebastopol, which was as yet but lightly defended. Had the Allies launched an immediate attack, in all probability the fortress would have been carried by assault ; but Canrobert (St. Arnaud having died on September 29) and Lord Raglan delayed until October 17, and were then repulsed.

The situation of the allied forces was an anxious one, for not only had they to lay regular siege to the fortress but also to protect their right flank which was open to attack. On October 25 came the attack which led to the two famous charges of the British Heavy and Light cavalry brigades. Then, on November 5, was launched a more formidable attack at Inkerman.

Inkerman has been called "a soldier's battle" and there have been many like it ; there was little or no direction and no control. On the Home Ridge, where the severest fighting took place, exposed to the full blast of the enemy's fire stood Lord Raglan and his staff. Eight British generals were killed, and, at the Sand Bag Battery, General Bosquet exclaimed "What a slaughter-yard !" The moral ascendancy of the British soldier was astonishing, Fortescue says :

"They met every attack virtually with a counter-offensive, and hesitated not to encounter any number whether with bullet, bayonet or butt. There never was a fight in which small parties of scores, tens and even individuals, showed greater audacity or achieved more surprising results. They never lost heart nor, by all accounts, cheerfulness. The enemy might be in front, flanks or rear, or at all three points together : it mattered not. They flew at them, quite undismayed and bored their way out. . . . Never have the fighting qualities of the British soldier been seen to greater advantage than at Inkerman. But it was wrong to call Inkerman, as it was styled, a soldier's battle. It was a regimental officer's battle, and to the regimental officer belongs the credit." [3]

Winter now came, yet no preparations had been made. From November 10 the rain poured down on troops without clothing, without camp kettles and without fuel; troops who had to eat their salt pork raw. The roads in the camps were seas of mud; a ham cost two guineas and beer three shillings the bottle. The men died by scores and hundreds daily of diarrhœa, dysentery and cholera. The medical services were strangled by red-tape, and when, on November 4, Florence Nightingale arrived at the Barrack Hospital, she found it standing in " a sea of sewage." With fierce resolution and courage she set to work and reduced the death rate from 42 per cent. to 2, while the politicians at home, terrified by the reports they received, did their utmost to shift the responsibility on to Lord Raglan.

Meanwhile Colonel Todleben, the Russian engineer in chief, added work after work to Sebastopol. In 1855, on account of Louis Napoleon's persistent interference, Canrobert resigned and was replaced by Pélissier, a soldier of resolute character. In May this general captured Kerch, and by cutting the peninsular off from the mainland sealed the doom of the fortress. On June 7 an assault was made on the Redan, and another on the 18th. On September 8 the French under General Bosquet stormed the Malakoff, General Macmahon being one of the first to mount the scarp. Meanwhile, on June 28 Lord Raglan died, of whom Fortescue writes: " No commander was ever worse treated, but maltreatment only evoked from him the greater loyalty and the higher standard of duty." [4] On February 26, 1856, an armistice was arranged, and on March 30 hostilities were finally brought to a close by the Treaty of Paris, by which Russia's armaments were strictly limited in the Black Sea; Bessarabia, obtained by her in 1814, was relinquished; and the renunciation of all rights of intervention between the Sultan and his

Christian subjects was enforced. Nicholas did not, however, live to experience this humiliation, for he died on March 2, 1855, and was succeeded by his son Alexander II.

In all, this uncalled for war cost the Allied Powers 252,600 men, and the Russian not far short of 500,000. In money it cost Great Britain £69,000,000, France £93,000,000 and Russia £142,000,000.

By crippling Russia in Europe, the defeat she had sustained induced her to turn her attention to Asia in order to restore her prestige. This was certainly not to the advantage of Great Britain, whose gains from the war were insignificant. Napoleon III had won a silver-gilt glory, all he had aimed at, and at the Peace Conference in Paris he had befriended Russia and opposed England. In Prussia it was believed that he would soon endeavour to overthrow the order established in Europe in 1815, and from about this date, as we shall see in Chapter V, Prussia began to set her military house in order and to prepare for the worst.

TACTICAL INVENTIONS

From the military point of view this war was remarkable for several reasons. Chloroform was used for the first time. And the Press began to exert an influence which made statesmen and generals tremble. It was the Press in England which clamoured for the siege of Sebastopol, thus stirring the imagination of the people and in turn influencing the Government. For the first time in the history of war newspaper correspondents accompanied the army to the front; and as witnesses of the appalling condition of the hospitals and the insufficiency of the supply services there can be no doubt they were instrumental in forcing a change.

As regards the art of war there is little to learn from this campaign. Generalship was beneath contempt, leadership was of a low order and tactics were prehistoric. The powers of the Minié rifle, though unmistakable, were almost entirely misapplied by the English and the French and the old musket equally so by the Russians ; all three of them relying on the bayonet and shock tactics. As of old, column met line ; and though attacks started as orderly movements, the ground and the fire soon broke them up into groups of men under little or no control.[5]

More interesting than tactics are the developments which began to take place in armaments, developments which did not attain maturity for sixty years. Amongst them are the suggested introduction of armour, and the use of lethal gas and the submarine.

As early as 1837 Jomini, after recounting the terrible destruction wrought by military inventions, said : " If Governments do not combine in a congress to proscribe these inventions of destruction, there will be no course left but to make the half of an army consist of cavalry with cuirasses, in order to capture with great rapidity these machines ; and the infantry, even, will be obliged to resume its armour of the Middle Ages, without which a battalion will be destroyed before engaging the enemy. We may then see again the famous men-at-arms all covered with armour, and horses also will require the same protection." [6]

Such a suggestion was useless without mechanical power, and such became possible when, during the Crimean War, Boydel steam engines fitted with footed wheels were sent out to negotiate the Balaklava mud. There can be little doubt that these traction engines suggested the idea of an armoured fighting machine to James Cowen, a philanthropist of this period, for he urged Lord Palmerston to use armoured traction engines fitted with scythes. " Like the Assyrian and British chariots their purpose was to mow a lane through the enemy infantry. This idea was, however, rejected as it was considered to be too barbarous." [7]

The suggestion of the use of lethal gas as a weapon is an even more interesting one. On May 12, 1812, the Earl of Dundonald placed a plan before Lord Melville

for " a new and most formidable method of attacking
and destroying an enemy's fleet . . . such a mode of
attack would be irresistible, and the effect of the power
and means proposed, infallible." [8] His idea was to
gas out the enemy's ships. Nothing came of this proposal ; but forty-two years later, in July 1854, he once
again submitted his " secret plan " to Sir James Graham,
First Lord of the Admiralty. His covering letter is
worth quoting ; he says : " Were it necessary—which
it is not—that I should place myself in an armchair on
the poop, with each leg on a cushion, I will undertake
to subdue every insular fortification at Cronstadt within
four hours from the commencement of the attack," and
Sebastopol could be as easily captured, he urged, " if
I am allowed to put my plans in execution." To the
possible objection of inhumanity, he wrote : " No
conduct that brought to a speedy termination a war
which might otherwise last for years, and be attended
by terrible bloodshed in numerous battles, could be
called inhuman, and that the most powerful means of
averting all future war would be the introduction of a
method of fighting which, rendering all vigorous defence
impossible, would frighten every nation from running
the risk of warfare at all." [9] Though the scheme was
not tried out, Dundonald predicted that gas as a weapon
" would ultimately become a recognized means of
warfare." [10] His day is not even yet.

The third of the " modern " weapons of war, the
submarine, also predates this period. In 1776 Bushnell
invented a submersible vessel which he called *The
Turtle ;* in 1797 Fulton invented another, and a
scheme was even suggested to rescue Napoleon from St.
Helena by an under-water boat. [11] During the war in
the Crimea Bauer, a German, built a large submarine
which he called the *Diable Marin* and offered it to
Russia. This is how this strange vessel arrived :

" In May, 1856, Bauer set out in his submarine for the harbour
of the fortress [Kronstadt] ; he was aided in his approach by a

very thick fog. The sentry on duty on the pier was amazed to see, emerging from the fog, a curious kind of vessel, of which only a small portion was discernible, and upon it stood a figure. At once the sentry challenged the stranger, and, to his amazement received in return the correct answer. This was altogether too much for the poor fellow, and throwing away his rifle, he ran from the ghostly visitant." (12)

It is strange to think that here in the first conflict of this new war period were suggested three weapons, the tank, lethal gas and the submarine, which influenced so largely the last war of this period. That they were not then used is not so strange, for, as far as war is concerned, statesmen and soldiers are generally two generations behind their times.

THE MUTINY IN INDIA

As the war in the Crimea died out, England found herself at war both in Persia and China, and, in 1857, was faced by the Indian Mutiny, which was a national uprising, its object being to cast off British rule. In 1757, the year of Clive's victory at Plassey, it had been predicted by Hindoo astrologers that this rule would last but a hundred years; and now, through the short-sightedness of the Government of India and the folly of Lord Dalhousie, the prediction was in part fulfilled and India began to regain her self-consciousness.

As early as 1817 Thomas Munro had pointed out that unless we admitted Indians into the government of their country we were riding for a fall. Lord Hastings expressed almost identical views in 1818; and Sir Henry Lawrence, in 1855, pointed out that " the natives had no outlets for their talents and ambitions as of old. . . . ' These outlets for restlessness and ability are gone; others are closing. It behoves us therefore now, more than ever, to give legitimate rewards, and as far as practicable employment, to the energetic few, to that leaven that is in every lump—the leaven that may secure our empire, or may disturb, nay even destroy it.' " [13]

Lord Dalhousie could not understand such liberalism, and, in the years immediately preceding the Mutiny, by humbling the Indian Princes and annexing their States he succeeded in making numerous enemies. During the conflict with Russia many troops had left India for the seat of war ; and in 1856 Canning, a weak man, who succeeded Dalhousie as Viceroy, upset the Indian Army by changing the recruiting regulations. All this was extremely foolish, for regimental mutinies had already occurred in 1843, 1844 and 1849.

The condition of the Army was normal ; that is to say it was rotten, for military efficiency is a rarity in India. The officers were inefficient and untrained, and were very much as they are described in the following letter addressed to Colonel Doyle, Military Secretary, on October 31, 1817, by a subordinate officer stationed at Agra :

" My dear Doyle,—The dawk [post] hour is approaching, so I must address you quickly. I had this morning for the first time a field day of instruction for my infantry brigade. . . .

" Commanding officers very rusty. One is deaf and blind— literally so. The second has never been before out acting with another regiment in line.

" A third has never been in command till within the last few days. The fourth has a voice like thunder, a figure like Lumbo Panjo, a seat in his saddle like a washball, but a clear head, and knows what he is about." [14]

In 1857, officers were sent out totally ignorant of the customs of the country. For instance, one engaging a servant asked him what his caste was, and got the reply : " Same caste as master, drink brandy sahib." Another, Colonel David Wood, of the Horse Artillery, " during dinner . . . turned gravely to one of the old Indian officers and said, ' Can you tell me what is a dhobie ? ' They all laughed, and it was explained that a dhobie was a man who washed your clothes. Wood, still grave, said : ' Oh, that accounts for the difficulty. I told mine to clean my horse and he refused.' " (15)

The Mutiny began at Meerut on May 11, 1857. The Crimean War was a fight in " a corner," but the Mutiny was a fight in " a continent." Its difficulties were not tactical but administrative and climatic. The enemy was beneath contempt, but the country was vast, only a hundred miles of railway existed, and the outward journey had to be broken at Suez, whither all water was brought by camels from the Nile nearly a hundred miles away. The nature of the fighting was frequently brutal. In June the massacre at Cawnpore took place, and retaliations naturally followed ; but it should not be overlooked that as all the prisons had been destroyed punishments for criminals were restricted to hanging and flogging.

With a few brilliant exceptions, such as John Nicholson, generalship was of a low order. Of Nicholson Fortescue writes : " It is remarkable that he seems to have been the first general officer who went everywhere and looked into everything with his own eyes." (16) Many of the others were far too old, being well in the sixties.

As regards the art of war there is little to learn from the Mutiny. " Every strategical and tactical principle was disregarded, and rightly disregarded, by the British commanders with practically perfect impunity ; "(17) but mobility was not one of the outstanding virtues of the army as it had been fifty years before in the days of Lord Lake. It is true, however, that in June, 1857, the Corps of Guides carried out the astonishing march of 600 miles in 22 days, and that General Rose's march of 1,000 miles to Kalpi and thence to Gwalior must always remain a memorable achievement, considering that it was carried out in the middle of the hot weather. " Men," writes one in an awful picture of one of Rose's marches, " began to talk of home and cool shady places and brooks as the hot wind begins to blow over them, parching up every drop of moisture in the body ; and dogs rush past with great raw wounds like sabre-cuts, caused by the sun, howling for water and shade."[18]

Generally speaking, however, movements were ponderous and slow. Thus Sir John Adye describes the approach of Sir Colin Campbell's army on Cawnpore on November 28, 1857 :

" What with the women and children, the wounded (amounting in all to 2,000 people) and the usual accumulations of camp equipage and stores which are inseparable from an Indian army in the field, his line of march extended for about twenty miles ; and when the strings of elephants, camels, bullock-waggons palanquins, etc., began to cross the bridge of boats the following day, the scene was more like the emptying of Noah's ark than anything else." [19]

In every way the Mutiny was an unfortunate event. Though, on February 17, 1858, it gave the British Army khaki uniform, it effaced from its memory the reverses of the Crimea and so had a reactionary influence on British military revival. Scarcely had it terminated than further trouble occurred in China which, in 1859, resulted in the French looting the Summer Palace in Pekin. The Taiping rebellion, yet another chaotic national movement, was then in its sixth year.

CAVOUR AND THE LIBERATION OF ITALY

In 1857, that is, immediately after the Crimean War, Napoleon III's position appeared secure enough. Russia lay defeated, England was embroiled in India, Austria was friendless and Prussia in the hands of a madman. Then in the following year came a change. On January 14 an attempt on the life of the French Emperor was made by Orsini, and though it failed it had a strange influence on the political situation. As the plot had been hatched in London, France accused England of sheltering political assassins. This led to the " Panic of 1859," the fear that France was about to invade England, and the Volunteer Movement of this same year. Then, on February 11, Orsini wrote to Louis Napoleon exhorting him to support Italian freedom. The Emperor, thoroughly terrified, thus came to believe that unless he took up arms in favour of Italy other attempts on his life would follow. Orsini had attacked him because he was an autocrat, and this attack had turned him into a democrat. Seldom, if ever, has a would-be political assassin so completely gained his point. And in the meanwhile other influences were at work.

From the fatal field of Novara onwards, Cavour, that " scientific intriguer," never for a moment changed his purpose—the driving of the Austrians out of Italy. Italy could not do so single-handed, an alliance was essential, and to gain an ally he plunged Sardinia into the Crimean War. It was a premeditated act to liberate Italy, and it had nothing whatever to do with maintaining the Ottoman Empire. Of it Fyffe writes :

" His Crimean policy is one of those excessively rare instances of statesmanship where action has been determined not by the driving and half-understood necessities of the moment, but by a distinct and true perception of the future. He looked only in one direction, but in that direction he saw clearly . . . every Italian whom Cavour sent to perish on the Tchernaya or in the cholera-stricken camps died as directly for the cause of Italian independence as if he had fallen on the slopes of Custozza or under the walls of Rome." [20]

As Cavour found it impossible to establish an alliance with England he somewhat reluctantly turned to France. Louis Napoleon wanted to regain Savoy and Nice, which had been incorporated by the French between 1792-1814 ; he also wanted Belgium and the Rhine provinces so as to re-establish the Rhine-Alps frontier. In the summer of 1858 he and Cavour met at Plombières where it was arranged that :

(1) Piedmont should pick a quarrel with Austria.
(2) France should act as her ally.

(3) Austria should be expelled from Venetia and
        Lombardy.
(4) Victor Emmanuel should become King of Northern
        Italy.
(5) The remainder of Italy, less the Papal States,
        should constitute the kingdom of Central Italy.
(6) These two kingdoms with Naples and Rome
        should form an Italian Confederation under the
        Pope.
(7) France was to receive Savoy and possibly Nice also.

In January, 1859, Napoleon III antagonized Austria
by saying that he regretted that the relationship between
the two countries was not so good as heretofore; and
Victor Emmanuel started the ball rolling by saying that
he could no longer be insensible to the sufferings of his
countrymen. Austria demanded that Sardinia should
disarm, and as Victor Emmanuel refused, on April 30
the Austrian troops under Gyulai crossed the Ticino.

THE FRANCO-ITALIAN WAR OF 1859

Gyulai was a most indifferent general. Instead of
pushing on and attacking the Sardinians before the French
could support them, he dawdled about; and the saying
that " he who does not know what he wants yet feels
that he must do something, appeases his conscience by a
reconnaissance in force " is applicable to his first action,
on May 20, at Montebello. There, Count Stadion, not
knowing what to reconnoitre, engaged fractions of his
corps, 24,000 strong, against 8,000 French, and was
severely beaten. Gyulai then fell back towards the
Quadrilateral. Louis Napoleon followed him up and a
battle took place at Magenta, some fifteen miles west of
Milan, where, on June 4, 54,000 allied troops defeated
58,000 Austrians, the French losing 4,000 killed and
wounded and the Austrians 5,700 besides 4,500 prisoners.
Four days later the French Emperor and Victor
Emmanuel entered Milan. On the same day the First

and Second French Corps, under Marshal Baraguay d'Hilliers, attacked the Austrian rearguard at Melegnano, a typical action of this period. The attack was a direct frontal " à la baïonnette " affair and without preparation, as simple and as crude as that of the Swiss carried out on the same field, at the Battle of Marignan, in 1515.

After this battle contact with the Austrians was lost ; war clouds were gathering in the north, for Germany was afraid that the conquest of Italy would be followed by the conquest of the Rhine. The Austrians meanwhile disappeared into the Quadrilateral ; then, on July 23, they turned about, recrossed the Mincio, and the next day ran into the greater part of the French army at Solferino where a purely encounter battle took place in which the Austrians were defeated losing 22,500 men to the Allies' 17,200.

The effects of this battle were profound. It awoke Italy, and, in awakening her, it awoke Napoleon from his dream of an Italian Confederation under Papal control. He therefore called a halt, and interviewed the Emperor Francis Joseph at Villafranca, where, on July 11, treaty of peace was signed. Austria though willing to give up Lombardy refused to part with Venetia. In March, 1860, Tuscany, Parma, Modena and the Romagna were united under Piedmont, Savoy and Nice being handed over to France. Thus was Italy, with the exception of Venice and Rome, united under Victor Emmanuel.

PROGRESS IN THE ART OF WAR

This war is noted as the first in which railways were extensively used for troop movements, and also as the first in which use was made of rifled cannon, the smaller fragmentation of its shells proving more effective than the old spherical ones. As the Austrian Lorenz rifle was a superior weapon to the French Minié, Louis Napoleon had instructed his troops that " arms of precision are only dangerous at a distance. They will not prevent

F

the bayonet being, as in former days, the terrible weapon of the French infantry,"[21]   At Solferino, according to Marshal Niel, " So long as it was a musketry fight I lost ground, owing to the enemy's advantage in numbers.   Then I formed a column of attack with one of the battalions of my reserve, and we won back with the bayonet more than we had lost with the fusilade."[22] This remark was probably intended to reach the French Emperor's ear ; anyhow, it had a misleading influence on the tactical lessons of the war.

It is true that the French method of attack was normally an impetuous rush, a " fuite en avant " as it was called, but their rifled guns enabled these attacks to be covered by fire.   Further, the French protected their attacking columns by swarms of skirmishers who took every advantage of the ground to creep close to their enemy and so make good the inferior range of their rifles.   Of the French attack at Solferino Colonel Chesney says : " The capture of the hill at Solferino was the fruit of long light infantry training, improved by experience in rough Algerian skirmish, and stimulated to the utmost quickness consistent with order by the example of the dashing Zouave . . . and by the natural intelligence of the French recruit ; "[23] and Moltke says : " The French distinguished themselves by tactical skill, good use of ground, and above all by a vigorous offensive,"[24] which, in the circumstances, was undoubtedly correct, seeing that the Austrians were utterly lacking in energy and initiative.

While the French, since the close of the Napoleonic wars, had occupied themselves little with the science of tactics, and had cultivated a high sense of leadership in Algeria, the Austrians fought their battles in accordance with the rules of the methodical fight as recommended in German military literature.   According to this school of thought the firing line was to be gradually nourished until the decision arose and an assault could be made. " But," as one critic truly says, " this moment never arrives, because the ' nourishing ' the fight causes new brigades to be brought up from the reserves, and the latter consequently dwindled so, that in spite of all the original superiority, nothing remained at the end to deliver the decisive blow with."[25]   This writer further adds that the French tactics " were neither entangled in theories, nor were they cleared up by definite maxims ; it was simply the natural emanation of their military skill which had been greatly increased by experience."[26] In short, the soldier will fight better left to himself than when trained under obsolete dogmas.   Out-of-date theories have consistently proved the ruin of armies.

CHAPTER IV

THE FIRST OF THE MODERN WARS, 1861-1865

The Origins and Nature of the American Civil War. The Grand-Strategy of the War. The Strategy of the War. The Tactics of the War. Military Inventions. Influences of the War on European Armies.

THE ORIGINS AND NATURE OF THE AMERICAN CIVIL WAR.

BARELY had the thunder of the guns died down at Solferino than the war clouds gathered in the West; and though at first it may seem that the stupendous civil war which was about to rock the continent of North America has little or nothing to do with events in Europe, on second thoughts it will be realized that the causes of this war were the same: They were a struggling upwards of the spirit of nationalism whose birthday dates even more truly from the signing of the Declaration of Independence on July 4, 1776, than from the storming of the Bastille on July 14, thirteen years later.

In the War of the Rebellion, 1775-1783, the American Colonies found liberty, a freedom endowed with the spirit of nationalism, which did not find solidarity; that is, it did not evolve into full nationhood, until the spirit of the Great Rebellion, the individual selfishness of the North and the South, had been squeezed out of the hearts of the people in the greatest civil war of modern times.

This titanic struggle within the frontiers of a divided people was in every way a modern conflict; it was the first of the great wars begotten by the industrial revolution; the second, in my opinion, being—the World War of 1914. In both, the origins of strife were at bottom economic; for, as Stephen Vincent Bénet dramatically proclaims, this war was

> "The pastoral rebellion of the earth
>   Against machines, against the Age of Steam,
>   The Hamiltonian extremes against the Franklin mean."[1]

The war with England, in 1812-1815, had thrown the Northern States on to their home industries, and, as is always the case, economic deficiencies were made good by war demands. Meanwhile, the Southern States remained predominantly agricultural, when, in 1820, the first decisive clash came with the " Missouri Compromise " which, as Bryce says, was in reality a truce between antagonistic revenue systems. Then, between 1824 and 1828, the tariff laws threw the main burden of taxation on to the Southern people who were consumers and not manufacturers, thus leading to a definite split in 1832, when South Carolina entered a protest against tariffs in the form of an Ordnance of Nullification. Then, this same year, into the controversy was thrust the question of slavery, and, " like the Trojan horse, it offered a very convenient vehicle by means of which to introduce discord and confusion into the heart of the edifice of the Constitution."[2] Though slavery gave leisure to the ruling class of the South it kept this class conservative and stagnant. " Wherever slavery was established, society took and kept a single and invariable form ; industry had its fixed variety and pattern ; life held to unalterable standards."[3]

The shifting of the economic causes of the war to the political sphere through the emotionalism begotten by the Abolitionist, or anti-slave, movement under Garrison and other fanatics, at once accentuated the importance of State rights. From the purely legal point of view each State was virtually autonomous ; consequently, when the Southern States seceded in 1860-1861 they had the law on their side. But what Jefferson Davis, the President of the Southern Confederacy, did not see was, that the industrial revolution was rapidly merging the

States into one great consolidated State, and that the force of circumstances had in fact replaced law; for between 1789, the year the Constitution was finally agreed upon, and 1861, the year in which the Civil War broke out, a new people had unconsciously been created by changes in environment. Strictly speaking, the North rebelled against the Constitution and the South against the Spirit of the Age.

As regards the nature of this conflict; it was a war within a half-formed nation, in which the North was fighting not a hostile army but a hostile people, and in which both sides were equally imbued with the justice of their cause. A war fought on the one side to maintain national unity, and on the other to retain State independence. For the North it could be no other than a war of conquest; it could end in no treaty, no argument, no terms, except unconditional surrender or separation. In its toils were gripped not only the future of America but the future of Western civilization; for the disruption of the United States would have resulted, rapidly or slowly, in changing the entire political and economic structure of Europe. [4]

THE GRAND-STRATEGY OF THE WAR

The destiny of this stupendous struggle lay in the hands of two men, Jefferson Davis on the one side and Abraham Lincoln on the other; and two such different men have seldom faced each other in the history of war. Lincoln was the son of the soil, Davis the artificial product of the study. The one had breathed into his soul the freedom of nature and, like primitive man, could best express his inner feelings through parables. The other had breathed the air of the cloister, and his soul had grown stiff as the parchment it had fed upon. The one was a democrat of the noblest type, the other an autocrat of unbreakable courage. Yet they had one thing in common; they both lacked knowledge of strategy. Nevertheless Lincoln grew to realize his ignorance, whilst Jefferson Davis until the end stood on the pedestal of his gigantic conceit.

As regards the grand-strategy of the war the problem was complexity itself ; for since neither side was in any way prepared for the conflict both had to start from the beginning. Further : both had to consider the possibility of European intervention ; and at the time Napoleon III, believing that the rising power of the United States was a direct menace to French trade, took the opportunity the war offered him to land an army in Mexico under Marshal Bazaine in order to support his protégé, Maximilian, who was crowned Emperor of Mexico in 1863.

On both sides the political object of the war was clear. The aim of the South was to regain recognition as an independent nation, or rather as a fraternity of States ; that of the North was to prevent this by compelling the South to re-enter the Union, and either abandon slavery or accept compensation instead. To defeat the North was scarcely possible ; consequently the only courses open to the South were either to tire the North out or to induce Europe to intervene and stop the war. Jefferson Davis had, however, no settled policy outside a rigid defensive broken by useless attacks, for which General Lee was mainly responsible. Davis believed that " cotton was king," and that lack of cotton would force European nations to intervene.

Except for the question of slavery, the grand-strategical problems which faced the Union Government were very similar to those which confronted the Allied Governments in 1914. The grand tactical idea of the North was to lay the entire Confederacy under siege, and slowly strangle it to death. Four grand-strategical problems faced Lincoln : The blockade of the Confederacy, the coast line of which stretched from Chesapeake Bay to the Mexican frontier, a distance of 3,500 miles ; the recruiting of the army and navy which was tackled with amazing success, seeing that nearly 3,000,000 men were enrolled and the navy increased from 40 steamships and 7,600 officers and men to 671 vessels, mostly steamers and many armoured, with a personnel of 51,000 ; the control of the army which was not successfully solved until the spring of 1864, when General Grant was given the supreme command ; and the emancipation of the slaves, in order not only to consolidate the country but to win over European opinion. It was not until January 1, 1863 that Lincoln was able to publish his Proclamation of Emancipation ; which date, in the opinion of Colonel Livermore, " marks an era in the history of the United States of America, second only to the 4th of July, 1776." [5]

The effects of this Proclamation were immediate. The moral victory was now won by the north, and in strategical effect the liberation of the slaves compensated for all the Confederate victories of 1861-62. Except for France, world opinion was now behind the North. In the World War of 1914-1918 a somewhat similar turning point was reached when the Germans torpedoed the *Lusitania*.

The political theatre of the war, the whole of the United States, some 3,000,000 square miles in extent, was inhabited by 31,000,000 people, of whom 9,000,000 were in the seceded States, and of these 3,500,000 were slaves. The tactical theatre, that is, the zone in which battles were fought, covered about a third of this area. It was bounded on the north by the rivers Missouri, Ohio and Potomac ; on the east by the Atlantic ; on the south by the Gulf of Mexico ; and on the west by the western boundaries of Louisiana, Arkansas and Missouri. In this area 2,200 combats were fought, 149 being important engagements ; on its coasts 1,504 blockade-runners were captured or destroyed, and during the four years of conflict approximately half a million men were killed or died of disease. To the North alone the war cost $4,750,000,000.

The entire theatre was by nature divided into three geographical areas : From the Atlantic to the Alleghany mountains ; from these to the Mississippi river ; and from that river to Mexico and the Pacific Ocean. The first was the area of the great political operations, the

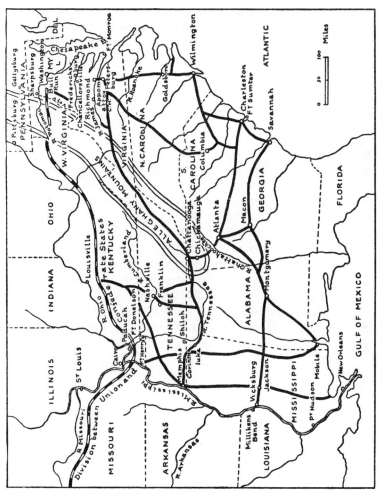

AMERICAN CIVIL WAR, 1861–1865.

attacks on the capital cities—Richmond and Washington ; the second was the scene of the great strategical operations based on the Mississipi and Tennessee rivers ; and the third was of minor strategical importance.

The country was badly roaded, a country suited for guerilla warfare and most difficult for a large organized army to operate in. Railways being few assumed a high importance, the waist of the whole Southern railway system, east to west, passing through the area Chattanooga—Atlanta—Macon. North of this lay the Alleghany range stretching for a thousand miles from Alabama to New York, separating the eastern political from the central strategical area.

The last of the great geographical factors which influenced strategy was the Mississippi. To the North its value was three-fold : it cut the Confederacy in two, severing the eastern States from the western ; it formed the main water-way from north to south, and, including the Ohio river, as far as Pittsburg in Pennsylvania. Once in Federal hands, it protected the right flank and rear of any army operating from Nashville round the southern extremity of the Alleghanies, and so towards the rear of the eastern political area, and towards Richmond. Strategically Chattanooga was the yard gate and Atlanta the back door of Virginia.

THE STRATEGY OF THE WAR

When, at half-past four on the morning of April 12, 1861, General Beauregard challenged the North to combat by firing upon Fort Sumter, Colonel Robert E. Lee still held his commission in the United States army, and Captain Ulysses S. Grant was seated as a clerk in his brother's leather store at Galena, Illinois. On May 10, Lee, for a brief space, was made Commander-in-Chief of the Confederate armies, and about the same time Grant offered his services to the Federal War Department, but his letter was not even answered. Yet, as fortune had it, on April 9, 1865, at Appomattox Court House, Lee in the full uniform of a General

surrendered to Grant who was dressed as a private
soldier. Not only was this surrender a triumph of
democracy over autocracy but of sound over indifferent
strategy.

The problem of the North was to crush the South
and occupy half a continent. How immense an army
was demanded by such an operation was not realized
until after the First Battle of Bull Run, fought on July 21,
1861. In this fight, which took place almost under the
entrenchments of Washington, the Confederate Government unwittingly started out on an admirable strategy ;
for the rout of the Federal forces so terrified Lincoln
and his ministers that for more than two and a half
years the security of Washington obsessed the Northern
political brain to such an extent that it distorted the
whole of the Union strategy in the East.

The first result was that Lincoln gave General
McClellan command of the army. This soldier, though
an able strategist and administrator, possessed little
fighting instinct. He saw that the protection of Washington lay in threatening Richmond, and that to defeat
the South demanded a highly organized army. His plan
was to transfer by sea 100,000 men to Fortress Monroe,
to advance this army on Richmond, whilst another army,
40,000 strong, under General McDowell advanced from
Washington southwards. McClellan's advance was
methodical in the extreme, and by the time he was in
sight of Richmond Lee was sending Jackson into the
valley of Virginia, which so played upon the nerves of the
Federal Government that McDowell's army was withdrawn. This wrecked McClellan's plan ; he was defeated
in the Seven Days' battle and retired to the river James
to reorganize.

The terror in Washington was so great that it was
decided to withdraw McClellan, and meanwhile, in order
to protect the capital, an army was hastily assembled
about Fredericksburg under General Pope. Lee, learning that McClellan was to be withdrawn, at once moved
north, and by a brilliant outflanking manœuvre forced

Pope back and defeated him at the Second Battle of Bull Run, on August 29 and 30. Then he committed a blunder of the first order ; he abandoned his defensive strategy and decided to invade Maryland and carry the war into the enemy's country. In his enthusiasm to save Virginia he cast strategy to the winds and sought a tactical decision. What he should have done was what General Nathaniel Greene did in North Carolina in 1781—avoided pitched battles and relied on rapidity of manœuvre to strike at weakness and at his enemy's lines of communication. The result was that with an army half clothed and half-fed, (for Lee was a most indifferent administrator), on September 17 he was defeated by McClellan at the battle of Antietam (Sharpsburg), and was compelled to with-draw south.

From now onwards throughout the remainder of 1862 and the whole of 1863 the strategy of the Federal Government was pivoted on the capture of Richmond, not so much in order to win the war as to prevent Lee operating against Washington. On December 13, General Burnside, who had superseded McClellan, was severely repulsed at Fredericksburg, and on May 2-3, 1863, Hooker, who had superseded Burnside, met a similar fate at Chancellors-ville. And then Lee committed his second strategical blunder. Having learnt nothing from his Antietam campaign, he decided once again to invade Maryland. He did so in June, and was defeated at Gettysburg by General Meade on July 1-3.

Meanwhile, what was happening in the West ? Here trial and error, those gropings in the dark, were by geography forced into line and compelled to march forward according to a fixed strategical plan. This plan was initiated by Grant when as a brigadier-general he occupied the city of Cairo on September 4, 1861. From there he saw the strategic value of the Mississippi, and without awaiting orders he occupied Paducah which blocked the mouth of the Tennessee river. The struggle for the Mississippi had begun, and out of it grew an amazing strategical plan.

Early in November Grant urged Halleck, his commanding officer, to move on Forts Henry and Donelson, two
works built by the Confederates to block the Tennessee
and Cumberland rivers; yet it was not until February 1
that Halleck gave Grant orders to make the movements,
which he did on February 6 and 16 respectively. The
fall of Donelson was the first decisive success gained by
the Federals during the war. It won Kentucky and laid
Tennessee open to invasion; it swept back the whole
Confederate line, depriving the South of an area which
would have supplied it with at least 100,000 soldiers.

The loss of Donelson compelled the Confederates to
abandon the Mississippi between Cairo and Memphis,
and led to the battle of Shiloh, on April 6-7, in which
Grant was surprised and only saved himself from defeat
by his courage and tenacity. Then followed the occupation of Corinth, and the capture of New Orleans on May
1, and, what was even more important, the removal of
Halleck on July 11, to Washington, which enabled Grant
rapidly to develop the strategy which ultimately won the
war.

After Shiloh Grant clearly saw that the next move
should be made on Vicksburg; for, Vicksburg won, the
entire Mississippi would be in Federal hands and the
Confederacy would not only be cut in half but completely blockaded. First clearing the area around
Corinth and Iuka, in November he moved south, but was
compelled to fall back on account of a raid which cut his
line of communications. Then he moved south again,
this time down the Mississippi, and, on January 30, 1863,
arrived at Milliken's Bend a little north of Vicksburg.
From here for three months he carried out a desperate
campaign among the swamps, and then decided to run
the gauntlet of the Vicksburg batteries, abandon his
communications, and attack the fortress on its eastern
flank. This he did early in May; and then followed one
of the most brilliant campaigns in history, Vicksburg
capitulating on July 4.

After Vicksburg Grant urged the Federal Government

to allow him to move on Mobile so as still further to
contract the Confederacy; but this was not allowed.
Then, early in October, he was ordered to Chattanooga
to relieve General Rosecrans, who, having been badly
defeated at the battle of Chickamauga on September
19-20, was now in a desperate situation. Grant arrived
there on October 23, and a month later decisively
defeated the Confederates under General Bragg, and was
planning to push on to Atlanta when, on March 3, he
was called to Washington to take over supreme command.

Here he at once got down to his plan. He decided on
an overland movement on Richmond, with the main
army, the Army of the Potomac, under General Meade,
flanked by two smaller forces, one in the Valley of
Virginia and one operating from Fortress Monroe. The
object of these armies was to force Lee to fight, and to
compel the Confederate Government to send every man
to his support. Whilst these three armies held Lee as in a
vice, Sherman, at the head of 100,000 men was to advance
from Chattanooga, drive the Confederate forces before
him, occupy Atlanta, advance on Savannah, and, once
based on this port, either move to Richmond by sea or
advance northwards through the Carolinas and so attack
Lee's rear and deprive the Confederacy of its administrative base of operations—its food supply.

This stupendous project was put into force on May 5,
1864. Rapidly Grant moved forward, and battle after
battle took place in Virginia—in the Wilderness, at
Spottsylvania, North Anna, Totopotomoy and Cold
Harbour, the last being fought on June 3. With con-
sumate skill Lee defended himself; then, on June 15,
Grant, with an audacity seldom equalled, swung across
his enemy's front, bridged the James river and lay siege
to Petersburg. Meanwhile Sherman moved forward,
entered Atlanta on September 2, carried out a campaign
against General Hood, marched through Georgia and
occupied Savannah on December 21.

Grant, having been held up before Petersburg during
the autumn and winter of 1864, in the spring of the

following year, as Sherman was approaching from the south, determined to move south of Petersburg and so prevent Lee from joining up with the forces opposing Sherman. This brought about the withdrawal of Lee and, on April 9, 1865, the surrender of his army at Appomattox Court House.

Such was the general strategy of the campaign, a vast encircling movement, and the eventual attrition physical, moral and economic of the entire Confederacy, a condition such as we do not meet with again until 1918.

THE TACTICS OF THE WAR

Tactically this war is an interesting one. Fighting opened much as it had done in the wars which followed the French Revolution, the Federals attempting to imitate regular soldiers and the Confederates naturally taking to a loose order of fighting. Throughout the war the rifle proved the dominant factor, the bayonet was little used and assaults proved increasingly costly. After Shiloh practically every battlefield was entrenched, and in the later stages of the war in Virginia field defences assumed an aspect similar to that seen fifty years later in north-eastern France. Thus did the defensive grow in strength. Colonel Lyman writes : " Put a man in a hole and a good battery on a hill behind him, and he will beat off three times his number, even if he is not a good soldier ; "[6] and Frank Wilkeson, a private soldier, says : " Before we left North Anna I discovered that our infantry were tired of charging earthworks. The ordinary enlisted men assert that one good man behind an earthwork was equal to three good men outside it."[7]

Battles may be said to have been ultra modern in their character. Here is a graphic description by Colonel Lyman of a " 1914 " battle fought in 1863 :

" I had taken part in two great battles, and heard the bullets whistle both days, and yet I had *scarcely seen a Rebel* save killed, wounded or prisoner ! I remember how even line officers, who were at the battle of Chancellorsville said : 'Why, we never saw any Rebels where we were ; only smoke and bushes, and lots of our men tumbling about ' ; and now I appreciate this most fully. The great art is to *conceal* men ; for the moment they show, *bang, bang*, go a dozen cannon, the artillerists only too pleased to get a fair mark. Your typical 'great white plain,' with long lines advancing and manœuvring, led on by generals in cocked hats and by bands of music, exist not for us. Here it is, as I said : 'Left face—prime—forward ! '—and then *wrang wr-rang*, for three or four hours, or for all day, and the poor bleeding wounded streaming to the rear. That is a great battle in America." [8]

" A fire fight between attacking and defending infantry almost always ended in the success of the latter." [9] Colonel Henderson once asked a veteran of the war " whether men could be got to advance shoulder to shoulder," and the answer he received was : " No, God don't make men who could stand that." [10]

Battles grew more and more prolonged, in truth we shall see nothing like this in 1866, 1870 and 1904. Why ? is not asked, and yet in the answer lies a world of knowledge. For instance, John Codman Ropes, whose knowledge of or interest in the war no man can doubt, has but a faint idea of its tactical nature. To him there is no trace of Marlborough, Wellington or Napoleon in Grant's last campaign—" its terribly bloody battles, its encounters of every day . . . the noble trees cut down by musket balls . . . the thousands upon thousands of brave men slain and maimed, and, above all, the indecisive results, amaze, terrify, repel, dishearten us." And again : " The experience of the Army of the Potomac in the campaign was in fact a new experience for soldiers. Sacrifices were demanded every day of the rank and file of the army which had hitherto been required only occasionally, and then only from those selected for some special post of honour or danger." These things he cannot understand : " To lie in a new-dug rifle-pit a hundred yards from the enemy for several days under constant fire is much like the experience of the engineer troops in a siege. To rush from the rifle-pit upon the enemy's works is the act of a forlorn hope, whose gallant performance is the admiration of a storming column, itself selected for a special and dangerous service. But it is not every day that the sap is pushed forward or the breach assaulted." [11]

Why cannot he understand them ? Why does he talk of Marlborough, of Wellington, of new experiences, of rifle-pits, prolonged battles, siege works and indecisive results ? Because he does not understand that the rifle bullet has completely revolutionized tactics. His knowledge enables him to place his fingers on the pulse of war, yet he cannot count its heart beats, nor can he diagnose its fever. He is blind to the reality of rifle warfare ; yet, though he wrote the above in 1884, he was no blinder than the majority of generals of thirty years later, or many of to-day. The rifle bullet utterly changed tactics, and unless this is understood all knowledge is a blank, or worse—a danger.

MILITARY INVENTIONS

It is, however, in the realm of military inventions that this war is so extraordinarily modern. In the half century preceding it what do we see ? Eli Whitney's cotton gin [12] transforming the South ; Fulton's steamships plying the waters of the Hudson, Delaware, Ohio and Mississippi ; railways developing apace between 1840 and 1860 ; the electric telegraph established in 1844, and McCormick's reaper conquering the prairies of the West.

During the war these inventions were followed by others. A breech-loading rifle was adopted ; even a magazine-loading rifle and a machine gun were invented. Torpedoes, land mines, submarine mines, the field telegraph, lamp and flag signalling, wire entanglements, wooden wire-bound mortars, hand-grenades, winged-grenades, rockets and many forms of booby traps were tried out. Armoured trains were used ; balloons were employed by both sides ; and though the Confederates did not think much of balloons they made one out of

G

silk dresses. To the sorrow of many a Southern beauty it was speedily captured, " the meanest trick of the war," so says General Taliaferro.[13] Explosive bullets are mentioned, and in June, 1864, General Pendleton asked the Chief Ordnance Officer at Richmond whether he could supply him with " stink-shell " which would give off " offensive gases " and cause " suffocating effect." The answer he got was ". . . stink-balls, none on hand ; don't keep them ; will make if ordered."[14] Nor did modernity halt here, for in sea warfare a complete revolution was established, the *Merrimac* and the *Monitor* in one day—March 9, 1862—rendering obsolete the wooden navies of the entire world ; ramming replaces boarding, and in England Sir John Hay said : " the man who goes into action in a wooden ship is a fool, and the man who sends him there is a villain." " A submarine was built by Horace L. Huntley at Mobile—twenty feet long, five deep and three and a half wide, which was propelled by a screw worked from the inside by seven or eight men."[15] On February 17, 1864, she sank U.S.S. *Housatonic* off Charleston and went down with her.

Colonel Lyman is as amusing when writing on war inventions as many a writer during the World War. On November 29, 1864, he jotted down in a letter :

" I did not have room to tell you of the ingenious inventions of General Butler for the destruction of the enemy. He never is happy unless he has half-a-dozen contrivances on hand. One man has brought a fire-engine, wherewith he proposes to squirt on earthworks and wash them down ! An idea that Benjamin [Butler] considers highly practicable. Then with his Greek fire he proposes to hold a redoubt with only five men and a small garden engine [a flame projector]. ' Certainly,' said General Meade ; ' only your engine fires thirty feet, and a Minié rifle 3,000 yards, and I am afraid your five men might be killed before they had a chance to burn up their adversaries ! ' Also he is going to get a gun that shoots seven miles and, taking direction by compass, burn the city of Richmond with shells of Greek fire. If this don't do, he has an auger that bores a tunnel five feet in diameter, and he is going to bore to Richmond, and suddenly pop up in somebody's basement, while the family are at breakfast! So you see he is ingenious. It is really summer warm to-day; there are swarms of flies, and I saw a bumble bee and a grasshopper."[16]

Life in camp and bivouac was equally modern though a little rougher. Newspaper boys were seen not only behind the battlefields but on them, and at least one regimental newspaper, *The Rapid Ann*, called after the Rapidan, was published.[17] "Delousing" was a frequent "operation of war," men "seated shirt in hand on the ground, endeavouring to pick the vermin off that garment."[18] This done, they would open tins of condensed milk[19] and brew their tea or coffee as they did in 1914-18.

INFLUENCE OF THE WAR ON EUROPEAN ARMIES

In Europe the lessons of this war were left almost entirely unexamined, for, with the exception of a book written by Sir Henry Havelock entitled *Three Main Military Questions of the Day*, published in 1867, little notice was taken of this war until 1898, when Colonel Henderson published his *Stonewall Jackson*. By continental Powers the whole struggle was looked upon as a kind of backwoodmen's affair; there was no spit and polish about it, it lacked the professional touch; consequently it was beneath the dignity of professional soldiers to examine it. To Graf von Moltke it was but a matter of "two armed mobs chasing each other around the country, from which nothing could be learned"; and in England Lord Wolseley so little appreciated its significance that, as late as 1898 in his introduction to Henderson's *Stonewall Jackson*, he could write: "Had the United States been able early in 1861, to put into the field, in addition to their volunteers, one Army Corps of regular troops, the war would have ended in a few months." Surely one army corps in the continent of America, confronted by the riflemen of the South, would in a few weeks have met the fate of Braddock and his Regulars on the Monogahela in 1755, or of Lord Percy and his Red Coats at Lexington twenty years later.

Moltke, however, did recognize this : " That the fire of stationary troops was so much more effective than that of troops advancing that it would be well to combine as far as possible a tactical defensive with a strategical offensive,"[20] and Havelock suggested [21] reducing the British infantry and forming a body of 7,890 mounted riflemen on the pattern of those used during this war. Nevertheless, the bayonet still dominated the minds of European soldiers, who took no notice of the fact that Federals and Confederates saw so little use in it that many men threw this weapon away, much as they did at the battle of Rocroi in 1643, when soldiers threw away their pikes and picked up muskets.

Yet during these years some progress was made. In 1862 Henri Dunant, a Genevese philanthropist, published a book entitled *Un Souvenir de Solférino* in which he described the sufferings of the wounded. It was this book which resulted in the assembly of a conference at Geneva in 1863, and the signing of the first Geneva Convention, on August 22, the following year.

In England the only military results of the war were that, in 1867, tinned mutton was issued to the Navy and nicknamed " Fanny Adams " after a contemporary murderess who disposed of her child by boiling it down ; and further, that the Minister of War began to stir himself and enquire into the work of his numerous subordinates. Whilst on one of his inspections he met a gentleman in the passage and asked him what hour he usually came to his duty.

" ' Oh ! ' said the gentleman in reply, ' I usually stroll in about eleven or twelve o'clock.' ' Stroll in ? ' said the minister, in surprise ; ' then I presume you do not leave until a late hour ? ' ' Well,' replied the gentleman, ' I generally slip off about three o'clock.' ' Slip off at three ? ' said the minister, much scandalized. ' Pray, sir, may I ask what department you belong to ? ' ' Certainly,' said the young man ; ' I come every Saturday to wind up the clocks ! ' " [22]

CHAPTER V

THE RISE OF PRUSSIA, 1861-1869

The Foundations of German Unity. The Seven Weeks' War. Lessons of the Seven Weeks' War. Decay of the British Army. The Prussian and French Armies.

THE FOUNDATIONS OF GERMAN UNITY

WHILE the conflict in America was being fought out to its bitter end crucial changes were taking place in Europe.

On June 24, 1859, the guns of Solferino had awakened Prussia to the reality which now faced her—the hegemony of France and the possible loss of the Rhineland Provinces; just as John Brown's raid on Harper's Ferry, on October 16 this same year, had roused the North and the South of the United States to an equally great reality. Still one more date must be mentioned in this memorable year: On November 24 appeared Charles Darwin's master work *On the Origin of Species by Means of Natural Selection, or the Preservation of Favoured Races in the Struggle for Life.* Its doctrines and speculations fitted the times as a glove fits the hand; so that consciously and unconsciously it was to be the oracle of contending nations, and its main idea was to be adopted as the leading doctrine of a prince, mystic, actor and egotist, then but eleven months old, by name Frederick Wilhelm Victor Albert, who in 1888 became William II Emperor of Germany.

In 1858 Frederick William IV of Prussia was becoming totally insane, and Prince William, who was born in 1797 and had been present at the battle of Arcis-sur-Aube in 1814, a soldier by instinct and education, became regent. On January 2, 1861, as King William I of Prussia, in his speech from the throne, he said: " The Prussian Army will, in the future, also be the Prussian Nation in Arms."

He at once set about to reorganize his army, for his

object was to create an effective war force of 371,000 men,
backed by a reserve of 126,000 and a Landwehr of 163,000.
To carry out this work he appointed Count von Roon as
his Minister of War ; Count von Moltke he had already
made Chief of the General Staff in 1858 ; and in 1862 he
selected Otto von Bismarck as his President-Minister.

Bismarck's policy was simple enough ; it was to drive
Austria out of Germany.   In the middle distance stood
France, a formidable adversary.   Russia was virtually out
of the picture.   In 1861 Alexander II, who had succeeded
Nicholas I in 1855, was occupied in reforming his people,
and giving the serfs the liberation which led to the Polish
insurrection of 1863.   Meanwhile, as if fate had ordained
it, Napoleon III emasculated his army by sending many
of his most efficient regiments to Mexico, where the bulk
of them remained until 1866-67.   Bismarck's road was thus
cleared, so he determined to travel along it at top speed.

THE SEVEN WEEKS' WAR

The settlement of the Schleswig-Holstein question in
1850 had never given Denmark complete satisfaction, and
when Charles IX succeeded to the Danish throne in 1863
the situation once again grew so acute that Saxon and
Hanoverian troops marched into Holstein.   Here was
Bismarck's opportunity.   He persuaded Austria to join
Prussia and restore peace : This action led to the
Schleswig-Holstein war of 1864, which, in October, was
concluded by the Treaty of Vienna, putting the Duchies
under the joint control of Austria and Prussia.

Bismarck knew well what he was doing.   Schleswig-
Holstein would become a bone of contention, and in
order to prepare for the inevitable war with Austria he
sought Italy as an ally.   Napoleon III stood in the way ;
so he promised him a free hand in Belgium, or part of the
Rhinish Provinces, if he in his turn would persuade
Austria to sell Venetia to Italy, which he knew Austria
would refuse to do.   Simultaneously, in order to annoy
Austria Bismarck reopened the question of German
federation.   As Austria would not part with Venetia,

a treaty of offensive and defensive alliance was signed by
Italy and Prussia on April 8, 1866 ; whereupon, trouble
arising in Schleswig-Holstein, to detach Italy, Austria
offered to cede Venetia, but it was now too late.

Seeing the gathering storm approaching, Louis Napoleon, believing that the time had come to obliterate the
treaties of 1815, was ready to join Prussia with 300,000
men in return for the Rhinish Provinces. Bismarck,
having no intention whatever of parting with them, in
order to precipitate the conflict now that Italy was an
ally, ordered troops into Holstein, whereupon Austria
broke off diplomatic relations on June 12.

The war which now took place is one of exceptional
interest. It was not a war of aggression in the common
meaning of the word, nor a war of conquest, but a war
of diplomacy—of rectification. The object of Prussia
was not to humiliate Austria or even to weaken her,
but to persuade her that the spirit of nationalism in
Germany was a living growing force which demanded
unity. Strategically the war was interesting, because
Austria was a veteran military Power, whilst, excepting
the Danish wars, few Prussian officers had any actual war
experience ; for Prussia had been at peace since 1815.

Tactically it is of equal interest, for though breech-
loading rifles and even repeating rifles had been used
during the American Civil War, this was the first war
in which one army armed with the breech-loader met
another armed with the muzzle-loader. In spite of the
fact that the Prussian needle gun was sighted to 400
metres whilst the Austrian Lorenz rifle was sighted to
1,000, it was the main tactical factor which led to the
Austrian defeat because it could easily be loaded when
the firer was prone, whilst the other could not be.
That this superiority could have been annulled by a
correct use of artillery was unrecognized by the Austrian
General Staff, in spite of the fact that the Austrian Army
had been re-equipped with rifled cannon in 1863, with
effective shrapnel range of 2,000 yards and case-shot
range of 500 yards.

The Austrian tactics were completely obsolete, reliance being placed on close formations and the bayonet. General von Horsetzky writes that in 1863 the Austrians taught the soldier " that the bayonet is not only useful for turning the enemy out of their positions, but that it should also appeal to the honour of brave men. . . ."[1] In 1859 they had watched the French successfully employ close quarter fighting, so they now decided to do the same, but they overlooked the fact that the advantage of closing lay not in range and accuracy but in rapidity of fire. They thus directly played into the hands of the Prussian riflemen.

Whilst the mind of the Austrian Staff floated in a nebulous past that of the Prussian probed into the future. This was the true secret of their success. Ever since 1852 Moltke had studied the use of railways for strategic movement, and also the telegraph, and by means of the latter he directed operations during the opening days of the war from Berlin. Further, he had saturated his mind with the doctrines of Clausewitz, which, right or wrong, endowed his strategy with a one-pointedness totally lacking in his opponent's.

His problem was by no means an easy one; for, besides his advance on Austria directly supported by Saxony, he had to wage a campaign against the Hanoverians, Bavarians, Hessians, Württembergers, Badensers and Nassauers reinforced by an Austrian division in western Germany. Fortunately for him Italy advanced into Venetia, and though, on June 24, Victor Emmanuel's army was defeated at Custozza, 80,000 Austrians were drawn away from the main theatre of war. In Italy this force remained until after Prussia's victory at Königgrätz (Sadowa).

Foreseeing that on account of railway communications his enemy would move on Olmütz, Moltke decided to advance two armies into Bohemia : the First, under Prince Frederick Charles, on Münchengrätz, and the Second, under the Crown Prince, on Trautenau-Nachod. These two armies were to unite in the vicinity of Gitschin.

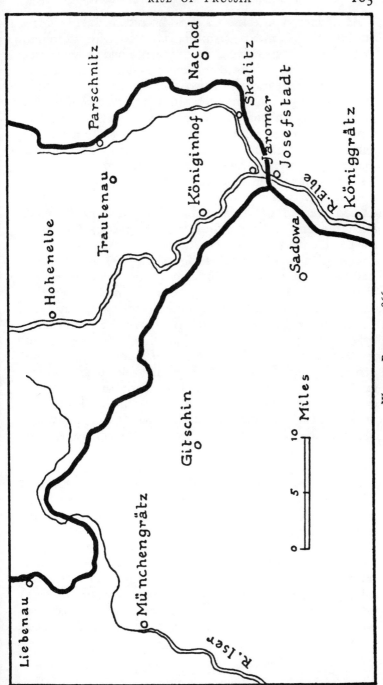

WAR IN BOHEMIA, 1866.

As Prince Frederick Charles neared Münchengrätz, the Austrians under Clam-Gallas retired to Gitschin, and the Crown Prince, having sustained a check at Trautenau and gained victories at Nachod and Skalitz, compelled Benedek, the Austrian Commander-in-Chief, to fall back on Sadowa. On June 30 the two Prussian armies were sufficiently close to unite at short notice. On July 3 the battle of Königgrätz was fought, the First Army engaging the Austrians during the morning and drawing them in, whilst in the afternoon the Second fell upon their right flank and crumpled it up. Though the victory was decisive, the Austrians losing nearly 45,000 men in killed, wounded and prisoners, Benedek with the greater part of his forces (150,000) got away, for the Prussian armies were in such an inextricable state of confusion that pursuit was out of the question. Moltke had issued orders on the 18th for a concentration around Wagram, of 1809 fame, when, on the 21st, an armistice was agreed upon, to begin at noon the following day.

The immediate result of the Austrian defeat at Königgrätz was that the Emperor Francis Joseph telegraphed to Napoleon III to intervene. On account of his wild goose chase in Mexico he could not afford to embark in a war; further, the rapid Prussian victories were entirely contrary to his expectations. Then, the armistice being signed, Bismarck demanded that Saxony, Hanover, Hesse-Cassel and other north German territory should be annexed to Prussia, and to gain the French Emperor's consent he hinted that France might take Belgium. Eventually, under the treaty of Prague, signed on August 23, though the integrity of the Austrian monarchy was preserved Venetia was transferred to Italy; Schleswig-Holstein went to Prussia; the States north of the Main were formed into a North German Confederation under Prussia, and those south into a separate southern union; Saxony was, however, left intact. The general results of the war were that Austria lost her Venetian encumbrance and had to pay an indemnity of £6,000,000; Victor Emmanuel gained the whole of Italy less Rome, and William I annexed Hanover, Hesse-Cassel, Nassau and the free city of Frankfort, and established a federal parliament which assembled in Berlin in 1869.

Meanwhile, a political party, the National Liberal, was formed. It demanded the union of south and north Germany. Such a fusion, in spite of a customs parliament now agreed upon by these two groups of States, would have taken a long time to effect had not the folly of the French Emperor brought such outward pressure to bear on the whole of Germany as to render it inevitable. He did exactly what Bismarck calculated he would do. Even before the signing of the Treaty of Prague he claimed the left bank of the Rhine in compensation for Prussia's gain in power, and this idea still obsessed him. The result was that fear of France threw the Southern States into the arms of the Northern, and a secret offensive and defensive alliance under the command of the King of Prussia was agreed upon. " A common war against a common enemy now appeared the surest means of welding the dissevered halves of Germany together, and for this war Bismarck steadily prepared." [2]

LESSONS OF THE SEVEN WEEKS' WAR

Though in war the moral to the physical may, as Napoleon said, be three to one, it must never be forgotten that the physical is the foundation of the moral, for it is weapon-power which creates fear. In 1866 this is clearly seen in the influence of the needle gun. " Our men," says an Austrian Colonel, fear " . . . the quick and easy loading the needle gun gives you; it is this which demoralizes them. In action they feel themselves disarmed the greater part of the time, whereas you [the Prussians] are always ready to fire." [3]

Against the massed Austrian formations protected by few skirmishers, its effects were terrible. At the battle of Nachod the Prussian advanced guard, six and a half battalions, held back twenty-one Austrian battalions for two hours and inflicted five times their own losses on them. At Trautenau it was much the same, for though the Austrians were successful they lost four times as many men as the Prussians. Again at Königgrätz, though for seventeen hours Benedek fought on the defensive with odds of five to three in his favour, yet the Austrians lost 18,000 killed and wounded to the Prussian 9,000. Of Trautenau Friedjung writes: " Seldom in military history has it happened that combatants who lost three or four times as heavily as their adversaries were yet victorious. This alone shows that it would have been impossible to go on fighting with the muzzle-loader against the needle gun ; in victory as well as in defeat the Austrians always lost three or four times as many men as the Prussians, while their rapidity of fire was by the same proportion less."[4]

Though the needle gun is quite sufficient to account for the failure of the Austrian cavalry, it must not be overlooked that against infantry its terrible effects were largely due to the excellence of the Prussian musketry training and minor tactics. Nevertheless in combined tactics the Prussians had much to learn. Their General Staff had studied the 1859 campaign with respect to infantry, but they had failed to take any notice whatever of the French artillery tactics. " The theory of making use of forces piece by piece, until the last intact reserve is reached [the methodical attack], with all its consequences, amongst which may be especially noted the splitting up of the artillery and the employment of the artillery mass for the first time in the final act of decision, was considered as the only valid one and as being alone suited to the nineteenth century." [5]

At Nachod the Prussians fought almost entirely without artillery, the guns being placed at the tail of the attacking corps. At Skalitz it was the same ; then the General Staff awoke to reality, a reality so well known to Frederick the Great and Napoleon. At Königgrätz the manœuvre battle replaced the methodical attack. To prepare the way the guns were brought forward and massed, and under cover of their fire the infantry advanced. Yet after the war the old theory fought hard for its existence, and though the breech-loader had disturbed all previous calculations, as Colonel Maude says : " No one stopped to inquire what would have happened had both sides been armed with similar weapons. Everyone put down the comparative immunity the Prussian Infantry had enjoyed to the fact that they fought as skirmishers—and not to the accident that they were able to load lying down." [6]

DECAY OF THE BRITISH ARMY

In 1864, when Prussia invaded Holstein, England could do nothing. By treaty she was bound to support the Danes ; but this was impossible, for her military forces, though not insignificant, were incapable of taking the field. In 1865 her Regular Army numbered 184,768, of which 66,130 were at home, supported by a Militia of 138,727 and a Volunteer army of 178,963 ; but efficiency had sunk almost to zero. The infantry were untrained, the army reserve numbered only 2,081 and was not liable for foreign service. Of the cavalry, Sir Henry Havelock writes : " *We* have just succeeded in knocking on the head and virtually abolishing for all good effect the small modicum of rifle instruction which had with infinite labour and fight against prejudice been introduced into our partially rifle-armed cavalry . . . proclaiming aloud that we pin our faith on spurs, lance and sabre." [7] Then he says :

" On the one hand, one of our jaunty, smart, burnished, ' well set up ' hussars, armed with his yard of blunt carving-knife (for what sword habitually kept in a steel scabbard is anything better), and his 500 or 600 yards rifle-carbine, intended to be harmlessly and playfully fired from the saddle, in *mounted* skirmishing from the back of a horse in perpetual motion, whose steadiness he cannot count upon for any fraction of a minute ; or that still more gorgeous anachronism borrowed from the Middle Ages, the British lancer, with his flag and pole. . . . Now, let anyone having a knowledge of this subject

contrast this sort of thing with—on the other hand—the destroying power of a horseman, armed with a breech-loader carrying
1,000 yards, and giving 10 to 12 shots a minute . . ." [8]

But Sir Henry was before his time; for the lance
lived on in the British Army until 1930, and the cavalry
sword is still with us and also its steel scabbard.

As regards artillery, the first breech-loading gun was
adopted by the British Army in 1859, and between
then and 1862 two and a half million pounds were
spent on re-equipment. Then, in 1865, these guns
were scrapped and a return was made to muzzle-loaders.
Nevertheless, the war of 1866 roused the spirit of enquiry.
It was at this time that General Peel, the Minister for
War, said : " The question now is whether the British
Army should be allowed to collapse." [9]

In 1867 the Snider breech-loading rifle replaced the
Enfield, and this same year the Ordnance Committee
actually tested out a new cannon at Woolwich Arsenal.
It was a small piece strapped broadside on across a
horse's back. The horse was tied to a post, the Committee standing on one side. The fuse was lit, whereupon the horse, somewhat startled, turned round,
pointing the muzzle at the heads of the interested
spectators. " Not a moment was to be lost ; down
went the chairman and members, lying flat and low on
their stomachs. The gun went off ; the shot passed
over the town of Woolwich, and fell in the Dockyard ;
the horse being found lying on its back several yards
away. The Committee were fortunately unhurt, and
gradually recovered their equilibrium, but reported
unanimously against any further trial." [10]   However,
as we shall see later on, the British Army was on the
eve of a great reformation.

THE PRUSSIAN AND FRENCH ARMIES

Though in the year year 1866 Prussia had accomplished
what she had set out to do, her General Staff, unlike
the French after 1859, did not rest. Imbued with the

spirit of Clausewitz they examined the war in the light of his doctrines. In 1869, Moltke issued a series of *Instructions for Superior Commanders of Troops.* In them we read :

." Very large concentrations of troops are in themselves a calamity. The Army which is concentrated at one point is difficult to supply and can never be billeted ; it cannot march, it cannot operate, it cannot exist at all for any length of time : it can only fight.

" To remain separated as long as possible while operating and to be concentrated in good time for the decisive battle that is the task of the leader of large masses of troops. . . . Little success can be expected from a *mere frontal* attack, but very likely a great deal of loss. *We must therefore turn towards the flanks of the enemy's position.*"[11]

The chaos of Königgrätz had terrified him, but the success of the great flank attack had elated him. Whilst Napoleon Bonaparte's idea had been " concentration before battle," masses had brought him to realize that he must " concentrate during battle." Further, he had learnt that the frontal attack could seldom be developed into a decisive attack. Even in 1861 he had considered that infantry were unassailable in front and he had compared an open plain to a wet ditch which cannot be rushed. Now he realized fully that a man who shoots at rest has the advantage over the man who fires advancing. The French also in part realized this. In their 1867 *Regulations* we read, " Fire has to-day acquired a preponderating effect on the battlefield," therefore frontal attacks are always dangerous, consequently the advantage is on the side of the defence ; yet we also read : When close to the enemy, there should be no fire, only " a determined advance to close on the enemy with the bayonet." [12]

The main difference between Prussian and French military thought was that the one was founded on the solid rock of Clausewitz, whilst the other was built on the shifting sands of many opinions,—experiences in Algeria, the Crimea, China, Italy and Mexico, none of which was analysed and lack of analysis led to a "valour of ignorance."

The French army was professional, not national, its General Staff was a permanent organization cut away from regimental life. As Boguslawski says: "the officers loafed about immensely." [13] In 1859, the general opinion in the ranks was "c'est le général soldat qui a gagné la bataille de Solferino." The valour of the man replaced the brains of his leader, contempt for the officer class arose, discipline consequently sank. It was the needle gun and not the Prussians which had beaten the Austrians; give the French soldier a rifle superior to this weapon; teach him to fire at long ranges; let the Prussians shatter themselves on this fire, then the valour of the French private soldier would settle the question.

Whilst Germany was being fused into one whole by her Custom's Union and the hostility of France, in 1867 the Garibaldians invaded the Roman States, and Napoleon III raised the enmity of Italy by dispatching a French force to eject him. Meanwhile, he aroused the suspicions of Great Britain with his Suez Canal project, and, when this canal was opeued in 1869, the British Government saw in it a threat to India and very naturally thought back to the ideals of his uncle in 1798. In place of winning over allies he antagonized all possible friends and this in spite of the fact that his military attaché in Berlin kept him well informed as to the state of the Prussian Army. In 1867 General Trochu tried to open the eyes of the people by publishing a book *L'armée française en 1867*, in which he pointed out its unpreparedness for war. Then, the following year, on January 2, during a sitting of the *Corps Législatif*, Marshal Niel proposed drastic military reforms; whereupon Jules Favre, pacifist and Deputy of Paris, exclaimed, "Vous voulez donc faire de la France une caserne?" To which the Marshal replied: "Et vous, prenez garde d'en faire un cimetière." Niel died in 1869, and with him died any hope of revitalizing the French Army.

CHAPTER VI

THE CONSOLIDATION OF GERMANY, 1870-1871

Origins, Mobilization and Plans. Battles and Sieges. The Tactics of 1870-1871.
Treaty of Frankfort.

ORIGINS, MOBILIZATION AND PLANS

THE causes which led to the outbreak of the Franco-
Prussian War were obvious to all ; but, as is the custom
in European diplomacy, they were not the ones which
actually detonated the conflict. France feared the
preponderance Prussia had gained in 1866, and Germany
saw in France a Power which would, if she could, restore
the old disgrace of the Rhenish Confederation ; she
intended therefore to smash French Imperialism. The
pretext was found in the vacancy of the Spanish throne
caused by the revolution of 1868. General Prim, the
revolutionary general, considered Prince Leopold of
Hohenzollern-Sigmaringen a suitable candidate, and this
Prince accepted the crown on July 3, 1870. At once
the French Press stormed against Prussia, demanding her
humiliation or war ; whereupon Leopold withdrew his
candidature.

Shortly before this democratic outburst, Napoleon III
had sent General Lebrun to Vienna to effect an offensive
alliance with Austria and Italy against Prussia, and
apparently reckoning on their support he demanded of
William I a guarantee that Leopold's candidature would
not be renewed. The reply he received was that the
withdrawal had been agreed upon and that this closed
the question. Bismarck, however, did not intend the
matter to rest here. On July 13 he published from
Ems an official telegram conveying the impression that
the King had refused to see the French Ambassador.
This set France on fire, and a vote for war was at once

H   113

carried by the French Government. "Whether the majority of the Assembly really desired war," writes Mr. Fyffe, " is even now a matter of doubt. But the clamour of a hundred madmen within its walls, the ravings of journalists and incendiaries, who at such times are the true expression of public opinion, what the Spanish Inquisition was to the Christian religion, paralysed the will and the understanding of less infatuated men." [1]

Thiers and Gambetta opposed the motion, and in only 16 out of 87 Departments of France was the clamour for war popular. The Emperor did not want it—he wept ; the Empress did—she rejoiced ; the *Marseillaise* intoxicated the people, and the boulevards of Paris roared with shouts of " A Berlin ! "

Democracies are madder than kings. In the eighteenth century kings generally knew what their armies were worth ; from the middle of the nineteenth onwards democracies never have known. Though the French Army was well found compared to what it had been in 1796, it was rotten at the head. " Men were in high places whose antecedents would have shamed the better kind of brigand," [2] whilst in the Prussian Army the " Fatherland " was all in all ; in fact the spirit of 1870 in Germany was what the spirit of 1792 had been in France.

Mobilization was at once set in motion, the " Krieg mobil " being telegraphed all over Prussia on the night of July 15. The Prussian scheme was based on system, the French on paper. The one was minutely arranged to be completed in a given number of days ; the French sent forward their formations unmobilized as they had done in 1859.

The Prussian plan was founded on the principles laid down by Clausewitz : Direction, Paris ; objective— the French Army wherever met. The French plan— on the nebulous agreement with Austria and Italy— was to cross the Rhine at Germersheim with 250,000 men ; move into Bavaria ; separate the Northern from the Southern States ; join up with the Austrian and Italian forces ; march on Jena and thence on Berlin. In absurdity this plan is rivalled only by the famous Plan XVII of 1914, and was wrecked even more rapidly ; for, on July 16-17, the Southern German States threw in their lot with Prussia and so annulled at one stroke the French triumphal march into Bavaria.

The Prussian forces were organized in three armies : The First, General Steinmetz, 60,000 ; the Second, Prince Frederick Charles, 131,000 ; and the Third, the Crown Prince, 130,000, and a general reserve of 63,000. On July 22 the French Army, about 250,000 strong, organized in seven corps and the Guard stretched from Belfort to Strassburg, still awaiting transport and supplies.

A word must now be said as regards armaments, especially because this was the first war in which breech-loader was to meet breech-loader, a war in which " killing by accident " was to become more important than " killing by intention." Further, a new weapon was to be used, namely, the mitrailleuse, a machine gun ; but its success was limited by misuse, the French employing it as a field gun.

In brief, the French rifle tactics were based on long range fire, so that the superiority of the chassepot might be fully developed ; then to dig in, await the enemy, and crush him by fire before attacking with the bayonet. These tactics compelled Moltke to assume the tactical offensive, which he had hoped to avoid, and he generally did so by holding his enemy's front and simul-taneously attacking a flank. Every tactical group from the company upwards was instructed to remain always on the offensive so as to give the French no breathing space—to hold by fire, attack by fire, outflank by fire and never cease fighting.

BATTLES AND SIEGES

The campaigns which now opened may be divided into two main periods : that between the declaration of war and the fall of the French Empire, and that under the Third Republic. Both of these periods may be divided into two series of operations : the first into the battles of the frontier and the overthrow of the French Army, and the second—the sieges of Paris, Metz, etc., and the people's war.

From the beginning the only hope of a French success lay in so rapid an advance that the German mobilization would be upset. This did not happen, because administrative deficiences held the French back ; yet, however necessary full equipment might be, seeing that the plan was to advance unmobilized, it may well be doubted whether the Great Napoleon, had he been in command, would have delayed his advance for the lack of cholera belts and camp kettles.

Hesitation at once put the Paris mob in charge of strategy. The boulevards were thronged, and shouts were raised demanding the instant invasion of Germany. This clamour forced the Emperor's hands, and on August 1 he initiated a movement on the Saar which led to the first engagement of the war, when the Second French Corps, under Frossard, met one battalion, two squadrons and a battery of the First German Army at Saarbrücken. The action took place on August 2 ; then, on the 4th, the Third Army at Weissenburg, throwing back a French detachment under Abel Douay, caused such a paralysis of the French Headquarters that the Emperor issued orders for a concentration of three corps at Cadenbronn, which necessitated the troops at Saarbrücken falling back to Spicheren close by. Steinmetz, quite unaware that the French were preparing to fight a great battle on the Saar, on the 6th came under fire of the enemy's guns at Spicheren, the sound of which drew every German unit within hearing towards the scene of action. Such were the first fruits of the offensive spirit inculcated during peace training.

This, the first major battle of the war is an interesting one. It was a chaotic jumble, and though the French could have massed a superior force they failed to do so. An account of the fighting was given to Archibald

Forbes, the well-known British war correspondent, by an eye-witness; this man said: "The German is a man of method and of stubborn pith. Under this death hail the dressing seemed as systematic as on the parade at Düsseldorf, the touch of man to man as accurate. Ever as a shell crashed through a company, or the mitrailleuse opened a lane and strewed it with dead and wounded, the men flanking the gap closed in with grim coolness which impressed one with the conviction that men who could act so could not be beaten."[3] But this order soon melted away.

The French under Frossard withdrew leaving the Germans in such inextricable confusion—the last fruits of the unlimited offensive—that no pursuit was possible.

After Weissenburg it had been much the same—there was no pursuit, and touch was lost with the French under MacMahon. Then, on the 6th, it was regained, the advanced guard of the Third Army coming up with the enemy at Wörth. Once again, directly the guns were heard there was a general stampede towards the scene of action. The French stood on the defence, and from time to time delivered a counter-attack. For example, at Elsasshausen: ". . . the fire became heavier, and a regiment of Turcos (Algerians), firing and yelling, came bounding through the smoke. This was too much for even Prussian grenadiers, and away they all went, followed by the Turcos."[4]

Overwhelmed by a superiority of nearly three to one, with both flanks turned, the French yielded, and MacMahon losing some 40 per cent. of his men escaped under cover of darkness, all touch with him being lost, for once again the German attacks ended in complete confusion.

The disasters at Spicheren and Wörth threw the Imperial Headquarters at Metz into a panic, and an order was issued to fall back on Châlons and there form two groups of corps under Marhals Bazaine and MacMahon. When this order became known in the

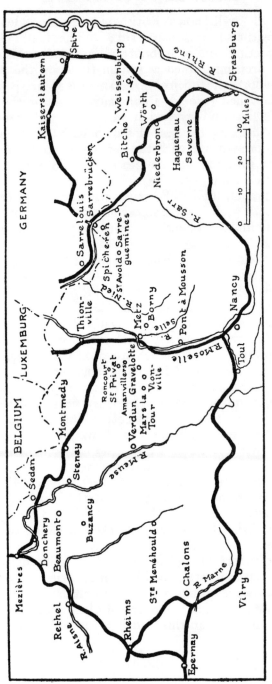

FRANCO-PRUSSIAN WAR, 1870–1871.

capital the Government declared that if the army fell
back Paris would revolt. Whereupon, on August 9,
the plan was changed, all troops east of Metz were
ordered to halt, and the fortress was to be held at all
costs. This resulted in a separation of forces, for whilst
Bazaine halted MacMahon fell back towards Châlons.

Meanwhile the German Second Army moved on
Pont-à-Mousson, south of Metz, with the First Army
on its right, when, on the 10th, to Moltke's surprise
Bazaine's army was discovered on the right front of the
latter. The Second was thereupon wheeled to the
right, and, on the 14th, once again the roar of the
cannon was the call for a general advance on Colomby-
Borny where a battle was fought and Bazaine driven into
Metz. Thus end the battles of the frontier.

Moltke, considering that the French were in full
retreat, pushed on part of the Second Army, under
General von Alvensleben, who, on the 15th, came in
contact with the enemy at Mars-la-Tour. Meanwhile,
Palikao, the Minister of War, telegraphed to Imperial
Headquarters from the capital : " If you desert Bazaine
there will be a revolution in Paris."[5] This resulted in
renewed panic, and Bazaine was turned about.
Consequently Alvensleben instead of finding him in
retreat found him with his five corps on his right flank.
In spite of being outnumbered by three to one, in order
to hide his weakness this determined Prussian general
decided to attack. On the 16th he did so at Vionville-
Mars-la-Tour. Then, on the 17th, reinforcements
arriving, the whole of the Second Army moved north,
with the result that, on the 18th, the German Ninth
Corps suddenly fell upon the centre of the French line
at Amanvillers, and so began the desparate battle of
Gravelotte-St. Privat.

On the German left, at St. Privat, the Prussian Guards
made a frontal attack and lost thirty per cent. of their
men, Canrobert's corps in two days (August 16-18)
expending 2,000,000 rounds of rifle ammunition, or
more than the whole of the number fired by the Prussian

Army in 1866. Though on the German right a preliminary bombardment prepared the attack, yet when the Germans issued from the woods, " they suddenly found that the French artillery and mitrailleuses had by no means been silenced—about two hundred pieces opening on them with fearful effect, while at the same time the whole crest blazed with a deadly fire from the ' chassepot ' rifles. Resistance like this was so unexpected by the Germans that it dismayed them ; and first wavering a moment, then becoming panic-stricken, they broke and fled, infantry, cavalry, and artillery coming down the slope without any pretence of formation, the French hotly following and pouring in a heavy and constant fire as the fugitives fled back across the ravine towards Gravelotte."[6]

The position at St. Privat being turned at Roncourt by the Saxons, the French resistance collapsed and a withdrawal was made towards Metz . Moltke hearing of this at once invested Bazaine in Metz, and with the rest of his forces followed up his retiring enemy. On the 29th he came in contact with MacMahon at Nouart, fought him at Buzancy on the 30th, and drove him into Sedan on the 31st. On September 1 the Emperor, his Marshals, 82,000 men and 558 guns, being completely surrounded and having no hope of escape, surrendered to William I of Prussia.

Archibald Forbes tells us that the night after the French disaster at Sedan he slept at the château of Belle Vue in the bed which had been occupied the night before by Napoleon III. Then he writes : " He had apparently been reading in bed, for a translation of Lord Lytton's *Last of the Barons* lay turned on its face, on a little table by the bedside." If that is not a piece of journalistic license then it is indeed a fitting close to a strange man's career.

With the capitulation of Napoleon the French Empire crashed to the ground, and, on September 4, a Republic was proclaimed under the leadership of Gambetta, To the Germans the war seemed won, for they did not then realize that the same spirit, the spirit of nationalism, which had carried them from the Rhine to the Meuse, was now by their very successes breathed into the heart of every Frenchman. " In 1848," wrote Blanqui, " Democracy stood alone and allowed itself to be destroyed ; in 1870 it has the country behind it, and this time it will defend itself with teeth and claws." (7)

Moltke had hoped that by the end of October he would be " shooting hares at Creisau." Instead, he was hard put to it at Paris. By the end of September the capital was surrounded and Headquarters established at Versailles. Meanwhile the French fortresses, Metz, Belfort, Strassburg, Toul, Verdun and Mézières held out and under their indirect protection thousands and thousands of Frenchmen were enrolled and added to the 500,000 regular soldiers, chiefly recruits and reservists, and 50,000 sailors and marines who were still in the country.

The " Défense Nationale " now began in dead earnest, campaigns being waged around Orleans, Le Mans, the Loire, the Sarthe, the Lisaine and about Belfort. Discipline, however, told against the want of it. At Spicheren a French soldier had said to a German : " Nos chefs ce sont des canailles," and a French officer had said : " Il n'y a plus rien à faire avec cette canaille là," (8) pointing to his men. All this had gone. Sedan had swallowed up the old arrogance and insubordination. But time was now against France ; for, as Napoleon Bonaparte had said, men must eat soup together for a long time before they can become soldiers. Strassburg and 17,000 men surrendered on September 28, then Toul with 13,000 men. Metz capitulated on October 27 with 3 marshals, 6,000 officers and 173,000 men, for Bazaine, in spite of his numerical superiority, could not break out, because no attack except a frontal one was possible. Here, towards the end of the siege, horse flesh was selling at two francs the pound, cheese at forty sous and bread at four and a half sous, which seems to show that starvation was not the only cause of surrender.

Verdun fell; then, early in January, Mézières. Still Paris held out, and with it Belfort.

Paris has for centuries been the idol of France. In 1870, as to-day, it was not the political centre only but the greatest road and railway centre in the country. He who holds Paris, it has been said, holds France. Paris was inhabited by 2,000,000 civilians and defended by 400,000 armed men; yet, on September 19, when the investment began, the German besieging force numbered but 200,000 rising to 240,000.

At Versailles, " There was the King's staff, with princes innumerable ; and there was the Crown Prince's staff, with ever so many more princes. . . . There was the Casino, there were the cafés. . . ." [9] In the distance could be seen the Mamelon of Montmartre, the towers of Notre-Dame, the Pantheon, the domes and spires and the Arc de Triomphe. Within the city was General Trochu, governor and commander of the garrison, Gambetta having escaped in a balloon on October 10. On October 31 a desperate sortie was made at Le Bouget, only to be beaten back. On December 17, the German bombardment was opened, in which much damage was done to the fortifications and still more to the nerves of the civil population. On January 28, 1871, an armistice was signed, and the following day, Paris, for two hundred years the centre of European politics, capitulated and Berlin for a while took her place.

THE TACTICS OF 1870-71.

Turning now to the art of war as experimented with during this period. On the part of the German Army we see a rapid progression from the methodical fight, as laid down in the text-books, to the manœuvre battle as demanded by ever-increasing artillery power. At Spicheren, owing to the fact that reinforcements arrived gradually, and that on the whole the *terrain* was unsuited to artillery, the attack was pushed in stages. At Colomby-Borny it was much the same ; but at Gravelotte it is otherwise : The German Seventh, Eighth and Ninth Corps held the French front whilst the French right wing was attacked in flank by the Guard and Twelfth Corps with the Tenth in reserve ; this attack being prepared by the fire of massed artillery. Sedan, in its turn, was essentially an artillery battle, a battle in which the German infantry played but a subordinate part. On this question of artillery a German writer says : " It was just the same later on, as regards the Republican levies, whenever the *terrain* in any way enabled artillery to be used. On every occasion when the infantry fight with its successive efforts was predominantly employed, as at Spicheren, Fifth Corps at Wörth, Third Corps at Vionville, Eighth and Ninth Corps at Gravelotte, the result was the complete dissolution of the body of troops engaged, divisions as well as corps, and extraordinary losses."[10]

The reason for this failure in the methodical attack, exept when purely a holding operation, was that fronts had become inviolable, and, as Colin says, " the Germans never succeeded in taking a position by a frontal attack, and still less so the French."[11] So does Boguslawski indirectly say the same thing when he writes : " In the greatest battles of the war, those of Gravelotte and Sedan, the turning tactics came prominently forward "[12] that is, they are by far the more important.

As regards the infantry soldier there was little to choose between the courage of French or German. Psychologically, the Frenchman develops his fighting qualities better in attack than in defence, and the German the other way round. Prince Hohenlohe asserts that " the German infantry is the most perfect that has yet been seen, or that can be imagined."[13] Hönig more honestly says that when they lost their officers they lost their heads ; and Meckel that the German dislikes dispersion, " he is confused by disorder, and by the withdrawal of his accustomed leaders. . . . It is not so with the soldiers of the Latin race."[14]

The French, contrary to their instincts, assumed the

defensive, and made constant use of rifle pits. They generally opened fire at from 1,000 to 1,400 yards, forcing the Germans to seek cover by ground at 400 yards' distance. At Wörth, in order to obtain the fullest rifle effect, the French occupied a forward slope and were pulverised by the German artillery. Under cover of this fire the German infantry advanced, and when within effective range one third of each company extended, the remainder following as supports and reserves in column of sections. The second line was stronger than the third, and advanced in line of company columns at deploying intervals. Once engagement took place, a swaying battle resulted, which, between 400 and 500 yards from the defender, swallowed up all three lines. Neither side ever succeeded in bringing troops in close order into the front line. " On both sides . . . the tactics of the drill ground and of peace manœuvres were completely altered as far as concerns the fire of the masses . . . Bayonets were never crossed in the open field, and but seldom in village or wood fights. . . . At Wörth, Mars-la-Tour, and Gravelotte, there was a surging backwards and forwards of the swarms of skirmishers on both sides." [15]

In this war the influence of artillery came more and more to the fore. The French did not mass their guns, the Germans did, and notably so at Gravelotte and Sedan. In 1866 the Germans had learnt their lesson, but from this campaign the French learnt nothing. Sedan was the greatest artillery battle of the war ; all the French attacks were brought to a standstill by gun fire, and most of them at 2,000 yards' distance, that is, outside effective rifle fire. At this battle " A French officer who was taken prisoner described the German fire as ' five kilometers of artillery.' " [16]

Cavalry steadily lost ground. Only one successful cavalry charge was made, namely, that of Bredow's brigade at Vionville. The French were, however, short of ammunition, yet in spite of this Bredow's losses were 33 per cent., and in some regiments 50 per cent. At

Sedan, General Gallifet attempted a most gallant charge with his brigade of " Chasseurs d'Afrique ; " but a single volley shattered it. Archibald Forbes gives a graphic and, I think, truthful picture of this exploit. He writes :

" Not a needle-gun gave fire as the splendid horsemen crashed down the gentle slope with the velocity of an avalanche. I have seen not a few cavalry charges, but I never saw a finer one. . . . It was destined to a sudden arrestment, and that without the ceremony of the trumpets sounding the ' halt.' The horsemen and the footmen might have seen the colour of each other's moustaches . . . when along the line of the latter there flashed out a sudden simultaneous streak of fire. Like thunder claps sounding over the din of a hurricane, rose the measured crash of the battery guns, and then a cloud of white smoke drifted away towards the chasseurs, enveloping them for the moment from one's sight. When it blew away there was visible a line of bright uniforms and grey horses struggling prostrate among the potato drills, or lying still in death. So thorough a destruction by what may be called a single volley probably the oldest soldier now alive never witnessed." [17]

Defensive field works were a novelty to the Germans ; but, on account of the tremendous power they added to the defence, they were not long in recognizing their value. Abattis played a prominent part at Metz as did wire fencing in the siege of Paris, during which gunboats were used on the Seine, and iron-clad wagons in more than one of the sorties.

Finally, the most important tactical lessons to be learnt from this war are : Firstly ; as Moltke says, " It is only the laity who believe that they can trace throughout the course of a campaign the prosecution of an original plan, arranged beforehand in all its detail and observed to the very close [of operations]." [18] In other words, a war of masses is a war of accidents in which genius is out of place. Secondly ; that the individual order of fighting has become the only battle formation for infantry ; in attack or defence in the field it is skirmishers only who can hold their own. Thirdly ; once engaged, the energy of infantry is rapidly exhausted, the moral shock of the breech-loader being as effective as its physical blow. Fourthly ; the cavalry charge is dead and with it the bayonet assault. Lastly ; whether the battle is to be fought methodically or by manœuvre the full power of artillery must be developed from the start, and not only must artillery be concentrated against a part of the enemy's position but it must be under the command of one man.

TREATY OF FRANKFORT

On January 18, 1871, ten days before the armistice was signed, an event of supreme importance took place in the Palace of Versailles, for there in the Hall of Mirrors, on the ceiling of which and at the base of the central painting, is inscribed " Le Roi Gouverne Par Lui-même," on the initiative of the King of Bavaria, the traditional ally of France, William I of Prussia was proclaimed Emperor of Germany. In July the year before France had gone to war to undo the work of partial union effected in 1866. Napoleon III had planned to march into Bavaria ; now its King put the coping stone on the work of the union. Further still, Russia, enchained by the Treaty of Paris, had burst her bonds by denouncing the clauses which forbade her maintaining war ships on the Black Sea. This had taken place on October 31, 1870 ; and on March 13, 1871, by the Convention of London this action was recognized by the Powers because they could not prevent it. The recall of the French garrison in Rome, which took place during the war, left the Eternal City unprotected, and directly the last French soldier had sailed from Civita Vecchia Victor Emmanuel marched on his future capital where the Papal mercenaries " laid down their arms at the breach of Porta Pia. Thus was the task of national union, to which three and a half centuries earlier Machiavelli had urged the princes of Italy, accomplished." [19]

If this complete overthrow of French policy were not bad enough—and it must be remembered that democracy had played a foremost part in its elaboration and the leading part in its disruption—the Parisian mob having ruined strategy now did its utmost to ruin peace. During the war the Germans had on the whole treated the French civilian population well. Archibald Forbes, an eye-witness, says : " The people . . . liked the Prussian way of doing business best. The hotel-keepers remarked that they got their bills paid as if the generals were tourists, whereas the French gave promises to pay when the war should be over." [20] Then came the armistice, and instead of showing a bold, proud and united front the *canaille* of Paris once again took charge. Women were stripped naked " who had dared to smile upon the Teuton satyrs,"—the German colours being painted on their flesh. A café was sacked " where a few German officers took supper," and " extensive use made of Condy's disinfecting fluid and chloride of lime in the Palais de l'Industrie, the theatres on the Champs Elysées, and other public buildings occupied by the Germans." [21]

This puerile vengeance took place immediately after the Germans had marched out of Paris on March 3— having entered it on the 1st. Then, on the 18th, the Commune was proclaimed. The Tuileries and the Hôtel de Ville were burnt, the archbishop of Paris assassinated, and fire and sword carried through the city. Once again was Paris laid under siege, and the victorious Germans, encamped on the heights overlooking the city, watched Frenchmen wage war upon Frenchmen, 30,000 men, women and children perishing in this fratricidal conflict. With such a contemptible spectacle before their eyes, it is a wonder that the peace treaty signed at Frankfort on May 5, 1871, and ratified by the National Assembly on May 18 was not severer than it was. Its terms were :

(1) The payment of an indemnity of £200,000,000.
(2) The right of Germany to be treated by France as the most favoured nation.
(3) The annexation of Alsace and eastern Lorraine.

Alsace was predominantly German, and had become part of France in 1697; Lorraine was predominantly French, but was not definitely incorporated in the Kingdom of France until 1766. The motive for their annexation was to block the French entrance into southern Germany. Immediately after the fall of Napoleon III in September, 1870, the historian Leopold von Ranke had said to Thiers, " ' It is against Louis XIV that we have now to wage war ' ; that is to say, we have now to fight against the country which has for centuries looked upon the defenceless condition of the Germans as the strongest bulwark of her own hegemony on the Continent. . . . The annexation, far from being a deed done on the spur of the moment by the caprice of an individual, was the inevitable outcome for both nations of several centuries of their history." [22]

Nevertheless, true though this is, would not it have been wiser, in place of humiliating a proud nation so indifferently represented by the Parisian scum—" half cat and half rabbit "—to have foregone the annexation of eastern Lorraine ? Because, by seizing it, the German Empire, as it has well been said, became burdened by a French mortgage [23] From now on every foreign enemy of the new born Empire could count on French support. The problem of Alsace-Lorraine thus became the problem of European peace.

PART III

PERIOD OF NATIONAL EXPANSION,
1872-1913

CHAPTER VII

POLITICAL AND ECONOMIC CONFLICT,
1872-1898

Foundations of a New World. The Controlling Factor—Economics. Expansion
by Colonization. Politics and Alliances. Nationalism and Materialism.
The Russo-Turkish War of 1877-1878.

FOUNDATIONS OF A NEW WORLD

FROM 1851 to 1870 France was the disturbing factor in
European politics. From 1871 to 1914 Germany replaced
her, and for the time being, through fear of her increasing
strength, combined with the weakness of France and the
rise of modern democracy and the consequent dearth of
great leaders, European affairs were stabilized. Under
the influence of this stability, unbroken by wars, except
on the confines of the continent, science, industry,
commerce and trade engendered such a stupendous
energy that the whole world was magnetized by Europe.
From this date, the history of Europe becomes the
history of the world, a prestige being established which
stands unrivalled since the days of Alexander the Great.

As Europe expanded, swallowing Africa, the Pacific
Islands, and thrusting her tentacles over eastern, western
and southern Asia, an inward recoil set in.

Between 1815 and 1848 two revolutionary waves had
swept over her many peoples, the clash between democratic freedom begotten by the French Revolution and
aristocratic autocracy as represented by the Metternich
school. Except in Eastern Europe, in Russia and the
Balkans, these two opposing ideals, though they had not
fully accomplished their work, had, by 1871, spent their
force. Thence onwards two new revolutionary waves
were destined in the greater part to replace them—

Capitalism and Socialism; both begotten by the industrial revolution. The one assuming the old autocratic form of pre-French revolutionary days, and the other assimilating the spirit of this revolution in an economic in place of a political form. The first was the product of James Watt and Metternich, and the second the product of James Watt and Jean Jacques Rousseau.

In this chapter it is my intention to trace the crooked path of these changing years, years during which were laid, not with foresight but in a haphazard manner, the foundations of the world in which we live.

THE CONTROLLING FACTOR—ECONOMICS

Until the year 1870 the monopoly of world trade was in the hands of Great Britain. No other nation even challenged her commercial supremacy; consequently her international politics were not based on armed force but on diplomacy, the aim of which was so to balance power in Europe that no nation would be strong enough to exert armed force against her. Militarily threatening none, economically she absorbed all. Then, in 1871, this balance of power was completely upset. Germany, hitherto a corn exporting country, began rapidly to become a manufacturing one. The French indemnity, though at first it dislocated the money markets, enabled her to emulate England. She stepped forth on the road travelled by England over a hundred years before, when the gold of Bengal, seized by Clive, fertilized the British industrial revolution.

In 1872 Germany demonetized her silver. This struck at French prosperity, as France, unsupported by Great Britain, was compelled to suspend her bimetallic system, and the result was that shortage of gold forced up commodity prices. Though this affected French trade during the first ten years after the Franco-Prussian War, under the stimulating influence of the Zollverein German industry developed vastly. Then, as it began to feel the competition of a reviving world, in 1879 Bismarck introduced trade protection, but neglected to create a colonial empire capable of absorbing over-production at home. Between the years 1880 and 1891 protection was extended, and what was the result ? The answer is given by Mr. Fullerton when he writes :

" The neighbouring nations exercised reprisals. The number of foreign markets diminished. Yet the German population was rapidly increasing. An industrial crisis ensued. Then it was that the Germans began to emigrate in droves. A fresh war might have helped to solve the situation. Instead, Germany decided to alter her economic policy. Between 1891 and 1907, accordingly, she followed the system of signing commercial treaties with the different Powers. Prosperity seemed to return. German manufactures once again launched forth on what appeared to be the route of a magnificent future. Now, instead of exporting her citizens—many of whom even returned from abroad—she lavishly dumped her products 'Made in Germany' upon all the world-markets." [1]

This ceaseless dumping and the rising arrogance of the German temper led to endless commercial friction, more particularly antagonizing British industry. " Tirpitz himself always stoutly maintained that it was the competition not of ships but of goods which changed the political face of Europe." [2] Economics became the fuel of politics, and in 1898 we find nations drawing together for economic reasons only. In that year the tariff war between France and Italy ended, France acquiescing in Italy's claim on Tripoli.

EXPANSION BY COLONIZATION

German energy being diverted from war to industrialization made easy for her by the discipline of her people, the remaining great European Powers, for the most part already industrialized or partially so, sought to increase their prosperity through colonial expansion. From 1870 onwards a veritable crusade was carried out by European nations in the name of Gold, every banker, statesman and merchant swearing on his cheque book for his personal

profit to " civilize " such portions of the world as could
not defend themselves against the white man's rifles and
cannon ; for " progress " to these people was synonymous
with "conquest." Having since 1815 freed themselves from
autocratic government, their one intention was to force
the absolutism they had rejected down the throats of all
peoples who happened to be any colour except white.
As regards aggression the years 1870-98 are only equalled
by the age of Ghenghis Khan. Between 1870 and 1900
Great Britain acquired 4,754,000 square miles of territory,
adding to her population 88,000,000 people : between
1884 and 1900 France acquired 3,583,580 square miles
and 36,553,000 people ; and in these same years Germany,
a bad last, gained 1,026,220 square miles and 16,687,100
people. There were many other nations besides who
acquired land ; but these three examples will suffice to
prove the stupendous and rapid progress of this crusade.

The three spheres of colonial activity were Africa, the
Pacific and China. Almost the whole of the first was
partitioned among the European Powers, their respective
spheres of influence being determined at the Conference
of Berlin, in 1884-85, and by subsequent Conventions.
Then the second was absorbed ; and when once the Pacific
Islands had been swallowed up the third was attacked.
The history of this gigantic movement is of the greatest
interest, but I can here give only a very brief outline of it.

Bismarck did not want colonies or a fleet, though during
the last four years of his supremacy he began to see the
necessity for the former. He was willing, however, to
back the French colonial policy, because he believed that
it would keep French eyes from " staring as if hypnotised
into the gap in the Vosges " ; meanwhile Russia looked
east and, in 1873, stormed and took Khiva.

Great Britain started the business of African partition
in 1875, quite unintentionally. To secure the route to
India, in November Disraeli bought up the Khedive's
shares in the Suez Canal. Then, in 1877, the Transvaal
was annexed ; and the Zulu War, which followed in 1879,
relieved the Boers of the fear of extermination. As with

the American Colonies after 1763, safety at home directly led to the Boers seeking independence, which itself led to the disastrous war of 1880-1881, when, at Majuba Hill, on February 27 of the last-mentioned year, a small force of British soldiers under Sir George Colley was routed. This war resulted in the Transvaal gaining complete internal self-government, and was a direct cause of the South African War of 1899-1902.

No sooner was the first Boer War at an end, than, in September, 1881, the Arabi revolt took place in Egypt. In November, Gambetta, then head of the French Government, invited Great Britain to discuss measures to secure the Khedive. In February the next year his Government fell and this proposal was abandoned, Bismarck declaring that " Egypt was the Schleswig-Holstein of the two Western Powers," and that " they would intervene together and quarrel over the spoils."[3] Though England acted single-handed he was right. On June 11, 1882, riots broke out in Alexandria. Great Britain asked France to co-operate with her in re-establishing order, but de Freycinet, now in power, declined, Italy also declining. On July 11 Alexandria was bombarded, and on September 13 Arabi was crushed by General Wolseley at the battle of Tel-el-Kebir. Drawn from Egypt into the Soudan, on January 26, 1885, occurred the Gordon tragedy. The conquest of this vast area was then suspended on account of the Penjeh crisis which arose over a boundary squabble with Russia in Turkestan and it was not revived until 1896, when the back of the resistance was broken by Sir Horatio Kitchener at the battle of Omdurman on September 2.

In 1882 Bismarck was delighted by the turn of events, and France, with the Napoleonic legend behind her, was furious. The result was that the Egyptian quarrel separated the two countries until 1904.

In 1886 Great Britain conquered Upper Burma, in 1894 she established a protectorate in Uganda, and in 1895 occurred the Jameson raid into the Transvaal which heralded the South African War.

The year 1881 is as important in French colonial history as in British, for in this year her Majuba was the massacre of Colonel Paul Flatte's expedition by Tuaregs in the Sahara. This same year she established herself in Tunis much to the annoyance of the Italians ; two years later she proclaimed a protectorate in Madagascar, annexing that island in 1896, after having already annexed Tongking in 1885.

In these land-grabbing operations she eventually fell foul of Great Britain ; for, in 1893, a dispute arose over the Siam boundary, which country was only saved from annexation by one side or the other because of the mutual jealousies engendered by their respective expansion policies. And, in 1898, another dispute arose on the lower Sudan, namely, the Fashoda incident, which brought the two countries to the verge of war.

Meanwhile, Belgium, 11,000 square miles in extent, being about to absorb the vast Congo territory (77 times her size), German pride and ambition could no longer stand the sight of the rapid partitioning up of the world ; so, in 1884, she annexed part of the Cameroons and Angra Pequeña (German South-West Africa) and the next year the Zanzibar hinterland which became German East Africa ; also in 1884 she annexed half of New Guinea. Later on, turning her attention to the Far East, in 1897, she leased Kiaochow from China ; whereupon Russia leased Port Arthur, Great Britain Wei-Hai-Wei and France Kwang-Chow-Wan. The following year, in order to gain a footing in the China Seas, the United States went to war with Spain and acquired the Philippine Islands.

Thus we see that though during this period the great Powers of Western Europe were at peace between themselves their war energy was in no way abated. Small wars abounded, wars of aggression in its most violent form, because the object of each war was conquest, and, generally speaking, the total suppression of any form of national or local government in the areas absorbed. To the white man nationalism stood for freedom ; to the black, the brown and the yellow man, it stood, in the white man's mind, for submission to his will. These wars cannot be examined here ; they were too many ; nor from the military point of view are they of much interest ; for, with the exception of a few disasters like Isandhlwana during the Zulu War ; Maiwand in Afghanistan in 1880, and Adowa in 1896, when in their last Abyssinian campaign the Italian lost over 4,500 officers and men killed and 1,500 captured, the weapons of science and civilization triumphed over the heroism and archaic equipment of barbarism—all men being barbarians who lived outside Europe and the two Americas. It was the history of Greece over again.

POLITICS AND ALLIANCES

With the ascendency of Germany over France, the whole of Western civilization underwent a profound change. Hitherto cosmopolitanism had been a European characteristic. Europe unconsciously felt herself to be a unit, a house of many rooms yet still one building, in which intercourse, social and commercial, was in no way greatly restricted. Now this unity became less and less tangible ; each room growing into a separate building was encompassed by tariff walls built not so much to foster home industries for peaceful but for war purposes. Thus was the idea of war injected into her political policies and stimulated by economic friction. Thus was the idea of freedom nationalized in a manner undreamt of in past ages, and then rationalized into an instrument for war. Gold and iron were now welded together, interfused and intermixed, and out of this seemingly magical metal was a new witchcraft, a new civilization, compounded. A civilization in which faith in self gave way to fear of others.

In 1871 France appeared down and out, yet in 1872 to the German eye once again did she appear threatening. In this year, to prepare for the eventual revenge she established compulsory military service, and through the newly created Committee of Defence she began to organize the whole country as a vast entrenched camp.

The result of this rapid and astonishing recovery was, that this same year, in order to isolate France Bismarck approached Russia and Austria and established an entente called the *Dreikaiserbund*, which endured until the Russo-Turkish War of 1877-78, when it became clearly apparent that Russia and Austrian interests did not coincide. Failing in this larger scheme, in 1879 he established a Dual Alliance between Germany and Austria, the main terms of which were, that each country would support the other if attacked by Russia, and that if any other country attacked, then a benevolent neutrality would be maintained.

Though this agreement lessened the likelihood of an Austro-Russian war it in no way prevented a Franco-Russian coalition. So in 1881, he revived the *Dreikaiserbund* idea, and became exceedingly friendly to England. Meanwhile, as we have seen, he encouraged France in her colonial enterprises, not only to compensate her for the loss of Alsace-Lorraine but to embroil her with England and Italy—this, as we have also seen, led to the French quarrel with England over Egypt and the French-Italian quarrel over Tunis. Italy now turned to Germany and Austria, and on May 20, 1882, a Triple Alliance was established between the three countries.

By 1883 Bismarck's policy had won through. The Triple Alliance had been established, England was friendly, and the *Dreikaiserbund* had been revived. Then came the first set-back. In November, 1885, Serbia attacked Bulgaria and was badly beaten at the battle of Slivnitza. Russia next stepped into the turmoil, her aim being to bring the divided Slav peoples of the Balkans under her influence. This at once started a quarrel with Austria, and led to the disruption of the *Dreikaiserbund ;* whereupon Russia, finding herself thwarted and isolated, in the summer of 1886 began to consider a Franco-Russian *rapprochement*. Bismarck scenting a rat, relations between Germany and France became strained, and in

1887 war appeared imminent. The next year the old Emperor William I died, and was succeeded by Frederick III who in his turn was succeeded by William II on June 15. Two years later the young Kaiser failing to see eye to eye with the old Chancellor dismissed him, and took personal charge of affairs. Then, in 1891, the French fleet visited Cronstadt, in 1893 the Russian fleet visited Toulon, and in 1895 an alliance between France and Russia was announced.

The fall of Bismarck and the rise of William II in his stead introduced a disturbing factor into European politics. The one stood for the establishment of German supremacy in Europe, the other for German supremacy in the world. This change in outlook was inevitable, and it was due not to any personal idiosyncracy on the part of the young Emperor, but to the fact that because Germany was rapidly becoming industrialized she was rapidly becoming a world power. Psychologically this change was strongly fostered during the eighties and nineties by the writings of Nietzsche and Treitschke who created a new Germanic spirit, which soon found its politico-economic expression in the idea of *Weltpolitik*, an outlook which gazed beyond the national frontiers out on to the world's markets with a greedy eye. In 1893 the Pan German League was formed.

On his deathbed the old Emperor William I had urged his grandson to remain friendly with Russia. Circumstances had prevented this, so he turned to England, visiting Queen Victoria in August 1889. The next year, with an eye on the future, he arranged the exchange of Zanzibar for Heligoland ; Stanley, the African explorer, saying at the time that " England had got a new suit in exchange for a trouser-button " ;[4] yet he knew what he was about. This friendship continued until 1894, when the defeat of China by Japan led to friction ; for though England was friendly to Japan, France, Russia and Germany compelled her to relinquish Port Arthur. Simultaneously friction arose in South Africa, in which country throughout 1895 Germany and Great Britain stood in open antagonism. Then, on December 30, 1895, took place the Jameson Raid, and on January 3 the Kaiser sent a telegram to President Kruger congratulating him on his success.

Meanwhile in the Turkish Empire and the Balkans new troubles were arising. The Armenian massacres of 1894 had shocked civilized nations and aroused national feeling, which in Greece was inflamed to such a pitch that the *Ethnika Hetairia*, a patriotic league, could no longer hold back its volunteers who, in April, 1897, accompanied by regular troops, crossed into Thessaly and so began the Græco-Turkish War which lasted until December the same year.

During this small war, William II, in place of joining in the general outcry against the " Great Assassin," urged forward by the economic impulse and seeing large markets for German goods in Asia Minor, sided with Turkey, and, in 1898, visited Palestine. There he delivered an inflammatory oration, saying : " May the Sultan and the three hundred million Mussulmans [70,000,000 of whom were in India] scattered over the earth be assured that the German Emperor will always be their friend." (5)

This same year he turned his attention to sea power, not because his intention was to threaten the security of the British Empire, but because it was imperative that German trade should be protected. Foolishly, he said : " I will never rest till I have raised my navy to the same standard to that of my army " ;(6) for this was a direct threat to the whole world and one which very naturally antagonized Great Britain. The Kaiser Wilhelm Canal having been completed in 1895, which itself was the foundation of German naval power as it linked the Baltic to the North Sea ; in 1898 the first Navy Act, providing for 12 battleships and 41 cruisers, was passed by the Reichstag, the Kaiser, on September 23, proclaiming " Our future lies on the water."

By 1898 the peace which had been established after the Franco-Prussian War had definitely transformed

Europe into an armed camp. Except in the Balkans, the urge of the nations was no longer towards liberty but towards security ; for as Spinoza had said over two centuries before : " Liberty or strength of soul are the virtue of private persons ; the virtue of the State is security." [7] A sure sign of the gathering war clouds was the assembly of the Hague Peace Conference in May to July, 1899 ; for when nations talk of peace they think in terms of war. Two of the conventions agreed upon are of especial interest, namely :

" (a) Prohibition of the launching of projectiles and explosives from balloons or by other similar new methods.

(b) Prohibition of the use of projectiles the only object of which is the diffusion of asphyxiating and deleterious gases." [8]

They are interesting because they are novel forms of war, and their restriction in 1899 in no way prevented, or hindered, their use in the World War fifteen years later.

NATIONALISM AND MATERIALISM

While the greater Powers were marshalling their forces and preparing for a war which was as unwanted as it was inevitable, the national urge, though obscured by these events, held its course steadily in the Balkans, in Bohemia, Hungary, Poland, Finland and Ireland, and was only waiting for a cataclysm to liberate it. Meanwhile, materialism advanced, and with it socialism. With Lincoln, Cavour and Bismarck the age of the great statesmen passes away ; the roads of national policy are no longer highways but tangled jungle tracks, often cut to no purpose, and frequently leading nowhere or to some impassable international morass. Politics enter the period of " swamp-warfare " of " forest-fighting," of " mountain skirmishes " ; the grand operations are no longer possible, for advancing democracy can produce only guerilla leaders and second-rate partisans.

Looking back on this age, in 1909 Mr. Stanley Leathers says in *The Cambridge Modern History* :

" The age has been prosaic and unromantic ; the enthusiasm for the mechanical and scientific triumphs of the early Victorian period has somewhat faded ; the belief in constitutional government and universal education as a remedy for all political and social evils has been shaken ; the blots on our economic and moral order have been relentlessly drawn to light ; self-complacency is no longer fashionable ; it is more popular to decry than to praise the world in which we live. The consolations of religion have for the moment lost their efficacy in large sections of the European population. The zeal of the young and ardent is thrown into schemes of social regeneration. Such schemes are everywhere, whether they take the form of personal work among the poor and the sick, or trades-union politics, or visions of progressive legislation moving step by step towards an improved society, or propaganda leading up to the social revolution and common ownership of all land, machinery and productive organization ; or the blind schemes of murder and destruction nursed in garrets and basements by the half-mad apostles of militant Anarchism. All these schemes alike are materialistic in their aims ; their kingdom is of this world ; they seek for no spiritual compensations, they admit no spiritual rapture ; their professors represent all grades between the extreme of self-devotion and the culmination of hate, envy and greed. But the belief in the possibility of social reform by conscious effort is the most dominant in the modern European mind ; it has superseded the old belief in Liberty as the one panacea ; even Bismarck paid homage to it ; and no modern statesman can afford to ignore it. Its substantial achievements, and perhaps its disappointments, are in the future ; but its currency in the present is as significant and as pregnant as the belief in the Rights of Man about the time of the French Revolution." [9]

Thus we approached the end of one age and slowly emerge into the beginnings of another. An age drab and dull, under the pall of a leaden sky lit here and there by the flicker of distant lightning. An age which awaits the storm, possibly the cyclone.

THE RUSSO-TURKISH WAR OF 1877-78

Before ending this chapter it is necessary to deal briefly with the only extensive war of this period ;

namely, the Russo-Turkish War of 1877-78. Its origin must be sought in the consistent suppression of the spirit of nationalism in south-eastern Europe since 1856. In 1870 all Christians in the Balkan States, coming as they did under the spiritual jurisdiction of the Ecumenical Patriarch, were looked upon as Greeks and not as separate races. Then, on March 3, the Sultan Abdul-Aziz by creating the Bulgarian Exarchate laid the foundation of a new power which though Christian was no longer Greek ; hence rivalry arose between the Christian races. The immediate cause was an agrarian rising in Herzegovina in 1875. From there the spirit of revolt spread into Bosnia and thence throughout the Balkans. England took little notice of it, Russia was interested ; then incensed by his subservience to Russia, Abdul Aziz was deposed and murdered. He was succeeded by Murad V, who in his turn was deposed and succeeded by Abdul Hamed II in August, 1876.

Meanwhile, in June, an insurrection broke out in Bulgaria which was suppressed by the Sultan with atrocious cruelty ; whereupon, on July 2, Serbia and Montenegro declared war on Turkey and were defeated. Thereupon Russia, in spite of the fact that England supported Turkey, resolved to free the Slav races. The result was that on April 24, 1877, war was declared on the Ottoman Empire.

The main interest in this war lies in its crudeness. Since the advent of the rifle and the rifled cannon neither Russian nor Turk had learnt anything of war. The Czar's total forces numbered 1,500,000 ; the Turkish maximum being about one-third of this figure. As regards armaments, the Turks were equipped with Krupp breech-loading artillery far superior to the Russian bronze cannon ; also their Peabody-Martini rifle, with an effective range of 1,800 yards, was superior to the Russian Krenk rifle with a maximum range of 1,200.

As regards strategy, the Turkish commanders fought on the defensive, the Russians being the aggressors. As regards tactics, the Turks rightly relied on the trench, and the Russians wrongly on massed frontal attacks. Kuropatkin, at the time Skobeleff's chief of staff, says : "Even when we had arrived within 600 paces of the enemy we made but little use of our rifles, and attempted to advance without firing a shot, without taking advantage of the natural cover which the ground afforded"; [10] and in spite of the terrible losses the Russians sustained, after the war we find their leading tactician, General Dragomiroff, writing : "The conclusions of the Prussians must not be applied to our men, who are well known to prefer fighting shoulder to shoulder. . . . What the bullet cannot do the bayonet will." [11]

Avoiding the Turkish fortresses of the Quadrilateral— Rustchuk, Silistria, Shumla and Varna—the Russians decided to cross the Danube between Rustchuk and Nikopol, mask the Quadrilateral, cross the Balkans and advance on Adrianople. Clearing the Danube, at the vicinity of Zimnitza they bridged the river. Meanwhile Abdul Kerim, the Turkish Commander-in-Chief, considering the whole movement a feint, lay inactive in the Quadrilateral. On July 3 General Gurko occupied Tirnova, outflanked the Shipka pass by crossing at the Hanikoi pass, and so freed the Shipka of the enemy ; whereupon the Sultan relieved Abdul Kerim of his command, replacing him by Mehemet Ali, and directed Osman Pasha, then uselessly garrisoning Vidin, to move with his 30,000 men towards Plevna, where he arrived on July 15.

On the 18th Nikopol fell, and the Russians, pushing on, attacked Osman on the 20th and were repulsed. As Plevna lay on the flank of the Russian advance south, it was essential that it should be taken, so a general assault was made on the 30th. Once again were the Russians driven back with a loss of over 7,000 officers and men to the Turkish 2,000. Breathing time having thus been gained, Herbert says : "An infectious desire, never relaxed till Plevna fell, seized the [Turkish] soldiers to dig themselves in like moles." [12]   Though

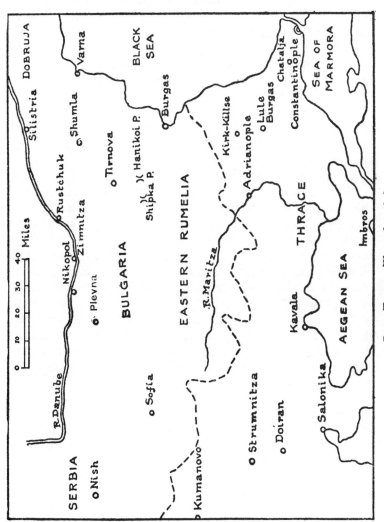

Russo-Turkish War, 1877-1878.

J

this remark is meant as a slight, it shows that however
untrained the Turkish soldiers may have been, and
however badly led, they were still unrotted by that
pseudo-professional spirit which considers defensive works
a symptom of cowardice.

The Turks should now have attacked the Russian
right flank, but they remained passive, when, on
September 11, Gurko having been recalled and the
Roumanians having joined in the war, 64,000 allied
troops supported by 440 guns, after a four days' artillery
bombardment, fell upon the Plevna works and were
once again repulsed, this time with a loss of close on
20,000, the Turks losing a quarter of this number, and
only 200 during the bombardment.

At length learning some wisdom, the Russians decided
to invest the fortress. This they did, and, on
December 10, Osman, unable to break out, surrendered
with 40,000 men. Whereupon the Serbians and Monte-
negrins joined in the war, and, on January 16, the
Russians occupying Adrianople the British fleet was
ordered to Constantinople, which action brought Great
Britain and Russia within a hair's breadth of war.

On January 31 an armistice was arranged, and on
March 3 the Treaty of San Stefano followed, creating
an enlarged Bulgaria, and a free Serbia, Montenegro
and Roumania. At once the jackals gathered around
the dismembered Turk. Austria and Great Britain,
scenting Russian supremacy in the East, set aside the
claims of nationalism and determined on a strictly
reactionary course. This resulted in the assembly, on
June 13, 1878, of the Congress of Berlin under the
presidency of Bismarck. The Treaty of San Stefano
was set aside, and a series of half-measures adopted
which satisfied no one and irritated all, establishing a
veritable cancer in the Balkans. The main points
decided upon were the following:

(1) Bulgaria, reduced in size, was constituted an
autonomous and tributary principality under
the Sultan.

(2) Eastern Rumelia was to remain under the direct political and military control of Turkey.

(3) Bosnia and Herzegovina were to be administered by Austria, the Sanjak of Novi-Bazar remaining under Ottoman administration.

(4) The independence of Roumania was recognized and that of Serbia and Montenegro defined.

To Great Britain the immediate result of her having thwarted Russian ambitions and ideals was the outbreak of the Second Afghan War in 1878. In 1873 the Russian conquest of Khiva had frightened Afghanistan, and the Amir Shere Ali had turned to Great Britain who would not, however, agree to give any material assistance. Shere Ali then sought Russian friendship. Russia, baulked in the West, now turned to the East and secretly supported the Amir. In 1884 Merve was occupied by Russia, and the next year occurred the Penjheh affair already mentioned.

The truth is that British diplomacy, unintentionally though it may have been, by restricting Russian expansion fostered war— war in the Balkans, war on the North-West Frontier of India, and eventually war in Manchuria by diverting Russian energy to the Far East. It was a pacific policy based on maintaining the *status quo* in order quietly to continue her trading. All policy, however, which is formed on maintaining the *status quo* is septic with a danger of war ; because the maintenance of the *status quo* dams up irresistible forces which if they cannot find an outlet in a pacific channel will eventually flow over the dam and wash it away. British hostility to Russia was, though less clearly seen, as much a forerunner of the World War as the hostility between France and Germany begotten by Alsace-Lorraine.

CHAPTER VIII

TRADITIONAL MYTHS AND MILITARY REALITIES, 1872—1898

Traditionalism and the Cardwell System. German and French Reaction. The
Mechanization of Morale. Military Reality.

TRADITIONALISM AND THE CARDWELL SYSTEM

In the slow and painful evolution of the art of war,
tradition and not experience has played the leading
part. To-day we wonder at the folly of the Chivalry
of France when for a hundred years they charged the
English bowmen without gaining a tactical success.
To-day we seldom wonder at the folly of attacking the
bullet by means of the bayonet, a folly which exceeds
that of the knights of France at least ten-fold. After
all they were clothed in armour though their horses
were vulnerable to arrows, and after all they had only
to meet bowmen and not riflemen and machine gunners.
So it happens that when we ponder over these things
we begin to realize that warfare is closely related to
lunacy. Not only do most wars find their outbursts in
pretexts which are quite irrational, but those who wage
them—the professional soldiers—being never less than
a generation out of date, and frequently several, are no
better mentally equipped to deal with them than was
Frederick's famous mule.

Frederick the Great, who was not a professional, that
is a traditional, soldier, for he broke every canon of the
professional and traditional art, once said to a gathering
of generals : " The great mistake in inspections is that
you officers amuse yourselves with God knows what
buffooneries and never dream in the least of serious
service. This is a source of stupidity which would

become most dangerous in case of a serious conflict.
Take shoemakers and tailors and make generals of them,
and they will not commit worse follies." [1]   This is
why the French Revolutionary Wars, the Napoleonic
Wars and the American Civil War produced such a
galaxy of leaders.   Many were shoemakers and tailors,
and very few were regular soldiers.

After 1870 military organization became more and
more professional and completely democratized.   After
this date no great generals appear, just as no great
statesmen appear.   In France, as elsewhere, conscription
is vastly unpopular ; and when a subject, or a duty, is
distasteful its progress is unenthusiastic.   Yet this actual
age demanded military enthusiasm as much if not more
than any past one.   Changes were taking place in civil
life which must influence war : new inventions were
appearing and new weapons were being produced.   In
1890-91 the magazine rifle was issued to the German
army with a bullet propelled by smokeless powder.
Cover by smoke was no longer possible, and aimed fire
was increased at least four-fold.   What did these changes
mean ?   As I will show a little later on, they meant a
return to bayonet tactics !

Meanwhile, in England, between the years 1861-71
the great wars of this decade shocked public opinion
into taking some interest in military affairs, and this
interest, coupled with the fact that the rise of Germany
had upset the balance of world power, resulted in the
reforms carried out by Lord Cardwell, Secretary of
State for War between the years 1869-74.   Returning
to the system of the Duke of York, the main changes
he introduced were the following ; Short service of
seven years with the colours and five with the reserves ;
this brought the old long service army, which had existed
since 1660, to an end.   Purchase of commissions was
abolished ; manœuvres were instituted, and eventually,
in 1881, two-battalion regiments bearing territorial
titles were created ; the object of this " linked-battalion"
system being dictated by the necessity of maintaining

the overseas garrisons at full strength ; the battalions at home becoming depot units for those in India and elsewhere.

In 1871 the British Army was re-armed with the Martini-Henry rifle, and in 1888 with the Lee-Metford magazine rifle. Strange as it may seem, company, battery and squadron training were unknown before the eighties, the men being trained, which meant drilled, by the adjutant and the sergeant-major ; yet it was not appreciated, and has scarcely been appreciated to-day, that the fighting power of an army is *the product* and *not the sum* of the arms composing it.

GERMAN AND FRENCH REACTION

Every war is a grim reality, and tactically every modern war, that is a war since 1850, has been a war of surprises. The leading lesson of 1870-71 was the stupendous importance of fire power. Meckel, an acute observer, said : " The foundations of success in the infantry combat consists in fire action, but the laurels of victory still hover on the points of the bayonets." [2]   Fire power for full development means manœuvre and control ; manœuvre demanding intelligence and sound tactical handling on the part of the subordinate leaders, and control, intelligence and strategical insight on the part of their commanders. As armies grew in size, as they did during these years, numbers demanded simplicity and intelligence was obscured by method. After the 1866 war a writer had said that " the correct course for infantry to follow was to fight in future ' like a horde of savages ! ' " [3] What he really meant was, in controlled and intelligent disorder. But disorder is antipathetic to the professional soldier, especially to the German ; and even in 1871, before Paris had fallen, " the Germans were drilling in their spare hours with redoubled intensity," [4] and immediately after the war, William I, not liking the loose order as it was difficult to control, in the revised

German *Drill Book* of 1873 did his utmost to discourage it.

As masses of men in close order can move only forwards or backwards, Scherff, in 1872, to overcome, as he thought, the complexities of command, established a most pernicious maxim, namely : " You can never be too strong when making an attack," a maxim which, as we have seen, was exposed as a dangerous fallacy during the Crimean War. Then he added : " An attack made with only part of your force at once awakens the idea of the possibility of non-success," [5] as if to provide against mishap were a detriment in generalship. It was this noted writer, basing himself upon Clausewitz, who initiated what may be called the bull-ring system of attack, head down and straight forward at anything—picador, matador or post-rail.

The French learnt better than their victors. Their *Regulations* of 1875 point out the preponderating importance of fire, and that no formations can move under effective fire, consequently fighting is by skirmishers only. Their artillery tactics, however, remained defective. They could not see that the bombardment was useless unless sustained up to the assault. Their *Infantry Regulations* from 1875 to 1900 do not even mention artillery, it being assumed that the guns have finished their task once the infantry begin to advance. There was no co-operation between artillery and infantry, and in all European armies it was the same.

Then came the 1877-78 War, and from it German and French soldiers, now beginning to forget the reality of 1870-71, read into it the lessons they wanted to read. So, in place of studying the war with an open mind, they turned it upside down, fondly imagining that in its romantic dregs they could find tactical salvation.

Skobeleff, a courageous swashbuckler with the mind of a corporal of grenadiers, had said : " The bullet is a fool, the bayonet is a hero"—here was something to bite on to. Had not a German eye witness written of Pevna:

" The Russian troops commenced to move. When they were
within easy range we hailed them with a quickfire of two to
three minutes' duration. I noticed deep gaps in their lines
which were promptly filled up. They were allowed to approach
as far as the foot of the hill. Then one bugle sounded the
charge ; a dozen others responded. . . . Nearer and nearer we
came ; we heard the Russian ' Hurrah ! ' ; wild cries of ' Allah ! '
were started and drowned individual voices ; commands
became useless. Now only a hundred paces between the
charging lines—they uphill, we downhill—and at last there was
a collision like that between two railway trains. . . . A chaos
of stabbing, clubbing, hacking, clutching, shouting, cursing,
screaming men." [6]

When danger does not exist, this is the type of fighting
which instinctively fascinates every soldier ; but when
danger is present, when it comes to war itself, this is
the type of fighting which instinctively every soldier
shuns. I do not suggest that this dramatic picture is a
pure invention, for the bayonet was at times used in
this war. But I do suggest that the reason for its use
should have been examined, which was that both sides
were such miserable rifle shots that at times the bayonet
could be used with effect.

In the French Army considerable attention was paid
to the writings of Dragomiroff. In 1884, the *Regulations*
of 1875 were re-written. Now the supreme object in
the attack was to get forward as rapidly as possible.
The duty of the supports and reserves was to sustain
movement rather than to protect movement by fire.
Intervals between skirmishers were reduced from six to
three paces. The firing line was to employ volley firing
by sections, and finally the charge was to be made in
two ranks shoulder to shoulder.

In the 1895 *Regulations* we read :

" As soon as the battalion has arrived within 400 metres of the
enemy, bayonets are fixed, and individual fire (without maga-
zines) of the greatest intensity delivered. The portions of the
reserve that are available are advanced. . . . The battalion

in second line in the meantime gradually advances closer. The advance is made by successive rushes followed by a quick fire of short duration. The fighting line reinforced by the reserves, and if necessary by the battalion in second line, gradually reaches to within 150 or 200 metres of the enemy. At this distance magazine fire is commenced, and all available reserves, and if necessary the second line, close up for the assault. At a signal from the Colonel the drums beat, and bugles sound the advance, and the entire line charges forward with cries of ' en avant, à la baïonette.' " [7]

Reality is now completely lost in the clouds of romance. In these *Regulations* skirmishers virtually disappear and a return is made to linear warfare. The argument runs as follows : If skirmishers do the fighting, would not it be better to put all the rifles into line from the start ? The 1895 *Regulations* answer " Yes " ; consequently whole battalions shoulder to shoulder in single rank lines are called " skirmishing lines," and behind them whole brigades, or divisions, are held back for the decisive attack, and are called " troupes de choc " and " masse de manœuvre." [8]

In the German *Regulations* of 1889 we find a similar madness. We read :

" Generally, however, the commander of the fighting line should bear in mind that the order for assault shall be given by him, and at the right time. When the fighting line has arrived to within short range of the enemy, and, having been sufficiently reinforced, has paved the way for the assault by the highest attainable fire action, the bodies of troops écheloned in rear should be brought up to the foremost line without a halt, and together with it should deliver the final blow. The drums of all closed bodies commence beating from the moment that the advance to the assault can no longer be concealed from view. Whether the closed bodies find themselves alongside or in rear of each other, what their formation is, and whether the commander should still retain a reserve depends entirely on circumstances. In the most decisive moment of the attack there is only one watchword for the fighting line, and that is ' Forward ! Forward ! straight for the goal ! ' The beating of

drums, the continuous sounding of the ' Rapid advance ' by all
the bugles, sets everybody, even the hindermost, in motion,
and with cheers the assaulting troops throw themselves upon
the enemy." [9]

Here again we are back in the realms of military
mythology. For such a form of fighting in face of the
rifle bullet one thing only was missing ; to make men
all but immortal, like Achilles they must be dipped into
the river Styx.

THE MECHANIZATION OF MORALE

It was obvious even to the writers of this criminal
nonsense that the problem could be solved only by
magic. If the instinct of self-preservation could be
suppressed, the man would become a machine ; how
was this Robot to be fashioned ? Something must cancel
out fear, and this something was discovered in the
magical word " morale." Had not Napoleon said that
" the moral is to the physical as three to one " ? Well
then, the answer was obvious : Moralize the soldier
and he will cease to be afraid ; therefore in spite of
danger the larger herd of men will swamp the smaller.
How simple was the solution—it was a mere matter of
elementary arithmetic.

In the Franco-Prussian War there died a very gallant
and uncommon soldier, for he was a " human " philosopher—his name was Ardant du Picq. He had seen
much service, and before 1870 he had jotted down his
reflections on war in a haphazard way. After the war
they were published in book form, were studied and,
as we shall see, were turned upside down and converted
into a veritable river of death. His philosophy may be
outlined by means of quotations. [10]

His starting point in war is the human heart as it
palpitates on the battlefield. " Absolute bravery, which
does not refuse battle even on unequal terms, trusting
only to God or to destiny, is not natural in man ; it is

the result of moral culture." This would seem to suggest that absolute bravery can be cultivated, yet du Picq does not really mean this, for later on he says: " Man is capable of standing before only a certain amount of terror. To-day there must be swallowed in five minutes what took an hour under Turenne " ; consequently the man who can swallow the greater amount of terror will dominate the field, because " the human heart in the supreme moment of battle is the basic factor."

Numerical strength divorced from quality was anathema to him ; he says : " The theory of strong battalions is a shameful theory. It does not reckon on courage but on the amount of human flesh. It is a reflection on the soul. . . . In the masses, man as an individual disappears, the number only is seen. Quality is forgotten, and yet to-day as always, quality alone produces real effect." And again : " What good is an army of two hundred thousand men of whom only one-half really fight, while the other one hundred thousand disappear in a hundred ways."

Quality means moral discipline ; thus : " Four brave men who do not know each other will not dare to attack a lion. Four less brave, but knowing each other well . . . will attack resolutely." " The purpose of discipline " is not obedience, but " to make men fight in spite of themselves." Instinct is not to be killed, but to be cultivated, because " War, so long as man risks his skin in it, will always be a matter of instinct." In its cultivation man must be taught how to be alert and " alive "—" The less mobile the troops, the deadlier are battles."

As regards weapons, he says : " Does war become deadlier with the improvement of weapons ? " And he answers this question with " Not at all " ; which is true, and why ? Because " Modern weapons have a terrible effect and are almost unbearable by the nervous system " ; that is to say : Their moral effect is so great that man fearing to face them reduces their physical effect by shunning them ; consequently, as the bullet keeps the attacker at arm's length, "bayonet attacks are not so easily made to-day."

As regards shock tactics he writes : "Guilbert says that shock actions are infinitely rare. The moral impulse which estimates the attacker is everything. The moral impulse lies in the perception by the enemy of the resolution that animates you. They say that the battle of Amstetten was the only one in which a line actually waited for the shock of another line charging with the bayonets." Then his French temperament and his studies of Classical warfare carry him away ; he says : "This moral effect must be a terrible thing. A body advances to meet another. The defender has only to remain calm, ready to aim, each man pitted against a man before him. The attacking body comes within deadly range. Whether or not it halts to fire, it will be a target for the other body which awaits it, calm, ready, sure of its effects. The whole first rank of the assailant falls, smashed. The remainder, little encouraged by their reception, disperse automatically or before the least indication of an advance on them. Is this what happens ? Not at all ! The moral effect of the assault worries the defenders. They fire in the air if at all. They disperse immediately before the assailants, who are even encouraged by this fire now that it is over. It quickens them in order to avoid a second salvo." Then a little later on he adds : " It is well known to everybody, to all nations, that the French have never met anyone who resisted a bayonet charge."

That all this is complete and unadulterated nonsense a little historical research should have revealed to him. For instance, Marshal Bugeaud says of an attack on the English during the Napoleonic Wars :

" The English remained quite silent, with ordered arms, and from their steadiness appeared to be a long red wall. The steadiness invariably produced an effect on the young soldiers. " Very soon we got nearer, shouting ' Vive l'Empereur ! en avant ! à la baïonette ! ' Shakos were raised on the muzzles of the muskets ; the column began to double, the ranks got into confusion, the agitation produced a tumult ; shots were fired as we advanced.

" The English line remained still, silent and unmovable, with ordered arms, even when we were only 300 paces distant, and it appeared to ignore the storm about to break.

" The contrast was striking ; in our inmost thoughts, each felt that the enemy was a long time in firing, and that this fire reserved for so long, would be very unpleasant when it did come. Our ardour cooled. The moral power of steadiness, which nothing shakes (even if it be only in appearance) over disorder which stupefies itself with noise, overcame our minds. At the moment of intense excitement, the English wall shouldered arms, an indescribable feeling rooted many of our men to the spot, they began to fire. The enemy's steady concentrated volley swept our ranks ; decimated, we turned round seeking to recover our equilibrium ; then three deafening cheers broke the silence of our opponents ; at the third they were on us, pushing our disorganized flight. But to our great surprise they did not push their advantage beyond a hundred yards, retiring calmly to their lines to await a second attack." [11]

Ardant du Picq's error was that he was carried away by his emotions. He failed to realize the moralizing effect of order on the defence, and the demoralizing effect of disorder on the attack. Further, he entirely overlooked the moralizing effect of ground as cover behind which men can lie down and fire at those advancing. His theory was sound enough for the hand-to-hand combat of classical times, fairly sound for warfare with the musket, but most misleading for the rifle. This error was inherited by the Moral School of War, which originated in France during the last decade of the nineteenth century, and which cast its spell over every army.

Only twenty years after the Franco-Prussian War, in which cavalry had proved a dismal failure against single-loading rifles, we find a French writer extolling the cavalry charge. Here is his picture of the infantry defenders :

" Unnerved by anxiety, blinded by smoke, deafened by noise, agitated by a thousand different and violent feelings, these men who have not got in their hearts a cleverly adjusted piece of mechanism, but a heart accessible to every species of emotion —can they, when threatened by a charge of cavalry, judge distances correctly, adjust sights, or aim with precision ? "

Here is his picture of the cavalry attackers :

" The signal is given. Along the whole line the drums and bugles beat or sound the charge. A furious clamour replies : the cry of fear or frenzy of a delirious mass, which to use Souvarof's vigorous expression ' flies to the front ' ! Bounding and shrieking the human torrent rushes on ! " [12]

Am I wrong in suggesting that warfare is closely related to lunacy ?

The worst offender, not because he was the most miserable but because he was the most eminent, in mechanizing morale, was the late Marshal Foch, who, when an instructor at the French Staff College, gave a series of lectures since published under the title, *Des principes de la guerre*. [13] These lectures were read between the years 1894 and 1900. He opened them by complaining that the old teaching dealt with the material side of war and that the moral side was only glanced at ; yet throughout these lectures he materializes morale, his doctrine being a mixture of Clausewitz and du Picq. He rightly extols the study of war, quoting General von Willisen's famous saying : " Vom Wissen zum Können ist immer ein Sprung ; der Sprung aber ist vom Wissen und nicht vom Nichtwissen." He then says that knowledge " lies at the root of will," which is perfectly true ; but knowledge to be of real value must be transmuted into terms of understanding.

Clausewitz he knows well, but he does not understand him. He says : " It is because the whole of Europe has now come back to the national thesis, and therefore to armed nations that we stand compelled to-day to take up again the *absolute* concept of war." This is illogical, because though in Clausewitz's day it was necessary to arm an entire people in order that this people might be turned into a nation, it is not consequently necessary, once this nation has been formed, to continue with the absolute conception; this oversight led this great soldier into a most astounding error. To prove that any improvement in firearms adds strength to the offensive and that, consequently, the larger a force the stronger it becomes in the attack, he writes on p. 32 :

" Nothing is easier than to give a mathematical demonstration of that truth :

Suppose you launch 2 battalions against ..	1
You then launch 2,000 men against	1,000
With a rifle fire of 1 shot to a minute, 1,000 defenders will fire	1,000 bullets
With the same rifle, 2,000 assailants will fire	2,000 ,,
Balance in favour of the attack ..	1,000 ,,
With a rifle firing 10 shots a minute, 1,000 defenders will fire within 1 minute	10,000 ,,
With the same rifle, 2,000 assailants will fire ..	20,000 ,,
Balance	10,000 ,,

As you see, the material superiority of fire quickly increases in favour of the attack as a result of improved firearms." [14]

Is not this complete lunacy ? To mention one factor only, out of a large number omitted, as the defender offers but one-eighth of the target that the attacker does, the assailants' hits must be reduced by seven-eighths; therefore, in the above example, the balance *against* him is 7,500, and not 10,000 in his favour.

Carried away by this absurd calculation, he elaborates his doctrine of—" Attack ! attack ! attack ! " He writes : " No victory without fighting. . . . Tactical results are the only things that matter in war. . . . No strategy can henceforth prevail over that which aims at ensuring tactical results, victory by fighting. . . . To make war always means attacking."

Having out-Clausewitzed Clausewitz, he out-du Picqs du Picq. He quotes Joseph de Maistre as saying : " ' A battle lost is a battle one thinks one has lost ; for,' he added, ' a battle cannot be lost physically ? ' Therefore, it can only be lost morally. But then, it is also morally that a battle is won, and we may extend the aphorism by saying : A battle won is a battle in which one will not confess oneself beaten."[15] Then a little later on he adds : " The will to conquer : such is victory's first condition." True ; but not the *only* condition.

The fact is that Foch intended to have it both ways : if you attacked with superior numbers you would win ; and if you attacked with superior morale you would win. Therefore whatever the circumstances may be—attack ! attack ! attack ! On such principles for twenty years the French Army was trained and educated.

MILITARY REALITY

From what has been said it may seem that in my opinion Marshal Foch was an indifferent soldier. That is not so ; he possessed an unusual insight into modern war ; but on account of his Clausewitzian complex, which coloured all his thoughts, he was unable to translate it into tactical terms. He saw clearly enough the economic nature of war. He says : " We find to-day a third kind of national war arising," a war " bent on conquering economic advantages and advantageous treaties of commerce for each nation." In support he quotes the German economic gains after the Franco-Prussian War, and the Japanese after the China War of 1894. Again he says : " War to-day is a commercial enterprise undertaken by a whole nation. It concerns the individual more directly than did war in the past, and therefore appeals much more to individual passions . . ' The Stock Exchange has acquired such an influence that it is able to launch armies into war,' (von Moltke). Who was responsible for the Boer War ? Certainly not the Queen of England, but the merchants of the City."

" National egotism, breeding self-interest in politics and war, and making war a means of satisfying the growing cravings of the nations, these nations therefore bringing into the fight a growing concentration of passion ; a more and more excessive feeding of war, including the use of the human factor and of all the resources of the country—such is the picture of modern warfare." [16]

What he did not see was that Clausewitz's doctrine of absolute war was only profitable when an industrialized nation, or one struggling to become so, swallowed up an undeveloped one ; and that, on account of the growing interdependence of the industrial world, wars between industrialized nations were becoming increasingly un-profitable, because the destruction, moral, economic and financial, inseparable from absolute warfare, is anti-pathetic to industrial development.

At this very time, however, there was one man who saw this clearly, not a soldier, nor a statesman, but a banker—Monsieur I. S. Bloch, a Pole. In 1897 he published in three volumes an elaborate analysis of modern war, entitled : *The War of the Future in its Technical Economic and Political Relations*, which so interested the Czar, that in 1898, he was persuaded to suggest a peace conference, which evolved into the Hague Conference of 1899. In 1899 an abridged edition of this work was published in English [17] and it is from this translation, edited by Mr. W. T. Stead, that the following quotations are taken.

Agreeing with Clausewitz that war is a political instrument, the secret of his amazing prevision lay in the fact that, as politics had entirely changed during the preceding half century, passing as they had from the agricultural sphere to the industrial one, he realized that the instrument—war itself—must change with them. He says : " What is the use of talking about the past when you are dealing with an altogether new set of considerations ? Consider for one moment what nations were a hundred years ago and what they are to-day. In those days before railways, telegraphs, steamships, etc., were invented each nation was more or less a homogeneous, self-contained, self-sufficing unit. . . . All this is changed. . . . Every year the interdependence of nations upon each other for the necessaries of life is greater than it ever was before. . . . Hence the first thing that war would do would be to deprive the Powers that made it of all opportunity of benefitting by the products of the nations against whom they were fighting." And again : " The soldier is going down and the economist is going up. There is no doubt of it. Humanity has progressed beyond the stage in which war can any longer be regarded as a possible [? profitable] Court of Appeal." Consequently war between the great industrial Powers is nothing more than mutual suicide. The old conception of war as a business is therefore absurd ; to-day is it a mad kind of burglary— the plundering of one's *own* house.

Turning to modern weapons, which are the military expression of an industrial civilization, he says : " The outward and visible sign of the end of war was the the introduction of the magazine rifle. . . . The soldier by natural evolution has so perfected the mechanism of slaughter that he has practically secured his own extinction." Not through the deadliness of this mechanism but through man's fear of it, a fear which will prevent him closing with danger and so overcoming danger.

Thus he pictures the future battle :

" The distance is 6,000 metres from the enemy. The artillery is in position, and the command has been passed along the batteries to ' give fire.' The enemy's artillery replies. Shells tear up the soil and burst ; in a short time the crew of every gun has ascertained the distance of the enemy. Then every projectile discharged bursts in the air over the heads of the enemy, raining down hundreds of fragments and bullets on his position. Men and horses are overwhelmed by this rain of lead and iron. Guns destroy one another, batteries are mutually annihilated, ammunition cases are emptied. Success will be with those whose fire does not slacken. In the midst of this fire the battalions will advance.

" Now they are but 2,000 metres away. Already the rifle-bullets whistle round and kill, each not only finding a victim, but penetrating files, ricocheting, and striking again. Volley succeeds volley, bullets in great handfuls, constant hail and swift as lightning deluge the field of battle.

" The artillery having silenced the enemy is now free to deal with the enemy's battalions. On his infantry, however loosely it may be formed, the guns direct thick iron rain, and soon in the position of the enemy the earth is reddened with blood.

" The firing lines will advance one after the other, battalions will march after battalions ; finally the reserves will follow. Yet with all this movement in the two armies there will be a belt a thousand paces wide, separating them as by a neutral territory, swept by the fire of both sides, a belt in which no living being can stand for a moment. The ammunition will be almost exhausted, millions of cartridges, thousands of shells will cover the soil. But the fire will continue until the empty ammunition cases are replaced with full.

" Melinite bombs will turn to dust farmhouses, villages and hamlets, destroying everything that might be used as cover, obstacle, or refuge.

" The moment will approach when half the combatants will be mowed down, the dead and wounded will lie in parallel rows, separated one from the other by that belt of a thousand paces which will be swept by a cross fire of shells, which no living being can pass.

" The battle will continue with ferocity. But still that thousand paces unchangingly separate the foes.

" Who shall have gained the victory ? Neither."

Such is his forecast of the modern battle, and here is his prediction of modern war as a whole :

" At first there will be increased slaughter—increased slaughter on so terrible a scale as to render it impossible to get troops to push the battle to a decisive issue. They will try to, thinking that they are fighting under the old conditions, and they will learn such a lesson that they will abandon the attempt for ever. Then, instead of a war fought out to the bitter end in a series of decisive battles, we shall have as a substitute a long period of continually increasing strain upon the resources of the combatants. The war, instead of being a hand-to-hand contest in which the combatants measure their physical and moral superiority, will become a kind of stalemate, in which neither army being able to get at the other, both armies will be maintained in opposition to each other, threatening each other, but never being able to deliver a final and decisive attack. . . . That is the future of war—not fighting, but famine, not the slaying of men, but the bankruptcy of nations and the break-up of the whole social organization. . . . Everybody will be entrenched in the next war. It will be a great war of entrenchments. The spade will be as indispensable to a soldier as his rifle. . . . All wars will of necessity partake of the character of siege operations . . . soldiers may fight as they please; the ultimate decision is in the hand of *famine*. . . . Unless you have a supreme navy, it is not worth while having one at all, and a navy that is not supreme is only a hostage in the hands of the Power whose fleet is supreme."

He realized that in a war between the Triple and the Dual Alliances " there would be ten millions of men under arms," and that battle frontages would become so enormous that command would be impossible. That battles would grow longer and longer in duration, and more and more costly, costing at least £4,000,000 a day should the five nations of the two Alliances declare war on each other.

Cavalry he considered useless, the day of the bayonet past and gone, and artillery the predominant arm.

The only soldier of note who troubled himself to criticise this book, one of the most remarkable ever written on war, was the veteran—General Dragomiroff. He condemned it because it failed to prove that the bayonet was still supreme.

CHAPTER IX

THE LAST OF THE WARS OF EXPANSION, 1899—1905

The South African War, 1899-1902. Lessons of the War. The Russo-Japanese War, 1904-1905. Outline of the War. Tactics of the War.

THE SOUTH AFRICAN WAR, 1899-1902

WHILST European nations were wrangling this way and that, and whilst Russia, that pseudo-European empire, was slowly and irresistibly moving towards the rising sun, Great Britain strove to maintain the *status quo* in the East. Anxiously she watched her vast Indian possessions which under the pressure of industrial development were beginning to become heated with self-consciousness. Then a new empire began to take form. Far distant, in the southern extremity of Africa, one man, Cecil Rhodes, the Clive of his age, a man who as a statesman had sprung into prominence during the Bechuanaland annexation of 1884, dreamt of a vast United States of South Africa, an immense British Dominion pushed northwards into Central Africa until its margins struck the confines of the Congo and the Nile. One man stood in his path—Paul Kruger, elected President of the Transvaal in 1883. Then gold was discovered, and, in 1886, Johannesburg was founded, and the Witwatersrand with its sunken millions of yellow magic loomed up like a wizard invoking the apparitions of strife.

Rhodes stood for expansion, Kruger for isolation. In 1889 a customs union was established between Cape Colony and the Orange Free State, to which later on all the South African States, except the Transvaal, became parties. Kruger stood aloof, taxing all new comers, the Uitlanders as they were called, to such an extent that soon they were paying nine-tenths of the

State revenue, the franchise laws being so regulated that it was impossible for them to exert any political pressure. This oppression led to the Jameson Raid which ended disastrously on January 2, 1896, and, like John Brown's raid of 1859, set blazing the spirit of nationalism, which henceforth divided South Africa into two hostile camps—the British and the Dutch. Then, after vain attempts to gain justice, on October 11, 1899, at five o'clock p.m. came war.

Though the conflict which now followed is regarded by most continental writers on military history as a somewhat insignificant guerilla affair, it should not be overlooked that it was the first war in which small-calibre magazine rifles and smokeless powder were tested on a large scale ; that the theatre of war was spread over 800,000 square miles of undeveloped country ; that railways were few, roads almost non-existent, and that during its two and a half years' duration the British Empire put into the field 450,000 men against an enemy who never numbered more than 40,000 men, out of a possible total of some 90,000. This war cost Great Britain £200,000,000, and it is interesting to realize that the number of rifle rounds expended by her soldiers was 66,000,000, or twice as many as were fired by the Germans during the Franco-Prussian War. As far as casualties are concerned the results were insignificant, the British loss in killed totalled 5,774, and the Boer about 4,000. To understand this war, as to understand the American Civil War, it must never be forgotten that the stronger side, in this case the British, had to subdue a hostile people, and not merely a hostile army. Hence the length of the war and the bitterness it engendered.

Exactly a month before war was declared Lord Wolseley had said : " If this war comes off it will be the most serious war England has *ever* had." [1] These words, though true, were scarcely prophetic, for Great Britain was not only without a foreign friend but her policy of " splendid isolation " had morally so antagonized continental Powers that when war broke out the entire European Press was against her.

From the military point of view, her idea as to what such a war entailed was ludicrous. Her War Office had learnt nothing from wars in South Africa. In 1848 Sir Harry Smith with six companies of foot and two of Cape Mounted Rifles had routed 1,000 Boers at Boom-platz, the mounted rifles proving of the greatest value. In 1881 Sir George Pomeroy-Colley, who was killed at Majuba Hill, had said : " The want of good mounted troops told very heavily against us, and our soldiers are not as trained skirmishers and shots as the majority of these Boers, who from their childhood have lived in the country, and to a great extent by their guns, and are used to stalking and shooting deer." [2] And early in 1899 Sir William Butler, then Commader-in-Chief in South Africa, having warned the Government at home on the unpreparedness for war and the importance of mounted troops against a mounted enemy, was recalled from his command, because his views, sound as they soon proved themselves to be, were considered prejudicial to military discipline. Then, as war became all but inevitable, the Government decided to bring the army in South Africa up to 70,000 strong ; whereupon the *Standard* newspaper of October 9, 1899, exclaimed : " Against such an army of bayonets, sabres and cannon, what can General Joubert's half-trained mob of irregulars expect to accomplish ? "

This war may be divided into three main phases : the Boer invasion of Cape Colony and Natal ; the British invasion of the Orange Free State and the Transvaal, and subsequent guerilla warfare. The Boer stategy was purely defensive and their tactics were generally the same. Their fighting lacked resolution, their discipline was of the meagrest and unity of command conspicuous by its absence. In fighting they relied on pony, rifle and trench ; wisely avoiding frontal attacks, they made the greatest use of their mobility in order to outflank their enemy, as happened at the battles of Colenso, Spion Kop and Vaal Krantz.

In his turn the British soldier had been trained for

shock action, little weight being laid upon preparation of the attack by fire. Sections were to be advanced by rushes of 30 to 40 yards until within 300 or 350 yards of the enemy ; bayonets would then be fixed and further rushes made up to 200 or 250 yards, when the second line having joined the first, the position was to be assaulted. The whole attack was very similar to those of the Peninsula and the Crimean wars ; in fact little or nothing had been learnt from the fighting of the previous fifty years, and it was only when the British broke away from their prehistoric *Infantry Drill* of 1896 that they were able to accomplish anything worth accomplishing.

In Natal, Sir Redvers Buller, by no means an exceptionally inefficient officer, as officers went in those days, showed a lack of generalship which was amazing. He was " completely imbued with the conviction that, in the field, no task was too difficult for infantry if well led." [3]   His knowledge of tactics was nil. No attempt was made to establish co-operation between artillery and infantry in the attack. At Thaba-Myama, during the Tugela fighting, General Warren's views were that " the Artillery alone was to carry on the fire-fight while the Infantry was to settle matters finally with the bayonet alone." [4]   And on January 12, 1900, Buller issued a special order saying : ". . . the men must get to close quarters with the Enemy—that is the way to victory and to safety ! Any retirement is fatal. The only thing the Enemy cannot withstand is a hand-to-hand fight with us." [5]   As well tell a bird-trapper to catch snipe with a fire-tongs as issue such tactical nonsense. What did the British soldiers, the victims of this generalship, think and feel ?   Here is the answer :

"The astuteness and adaptability of their invisible foe, how cleverly he fought in all shapes, how rarely he committed himself, how rarely he was at a loss, were subjects of frequent discussion amongst them, and one heard more than one surmise as to what would happen ' if we were allowed to scatter over the country like the Boers do ! ' Poor fellows, the proposition was usually succeeded by a thoughtful silence, and a helpless look which argued ill for comfort in the verdict. Once a man actually and boldly averred what all had in their minds : ' They've got more brains nor we ! ' and the announcement was not negatived by his comrades." [6]

Here is yet another answer :

" In situation after situation where our soldiers were helpless the Boers were perfectly at home. It was this which made one Boer equal to three freshly landed British soldiers in everything except those hammer and tongs fights which, in such a war, are quite exceptional." [7]

It was indeed a matter of brains ; brains rendered useless by petty barrack routine, by pipe-clay and red tape, by the hunting and the cricket spirit, by anything and everything except a soldierly spirit and an interest in war. The British military tradition had emasculated the British Army, an army which if it had been well led, well mounted and well trained would have proved itself invincible, instead of having to rely on attrition to weary out the " embattled farmers."

LESSONS OF THE WAR

There is not the space here to examine the numerous small battles fought, the most important of which was that of Paardeberg, where Cronje and 4,000 Boers surrendered to Lord Roberts on February 29, 1900— the anniversary of Majuba ; nor would it be a very profitable task, so we will turn to the lessons which can be learnt from the fighting.

Like every war since 1850, this one produced its crop of tactical novelties, the greatest of which was " the emptiness of the battle-field " due to the wide extensions enforced by the magazine rifle and smokeless powder. The old terror of a visible foe gave way to the paralysing sensation of advancing on an invisible one, against whom no weapon could avail, an invisibility which fostered the suspicion that the enemy was everywhere. A universal terror rather than a localized danger now enveloped the attacker, whilst the defender, always ready to protect himself by some rough earth-work or stone-work, was enabled, on account of the rapidity of rifle-fire, to use extensions quite unheard of in past fighting and so to overlap every frontal attack. Thus, at the battle of Modder River, the Boers extended 3,000 men on a frontage of 7,700 yards; at Magersfontein, 5,000 men on 11,000, and at Colenso, 4,500 men on 13,200. Yet in spite of this human thinness, these fronts could not be penetrated.

The frontal attack, consequently, failed time and again; for against so mobile a foe it was almost impossible to manœuvre. Soon, however, the British generals began to realize that a mounted enemy must be met by his like, so that whilst his front is held by fire his flanks may be turned and enveloped. Though the cavalry under General French, some 6,000 strong, opened the road to Kimberley by a magnificent charge, in which they broke right through the Boer position at exceedingly small cost to themselves, only one officer and fifteen men being killed and wounded, it was mounted infantry and not cavalry which played the leading part in this war. Shock actions, such as that at Elandslaagte on October 21, 1899, were the exception; for it was by making use of the horse in outflanking movements and of the rifle when fighting on foot that the most profitable results were obtained.

The general lesson of this war is well put in the German Official History, which says: " In South Africa the contest was not merely one between the Bullet and the Bayonet, it was also between the soldier drilled to machine-like movements and the man with a rifle working on his own initiative. . . . War had been proclaimed between rigid formulas and untrammelled healthy common-sense." [8]   Inexperience in handling large bodies of men during peace time had " mechanized " the brains of the British Generals, who, being oblivious of the friction and difficulties which arise even during peace manœuvres, looked upon the masses entrusted to them as mechanical contrivances which could be moved forward by a word of command.

During this war, which, in spite of all its dissimilarity was on a very small scale a rehearsal for the World War of 1914-18, the British Generals, at least some of them, learnt : that extensions were an essential in the attack ; that discipline must become less mechanical ; that the defence was stronger than the attack, and that envelopment alone could produce profitable tactical results.   In Germany, in spite of the highly critical Official History already quoted, the General Staff considered that there was little to be learnt from it, and from General French's charge during the relief of Kimberley operations they deduced the entirely erroneous conclusion that great cavalry charges were still possible against highly trained European soldiers.   We read : " It was not the small-bore rifle and smokeless powder nor the loss of men (which was comparatively small) that caused such shrinkage from frontal attack ; it was the misgivings of the leaders about their own capacity, and consequently the shaken confidence of the troops in their leaders."[9]   As German leadership was considered above reproach, this conceit blinded their General Staff to a truth which should have been seen by a child.

The French, less obtuse, took a deeper interest in this war ; for in their new *Infantry Regulations*, issued in 1904, we find the importance of initiative stressed ; company commanders given a freer hand, and the skirmishing line replaced by small groups of men each under its own leader.

The greatest lesson was this (a lesson which concludes the German Official Account, yet one which no General Staff cared to learn, has ever learnt, or is ever likely to learn) : " Fortunate is that Army whose ranks, released from the burden of dead forms, are controlled by natural untrammelled, quickening common-sense." [10]

THE RUSSO-JAPANESE WAR, 1904-1905

Baulked in the West, mainly on account of the British Ottoman policy, Russia's energy flowed eastwards, and, as we have seen, halted at Port Arthur. This was a direct challenge to Japanese expansion, as also was the occupation of the Chinese ports by other European Powers who, in 1894, had been so insistent on the maintenance of the integrity of China. Japan, supported by the alliance with Great Britain, signed in 1902, which protected her from German, French or American interference, though her navy was inferior to the combined Russian fleets and her army less than half the total strength of her enemy's—which numbered 1,000,000 men—decided that the moment had arrived, a moment which might soon pass by, wherein to challenge Russia to single combat.

The main factors which governed her strategy were the gap in the Siberian railway at Lake Baikal, and the Russian naval base—Port Arthur. As long as the first existed she reckoned that Russian reinforcements would be seriously slowed down; and as regards the second she realized that if she could occupy this ice-free port before the ice-bound port of Vladivostok was open, not only would she be able to cut off the Russian war-ships at Vladivostok from those at Port Arthur, but that if the enemy fleet in the Baltic were sent to the China seas it would be denied an ice-free base of operations. Once Port Arthur was occupied, the military object was to gain a great decisive battle in order to convince Russia of the hopelessness of her task.

Russia, in her turn, had no plan; her unpreparedness was complete, her lethargy normal. East of Lake Baikal she had 135,000 troops split up over an immense area and under no centralized command; for though General Kuropatkin was Commander-in-Chief, he came under the orders of Admiral Alexeiev the Viceroy, an ignorant and incapable man. Kuropatkin's idea was to centre himself on Liao-yang or Mukden, and, under cover of a series of delaying actions, collect reinforcements, draw the enemy into the interior and there offer him battle. Sound though this strategy was, his distribution was faulty, being too scattered. His main enemies were not, however, the Japanese, but the government at home influenced by old Dragomiroff, then in his seventy-fourth year, who could not tolerate the idea of falling back before Orientals; the incapacity of Alexeiev who kept the Russian fleet land-locked in Port Arthur and when it was blockaded there imposed on Kuropatkin the responsibility for the fate of this fortress; and the disobedience of his subordinates, more especially General Zasulich who, against orders, fought the battle of the Yalu because, as he said, " it was not the custom of a knight of the order of St. George to retreat."

OUTLINE OF THE WAR

Negotiations broke down on February 5, 1904. Simultaneously the First Japanese Army under General Kuroki began to disembark at Chemulpo; and on the 8th, the main fleet, under Admiral Togo, sailed for Port Arthur and after a series of operations blockaded the Russian fleet. Advancing from Chemulpo over a roadless country, on May 1 Kuroki met General Zasulich and defeated him in the battle of the Yalu, which, as it has been said, was the Valmy of Eastern warfare, for though the Russians were in inferior numbers their defeat showed clearly that they were not invincible.

Under cover of this victory, the Second Army, under General Oku, landed at Pitszewo on May 5, and, on the 26th, defeating the Russians at Nanshan, drove them into the tip of the Port Arthur peninsula and so isolated the fortress. Meanwhile the Third Army, under General Nogi, landed at Pitszewo and relieved Oku, who moved north, whilst the Fourth Army, under General Nozu, was formed at Takushan.

These initial operations being entirely successful and

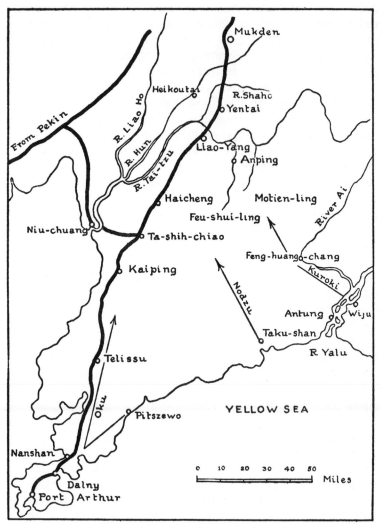

RUSSO-JAPANESE WAR, 1904-1905.

the Russian fleet neutralized, the Japanese plan was for the First, Third, and Fourth Armies to move northwards converging upon Liao-yang, whilst the Second Army operated against Port Arthur. Meanwhile, such pressure was brought to bear upon Kuropatkin that entirely against his wishes he was compelled to assume the offensive. This resulted in General Stakelberg and 35,000 men being sent southwards. Entrenching at Telissu, on June 14-15 he was attacked by Oku, who lapping round both his flanks severely defeated him. Pushing on, on July 24, Oku attacked General Zarubayev at Tashichiao, and was repulsed ; this was the first setback experienced by the Japanese since the initial landings.

When once Oku, who had the longer distance to advance, was well on his way, Nozu and Kuroki moved northwards fighting through a mountainous country, and, on August 24, the three armies began the last stage of their converging movement, Marshal Oyama having now taken over supreme command.

The Russian position at Liao-yang was a semi-circular one, with the city, now virtually a fortress, in its centre with a series of entrenchments stretching round it on its southern side, and their flanks resting on the river Tai-tzu. Oyama's plan, which was an exceedingly bold one, was to attack the western flank of the Russian position, and, under cover of a series of fierce assaults, advance the First Army across the Tai-tzu river east of the city, turn the enemy's left flank and fall upon his rear and so win a second Sedan.

Gaining information of this movement, Kuropatkin withdrew to Liao-yang in order to shorten his front and so collect sufficient reserves with which to counter-attack Kuroki, who was now separated from the Second and Fourth Armies and had his back to the river. This withdrawal was completed on September 1st ; whereupon, having collected 90,000 men, Kuropatkin delivered his counter-stroke, which after fighting of the severest nature was repulsed. Learning of a renewed attack on his right, the Russian Commander-in-Chief's resolution collapsed, and he ordered a general retreat on Mukden.

Liao-yang was in every sense of the word a great battle, and far more so than those which followed it during the remainder of 1904, the most important of which was the battle of the Sha-ho, fought on October 11. Meanwhile, Nogi with the Third Army had launched attack on attack against Port Arthur, and after losing over 90,000 men the fortress capitulated to him on January 2. Once relieved of this siege he was moved northwards to reinforce Oyama. On January 26-27 the battle of Heikoutai (Sandepu) was fought in a blinding snowstorm; then reinforced by Nogi and a new army—the Fifth—under General Kawamura, bringing his strength up to 310,000 men, Oyama, towards the end of February, attacked Kuropatkin at the head of a numerically equal force at Mukden, and by turning his right flank compelled him, on March 9, to abandon his position and retire on Harbin.

Whilst these operations were going on the Russian Baltic fleet under Admiral Rozhestvenski stood out from Libau on October 14, 1904; arrived at Kamranh on May 14, 1905; disappeared into the Pacific, and, on the 27th, met the Japanese fleet, under Togo, in the straits of Tsushima. By dawn the next day the Russian fleet had ceased to exist.

Defeated on land, destroyed at sea, and threatened by revolution at home, Russia was not loath to accept the mediation of the President of the United States; nor was Japan, for she was nearly at the end of her resources. Though the war drifted on through June and July, peace negotiations were opened on August 9, and the Treaty of Portsmouth (New Hampshire) was signed a fortnight later. By it Japan gained half the island of Saghalien, the lease of the Kwang-tung peninsula and Port Arthur, and the recognition of her rights in Korea.

TACTICS OF THE WAR

From so brief an outline of the more important events it is impossible to realize the extraordinary difficulties of this war ; the first great war fought by modern armies in an undeveloped country. The Russians were separated from their home base by thousands of miles, the Japanese from theirs by a precarious command of the sea. Both sides had but one railway to supply them ; yet in spite of all these difficulties, accepting the Russian strategy, or rather lack of strategy, as it was, it was the superior Japanese tactics and training which won the day.

The Japanese General Staff had been fattened on Clausewitz, and the army imbued with the highest patriotism. Facing them was a General Staff decadent, indolent and obsolete, and an army of magnificent animal substance, ox-like patient and powerful, but trained for warfare a hundred years out of date. Dogged and determined the Russian soldier was incapable of thinking, the officers were ignorant and intriguing ; in fact the whole army was a clumsy, cumbersome machine. Loaded up with 90 lbs. of kit, and thus turned into a pack-animal, it was next to impossible for the Russian soldier to undertake an offensive operation ; and yet it was for the offensive that he had been trained ; an offensive not such as depended on skill, on mobility, on cover by ground and on accuracy of fire, but on a straightforward frontal movement such as we have seen in 1854 and 1878. " The Russian Army had been brought up on the idea that shock tactics and close order were the best means by which to win battles, and it was really for moral reasons, and to frighten other countries, that a magazine rifle was issued to its troops. . . . The regulations certainly contained rules for firing lines, supports, and reserves, but this was mere vapouring, and was never intended to be taken seriously. It was the bayonet which was ' to do the trick.' " [11] Again

L

we read : " The Russian authorities acted as if troops were mere machines, and frankly said that no number of defeats would ever discourage their men "—indeed a comforting doctrine ! The result was mass attacks and massacre, a good example being the Russian attacks at the battle of the Shaho, where 8,000 dead were left upon the ground, the Japanese Second Army losing only 1,014 in killed.

Though the Japanese frequently made use of frontal attacks, especially in the Port Arthur battles where the area was generally too narrow for outflanking movements, they realized that their main object was to hold and not to break through the enemy, and this is most notice-able during the battle of Liao-yang. They put their trust in envelopment and won their battles by out-flanking. In the attack they first carefully reconnoitred the ground, then advanced to within about 800 yards' distance without firing, and either assaulted under cover of artillery fire which was maintained to the very last, or else dug themselves in, assaulted at night, or advanced under cover of night and continued the attack the next morning. At Mukden, where the ground was open and flat, the heaviest casualties occurred at about 400 to 500 yards' range. " Within 300 yards of the enemy," said a Japanese captain, " our losses are comparatively small." It must always be remembered, however, that the Russians were the most indifferent shots. This fact misled many of the foreign officers attached to the Japanese, who saw in this lessening of casualties a possi-bility of pushing in with the bayonet. They however overlooked the true reason for it, which was superiority of artillery fire. Major J. M. Home, a British officer attached to the Japanese Army, was one of the first to realize this. He says : " The denser the formation of infantry when launched to the attack the better, pro-viding the attacking guns can keep down the fire of the defence until they have to cease fire for fear of hitting their own infantry." [12]   The true reason, then, is to be found in the superiority of gun fire which compelled the Russians to keep down in their trenches and so slacken their rifle fire, coupled with the fact that the closer an attacker can advance the more nervous the defender becomes.

Guns and earthworks are the two main characteristics of this war, and not bayonets and bullets.   For though bullet casualties still vastly out-numbered those caused by shell-fire, whenever the guns were well handled (and in this war the quick-firing field-gun was first used), victory in nine cases out of ten was assured.   The gun in its turn forced the infantry to entrench, and the entrenched infantry forced the attacking guns to take cover behind sky-lines and make use of indirect laying, that is, of defiladed fire.   Defiladed fire demanded telephone communications, trenches demanded wire entanglements, and for enfilading purposes machine-gun fire, whilst cavalry in battle faded out of the picture. There is not one cavalry action of importance recorded ; yet in fairness to this ancient arm it must not be over-looked that the Japanese were but poor horsemen and the Russian Cossacks a mounted *canaille.*

It is true that the bayonet figured more conspicuously than it did in 1870-71.   The reasons for this are to be found in the fact that the broken and hilly country often made small surprise attacks possible, and as the plain lands were frequently covered with *kaoliang* (millet), which grows to a height of from eight to twelve feet, small parties of men and sometimes entire firing lines encountered each other unawares.   Further still, the Chinese villages, in which there was much fighting, being walled and divided up by a network of narrow lanes, could normally be cleared only by hand-to-hand encounters.   Generally speaking, however, the numerous bayonet attacks recorded were not assaults at all but merely occupations of positions from which the enemy had retired or had been driven out by shell fire.

The outstanding lessons to be learnt from this war are : the failure of frontal attacks and the success of envelopments ;   the enormous protective power of trenches, when well built, and of wire entanglements, as well as the increasing deadliness of the machine gun. The steady decline in casualties per hour and a corresponding increase in the duration of the battle is most noticeable. Thus, whilst in the eighteenth century the losses per hour were from 4 to 8 per cent.—under Napoleon 2 per cent., and in the 1866 and 1870 wars 1.5 per cent.—in Manchuria they were 0.1 to 0.2 per cent. But whilst in the eighteenth century a battle lasted generally 5 or 6 hours, in Manchuria we find it lasting several days. The battle of Mukden took 6 days, but in 1870 St. Privat was over in 8 hours.

The most important lesson of all, however, was the growing power of artillery, which is proved again and again. Thus, in the " Reports from British Officers," Colonel W. H. H. Waters says : " By the light of my new experiences I can see no reason why artillery should not often be the decisive factor, and it certainly was at Telissu." [13]   And Major J. M. Home writes :

" The great impression made on me by all I saw is that artillery is now the decisive arm and that all other arms are auxiliary to it. The importance of artillery cannot be too strongly insisted upon, for, other things being equal, the side which has the best artillery will always win. . . .

" So strongly am I convinced of the immense importance of artillery that it seems almost a question for deliberate consideration whether artillery should not be largely increased even at the expense of the other arms. Infantry can, if necessary, be trained in about three months, whereas artillery cannot be so improvised. . . .

" With the extraordinary development of artillery it begins to appear as though infantry fire action cannot usefully be employed at ranges beyond 600 yards, as beyond that distance the hostile guns ought to be able to prevent infantry from using their rifles." [14]

Thus do we see the gun gaining supremacy over the rifle, just as the rifle had gained supremacy over the bayonet, and on the blocd-red horizon of the Manchurian War is written for all who can read—a new tactics.

CHAPTER X

THE TURMOIL OF THE NATIONS,
1899—1913

Advancing Democracy. Influence of the War in South Africa. Influence of
the War in Manchuria. Influence of the Manchurian War on Military
Thought. The Economic Background. The Political Foreground.

ADVANCING DEMOCRACY

EXPANSION by conquest was virtually at an end, the
world had been divided up, tension had now set in and
distraction was about to follow. The rationalism of
the nineteenth century was fast dissolving into the
emotionalism of the twentieth ; statesmen being replaced by demagogues, and the social philosophers by
one-eyed fanatics. Since 1848 the Western world had
been turned upside down, the people had come into
their own, and, ignorant, envious and quarrelsome, they
attempted to discover a short cut to a social heaven by
building a second tower of Babel, this time founded
upon gold.

As the nineteenth century passes away we enter an
age of contradictions, of blood-red sunsets and glimmer-
ing false dawns ; of disquisitions on peace and war,
wealth and poverty, socialism and capitalism and this
thing and that thing, all girt about and riveted loosely
together by ignorance and opportunism, and fused into
an amorphous mass by a venal, sensation-loving Press
which stood for the spirit of democracy, and did in fact
fairly represent it, since it howled for action with one
voice and condemned it with the other.

It is an age of excessive spending. Thus, in 1872,
elementary education in Great Britain cost £1,500,000,
in 1908 it cost £16,000,000 ; the cost of the British
Army in 1892 was £17,000,000, and in 1906 £29,000,000.

From these figures we can clearly deduce one fact, namely that the increased education of the masses does not necessarily tend towards peacefulness. This fact is, I think, supported by history ; for if the period 1814-1914 is examined it will at once be discovered that during its first forty years there were thirteen wars of importance, and during its last sixty, thirty-three. This is scarcely an earnest of the peaceful nature of democracies.

Nevertheless, in 1907 the second Peace Conference assembled at the Hague, yet it accomplished so little that two years later Lord Rosebery said ; " Armaments are increasing, this calm before the storm is terrifying." [1] Between 1898 and 1908 the European war budgets rose by £100,000,000, and again between 1908 and 1914 by a similar sum. As expenditure on armaments tended towards war, so did expenditure on social reforms tend towards revolution. Both meant national and international bankruptcy. War, or revolution, which was it to be ? We will attempt to trace the answer to the question.

INFLUENCES OF THE WAR IN SOUTH AFRICA

The immediate result of the war in South Africa was to dislocate the balance of power in Europe. Engaged in one war, Great Britain was unlikely to become involved in another. This freed the hands of Germany, and the result was the Naval Bill of 1900, by which her fleet was nearly doubled, a programme being laid down for 38 battleships and 20 armoured cruisers. In 1901, from the steps of the Bismarck monument in Hamburg, William II exclaimed : " Our future is on the water." What he exactly meant by these words he left it to his listeners to guess. By Great Britain they very naturally were taken as a challenge to her own naval supremacy ; yet it must not be overlooked that, as Germany possessed few colonies, she had to guarantee for her trade free overseas markets, and that in the event of war this guarantee was impossible without a powerful fleet.

Economic necessity was in fact directing the Kaiser's policy quite as much as if not more than his naval enthusiasm and love for dramatic effect.

The result of this naval increase was that in 1904 Admiral Sir John Fisher persuaded the British Government to shift the centre of gravity of the fleet from Gibraltar to the North Sea, that is, within easy reach of Germany, which country was thus brought into the danger-zone. In October 1905, this able and far-seeing sailor laid down the first *Dreadnought*, and it was this same year that he predicted a war between Great Britain and Germany in August 1914.[2]

The British Army also was reorganized. Its incapacity in South Africa could scarcely be overlooked, especially now that a war spirit was creeping over Europe. In 1903 a committee of enquiry under the chairmanship of Lord Esher was assembled, and out of its recommendations arose two great changes, namely, the creation of the Committee of Imperial Defence, which dealt more with foreign policy than with defence and was in no sense an Imperial organization, and the abolition of the Commander-in-Chief and his replacement by the Army Council, a committee of equals formed out of the heads of the War Office departments with the Secretary of State for War as chairman. Its advantage was that it enabled the Cabinet to impose its will upon the Army without having first to wage a battle royal with the Commander-in-Chief supported by the military clubs. Its disadvantage was that as most governments, more particularly governments drawn from the Conservative party, possess no military policy outside economy in expenditure, it left the Army without a head to fight its battles. " Gentlemen, never give a decision," once said an Army Councillor of wit, " for if you do you will bitterly regret it." This saying shows clearly the limitations of this Council as a policy-making machine.

Once the Commander-in-Chief was out of the way, Mr. Haldane, who became Secretary of State for War in 1905, took the matter of reorganization in hand. He reduced the Regular Army in size and organized it as an Expeditionary Force of one cavalry division, six infantry divisions, and army troops. In addition he converted the Militia into the Special Reserve, and created the Territorial Force, as a second line army, out of the Volunteer Forces.

As regards the British Empire as a whole, the most far-reaching change was neither naval nor military, but political. The Empire had set out to crush the national spirit of two small republics. It did so for a brief seven years, when, in 1909, the Union of South Africa was established; but thereby the spirit of the republics passed into the body of the great Dominions. From 1903 onwards, having won their spurs of manhood in the war, the Dominions became all but nations in name, and the Empire became transformed into a Commonwealth. Simultaneously Mr. Joseph Chamberlain put forward his plan for tariff reform, partly to meet the expenditure on social reforms, and partly to establish a preferential system which would draw the Empire together by establishing an economic bond to replace the political one which had now broken. Though there were many in the country who desired Imperial unity, and more who desired social reforms, there were few who wanted to pay for either; consequently his plan was wrecked on public opinion deprived of all reason by Press and poster.

INFLUENCES OF THE WAR IN MANCHURIA

As the war in South Africa unhinged the old British Empire, swinging it into a loose-jointed federation of States, so did the war in Manchuria unhinge the balance of power in Europe through the crippling of Russia, which in the event of another Franco-German conflict in the near future meant that France would be deprived of her support. At once General von Schlieffen, Chief of the German General Staff, amended the war plans, and decided that as Russia was now crippled he would settle with France by moving through Belgium. In 1905 he completed his plan which remained substantially the same until 1913.

Ever since the Russian occupation of Port Arthur, the French Government had been fearful that Russia might become embroiled in a war with Japan ; and as early as June 1898, when M. Delcassé was appointed Minister for Foreign Affairs, a more friendly feeling was shown towards England. During the South African War no advance could be made, but shortly after its ending, as an answer to the German naval threat, King Edward VII, who had succeeded to the throne on January 22, 1901, visited Paris and by his charm and astuteness won the hearts of the French. A return visit to London was made by President Loubet, and a bargain having been arranged over the Egyptian and Morocco questions, a definite entente was established in 1904. This understanding shattered the German policy of setting France and England at loggerheads, so Germany turned to Russia.

On July 23, 1905, a meeting took place between the Kaiser and the Czar at Bjorko, and the following day, on board the *Hohenzollern*, William, in order to establish a coalition against England, persuaded Nicholas to sign a secret treaty pledging that " if any European State shall attack either Power the other will aid with all its forces." Nicholas was to make these terms known to France and " invite her to sign it as an ally." [3]

The Czar's ministers were astounded when they discovered what had taken place, and the treaty was scrapped because it was obvious that France would never agree to an alliance with Germany, as this would carry with it a recognition of the settlement made under the Treaty of Frankfort.

Great Britain then turned to Russia and an arrangement was arrived at in which the outstanding difficulties over Tibet, Afghanistan and Persia were settled. Thus was a Triple Entente established to face the Triple Alliance. As Mr. Gooch says : " The two parties— Great Britain and Japan on the one side, Russia and France on the other—had now made friends. Russia had no longer to think of the perils of the Far East, and could turn her undivided attention to the even more dangerous game of European politics."[4]   This year France and Japan agreed to respect the integrity of China, and Russia and Japan signed a similar treaty.

The political board of Europe was now set, but the table upon which it was laid out was so rickety that the slightest jar or jog might easily upset it.

INFLUENCE OF THE MANCHURIAN WAR
ON MILITARY THOUGHT

The war in Manchuria had not proved M. Bloch right, but it had not proved him wrong; for the war he had in mind was a war in Europe, and not a war in a corner of Asia.   It had proved, however, that many of his contentions were well founded : Such as the indecisiveness of modern battles ; the reduction of slaughter through weapon improvement ; the extensive use of entrenchments ; the supremacy of artillery, and the increasing probability of war being brought to an end by attrition and revolution in place of by force of arms.

Bloch's great work lay, however, beyond the horizon of the military mind. In any case, what could a banker know of war ? So it came about that the General Staffs set up their old idols upon their old altars and burnt before them the new incense of Manchuria. The French and the German Staffs (and it is these two I intend to deal with, for the remainder were but their disciples) revised their training manuals, unconsciously, or purposely, reading into the war what they wished it to prove. Both based their doctrines exclusively on the offensive, the bayonet assault remaining the pivot of their tactical ideas.

The main difference in the two doctrines now decided upon may be traced to national characteristics. Physically and intellectually the German is heavy and methodical, the French quick and cautious. The French, following

Napoleon, believed in attacking in order to uncover, and then, when full information had been gained, to manœuvre against the point selected *during* battle for the decisive blow. The Germans did not : They believed in marching direct upon the enemy once he had been located, to attack him *au fond* in front and simultaneously wash round his flanks and envelop them. Their system was Spartan, an advancing wall of men without a general reserve : that of the French was Roman, a lighter front supported by a heavy rear. The Germans recognized that fronts were inviolable, but must always be attacked in order to fix them, that is pin them down ; the French believed that a flank attack can always be anticipated whilst frequently a frontal one cannot be. In brief, the Germans, being methodical, believed in plan supported by brute force, and the French, being far more individual, believed in cunning adapted to ground. The Germans considered that the French method would lead to disorder, they pinned their faith on the General and his plan ; the French, on the other hand, believing that the German method would lead to excessive slaughter and a blunting of the weapon, pinned their faith on the initiative of their private soldiers.

As regards infantry tactics, the Germans believed in opening an attack with a dense firing line ; to advance it until the enemy's fire was felt, and then smother the enemy's position with bullets ; next to crawl forward from between 800 and 400 yards of the enemy and from that range gain fire superiority ; and then to advance again and at 100 yards assault with the bayonet. Should this last advance prove impossible, the forward movement would be made by night and the assault at dawn. In their *Infantry Regulations* we read : " At the break of day the fire of the infantry and machine guns in concert with that of the artillery will oblige the enemy to burrow in his trenches. One will thus be able to proceed with the destruction of the obstacles and deliver the assault." (5) The French theory was based on the doctrines of Ardant du Picq : To move forward under controlled fire to 400

yards' range, at which point no aimed fire being possible
losses will diminish ; then to advance and take the position
with the bayonet.

Both General Staffs studied carefully the artillery
tactics of the Manchurian War. The French considered
the reports on the preponderance of the Japanese
artillery exaggerated, and the Germans learnt definitely
that the artillery duel and the infantry attack are not
two separate acts of battle but one. Both believed in the
advantages of indirect laying for all guns not immediately
supporting the infantry attacker ; but the Germans on
the whole disliked defiladed fire, believing that, as their
artillery was numerically superior to that of the French,
by opening fire .from all guns simultaneously from
uncovered positions they would be able the more rapidly
to crush their antagonist. The main difference lay in
their respective outlooks on the howitzer. After Plevna
the Germans had adopted the light howitzer, after
Manchuria they adopted the heavy. The French did not
like howitzers ; they considered their 75-mm. field guns all-
sufficient. The heavy howitzer, they said, was a cumbersome weapon unsuited for mobile warfare, and though
the Germans acclaimed the tremendous moralizing
effect of its heavy shells, the French answer was : that
German troops required to be stimulated by noise,
whilst the French did not—they were too intelligent.[6]

Such were the theories propounded between 1905 and
the outbreak of the World War ; and of the two armies
it was certainly the German which had learnt most
from the Manchurian struggle. Both sides, however,
missed the main lesson : The preponderance of the projectile, bullet or shell, *on the defensive*, and its logical
consequence—field entrenchments. Neither could see
that on account of the bullet a war between millions
instead of hundreds of thousands of men must become a
war of entrenchments, and that a war of entrenchments
must result in an enormous increase of artillery and of
shell ammunition. A French writer says :

" In a war between France and Germany we do not anticipate a battle of such a nature [*i.e.*, an entrenched battle]. The fortified places are already quite numerous, and an army that would shut itself up in a permanent defensive position would be inviting destruction.

" The defence will always be only temporary and consequently will be made in a position hastily established, which the enemy will have to take quickly otherwise the motives which imposed a temporary defence will have soon ceased and the force on the defensive will pass to the offensive.

" Battles in entrenched camps as occurred at Plevna or Mukden will never take place in a war with the French army."[7]

This forecast should be compared with M. Bloch's picture given at the end of Chapter VIII. It is also of interest to compare with it the following outline of how the French looked upon the next great European conflict :

" The war will be short and one of rapid movements, where manœuvre will play the predominant part ; it will be a war of movement. The battle will be primarily a struggle between two infantries, when victory will rest with the large battalions; the army must be an army of personnel and not of *matériel*. The artillery will only be an accessory arm, and with only one task—to support the infantry attack. For this task it will only require a limited range, and its first quality must be its rapidity of fire, to admit of it engaging the manifold and transitory targets which the infantry will disclose to it. The obstacles which one will meet in the war of movement will be of little importance ; field artillery will have sufficient power to attack them. In order to follow as closely as possible infantry to be supported, the equipment must be light, handy, and easy to manœuvre. The necessity for heavy artillery will seldom make itself felt ; at all events, it will be wise to have a few such batteries, but these batteries must remain relatively light in order to retain sufficient mobility, which precludes the employment of heavy calibres and powerful equipments. A battery of four 75-mm. guns develops absolute efficiency on a front of 200 metres ; it is consequently unnecessary to superimpose the fire of several batteries. It will serve no useful purpose to encumber oneself with an over-numerous artillery, and it will suffice to calculate the number of batteries that should be allotted to the organization of formations on their normal front of attack."[8]

To-day, knowing what we do of the tactics of the World War, it would be difficult to concoct, even as a joke, a more faulty appreciation.

THE ECONOMIC BACKGROUND

Before turning to the political manœuvres and forays which led up to the World War, I will examine the economic background, not of the world, for that would be too immense a subject for a few brief pages, but of the part of it called Germany. I do so because I believe that since the industrial revolution the foundations of all political actions are economics. The civilization of 1899-1914 was economic, the origins of the war begotten by this civilization were economic, and the struggle itself was not so much a struggle between arsenals as between hostile manufactories. The link between all these economic forms was political—the expression of industry in the language of diplomacy.

After 1871, as I have shown, Germany became an industrial nation. After 1877 she became a highly protected one dependent upon free markets. Then, too late to achieve much, she turned to colonial expansion ; lastly she established a system of peaceful penetration which was counter-attacked by hostile tariffs. To enforce her economic policy upon her neighbours she had her immensely powerful army ; but to enforce her will on her overseas competitors her army was useless, so she built an immensely powerful fleet. Every time a hostile tariff was raised against her she said that she was being encircled, and demanded her place in the sun. When it came to argument she invariably laid a revolver upon the table before opening her mouth, and the result was that the nations became frightened and coalesced against her.

Her expenditure at home was enormous, not only because of her army and navy but because her social services were on a vast scale. Wealthy beyond dream compared with what she had been before 1870, her overdraft yearly grew in size. Behind her perilous banking system stood popular opinion—democracy. Whenever her policy was thwarted a wave of " foaming chauvinism " swept over the country. Though the German Government was pacific, popular opinion was bellicose, driving the Government along a precipitous path, and one which must lead to war. For a hundred and fifty years Europe had been endeavouring to deprive Kings and Governments of the right to make peace and war, and it was " thought that with the coming of an era in which war should depend on the people's will, peace would prevail throughout the world."[9] The exact opposite was the case. In Italy popular opinion caused the Tripoli War of 1911 ; in the Balkans popular opinion caused the Balkan War of 1912-1913 ; and it was popular opinion, and above all the German, which caused the World War, not in August 1914, but from Sedan onwards.

Debts reacting upon policy, from about 1910 until the outbreak of the war Germany was haunted by fear of bankruptcy. To keep solvent she borrowed heavily. Though interest was high, for a time she got what she wanted. Then came rumours of war and France ceased to lend. In October 1911, she required 300,000,000 francs, which, had it not been for the Agadir incident, France would have let her have at 3 or 4 per cent.; but France would not lend them, so she turned to America who loaned them to her at 6 or 7 per cent.[10] Thus she plunged towards the abyss, and as Mr. Fullerton writes in 1913 : " There are . . . many indications that the German rulers may eventually come to regard a war as the sole solution for the life and death economic problems with which they are confronted."[11]

The misfortune of Germany and of the world was that the industrial revolution came to her late. Had it come

to her when it came to Great Britain there would have
been no World War as we know it ; again, had there been
no coal in Germany, Germany as we know her to-day
would not exist.

THE POLITICAL FOREGROUND

Bearing in mind this economic background, the
understanding of which renders intelligible the shadow-
show which was played upon it, we will examine the
political foreground and see the outline of what was
taking place there.

Germany wanted markets ; Germany was powerful ;
Germany was arrogant. Her *Weltpolitik* had intoxicated
her people ; they wanted to make history as well as to
make trade. In the trade-war Germany was being slowly
encircled by a yearly strengthening of the hostile tariff
walls, and behind this encirclement she saw political
encirclement in the formation of the Anglo-British
Entente, and being a good disciple of Clausewitz she
realized that the army of France and the navy of Great
Britain were political instruments.

Her first problem was, consequently, to disrupt this
Entente, to separate Great Britain and France who, as
she thought, were held together only politically by their
mutual agreement over Egypt and Morocco. France
had agreed to respect the integrity of Morocco, but this
country was in anarchy, and, in 1904, France sent a
mission to Fez. Germany was annoyed, but she waited
until the Russian defeat was complete, and then, on
March 31 of the following year, the Kaiser visited
Tangier in order to " safeguard " German interests in
Morocco. In place of achieving the German aim of
separation, this visit strengthened the Entente, and in
January, 1906, led to the Conference of Algeciras which
Reventlow considered a German defeat.

Anarchy continuing, in 1911 once again French troops
were sent to Fez : whereupon Germany, declaring that
the Treaty of Algeciras had been infringed, sent a small

warship, the *Panther*, to Agadir. This action aroused Downing Street, and on July 21 Mr. Lloyd George, Chancellor of the Exchequer, hurled a bomb-shell into the German camp. He said :

" I conceive that nothing would justify a disturbance of international good-will except questions of the gravest national moment. But if a situation were to be forced upon us in which peace could only be preserved by the surrender of the great and beneficent position Britain has won by centuries of heroism and achievement—by allowing Britain to be treated, where her interests are vitally affected, as if she were of no account in the cabinet of nations—then I say emphatically that peace at that price would be a humiliation intolerable for a great country like ours to endure." [12]

Germany was at once thrown into a frenzy, and the immediate upshot was that, by demanding and obtaining a slice of the French Congo in compensation for abandoning her interest in Morocco, she undermined the Triple Alliance by practically compelling Italy to extend her sovereignty over Tripolitania and Cyrenica. This led to the Italo-Turkish War ; for had Italy missed this chance there was no saying what claims Germany herself might not lay to Tripoli.

Three years before the Agadir incident, Turkey having been thrown into turmoil by the Young Turkish party under Niazi Bey and Enver Bey, in October 1908, Austria annexed Bosnia which at once brought to a head the fanatical national feelings between Christians and Moslems in the Balkans. Russia, ever ready to help the Slav States, being still impotent, had to give way, and in the autumn of 1910 the Kaiser appeared in Vienna " in shining armour " which seemed well burnished in the light of Russia's humiliation.

Then came the Italo-Turkish War, the Italians occupying Rhodes and the islands of the Dodecanese. Here was the Balkan chance to drive Turkey out of Europe ; so Serbia and Bulgaria entered into an alliance early in 1912. Then Greece joined Bulgaria, and, on

M

October 8, Montenegro declared war on Turkey. Immediately Bulgaria, Serbia and Greece joined in the fray, the result being that the Turks were routed by the Bulgarians at the battles of Kirk-Kilisse and Lule-Burgas, the Serbians overrunning Macedonia and the Greeks occupying Salonika. Then came a check, at Chatalja the Turk were well entrenched, and all attacks failing an armistice was concluded on December 3.

Between the Allies it was agreed that Serbia should gain an outlet to the Adriatic in northern Albania. Austria objected, and a war between her and Serbia appeared imminent when Russia stepped in. As a war between Austria and Russia would have upset the alliances, France, Germany and Great Britain called together a conference, the upshot of which was that Serbian access to the Adriatic was blocked. This upset the arrangement between the Balkan States. Serbia demanded in compensation a slice of Macedonia. Bulgaria refused to yield and Serbia and Greece declared war on her. Then the Roumanian army entered the field, Bulgaria was overwhelmed and lost the whole of Macedonia and the Dobruja as well.

When the Peace of Bucharest was signed in August 1913, Turkey had virtually ceased to exist as a European Power. Since 1880 she had lost Bosnia, Herzegovina, Bulgaria, Thessaly, Macedonia, Thrace, Epiros, Albania and Crete. In Europe she still occupied Constantinople and Adrianople—and that was all. Roumania and Serbia had thrown off the last shreds of vassalage and Montenegro had grown in size. Cyprus had gone, Egypt had gone, Tunisia had gone and so had Tripoli. Thus was the work of Osman, Orkhan, Murad, Bayezid, Mahommed and the rest undone and done with. As late as 1683 the Turks had encamped under the walls of Vienna; now, in 1913, they were hanging on to the European shore-line of the Propontis with their finger-tips. The struggle with Asia was at an end; it was time a new struggle should begin, and Europe was ready for it. Stuffed with gold, weapons, explosives and political madness, her many peoples blindly slid towards the abyss.

A Zeppelin accidentally comes to ground at Lunéville, someone scribbles an obscene word on her envelope, and Germany is thrown into hysteria. Bernhardi proclaims the next war, and in the theatres and in the cafés of every European city the more chauvinistic a tirade the more frenzied the applause. The Press of all countries piles neuroticism like fuel upon the fire. Baron Beyens, Belgian Minister at Berlin, says : " Peace remains at the mercy of an accident."[13]   Colonel House says : " The whole of Germany is charged with electricity. . . . Everybody's nerves are tense. It only needs a spark to set the whole thing off."[14]   Francis Ferdinand and his wife are murdered in Sarajevo on June 28, 1914. Here is the accident, here is the spark which detonates the European volcano built by the two hostile camps fashioned out of 1871. The World War is upon us—the climax of the Franco-Prussian. Its flames are seen in every land, its ashes fall upon every country, and even as I write they still suffocate us with their stench.

PART IV

PERIOD OF NATIONAL CONSUMMATION
1914—1932

CHAPTER XI

THE GRAND-STRATEGY OF THE WORLD WAR, 1914—1918

The Governing Problems. 1914, The Breakdown of the German War Plan. 1914, The Change in the German Objective. 1915, The Year of Political Blunders. 1916, The Year of Physical Attrition. 1917, The Year of Moral Attrition. 1918, The Year of Decision.

THE GOVERNING PROBLEMS

THE war which now took place had two main characteristics : First, it was a European Civil War ; secondly, it was a World War ; for though it started as a local contest between two nations, the Austrians and the Serbs, who declared war upon each other on July 28, 1914, it rapidly sucked in most of the European Powers and finally nearly all the World Powers. The reason for both these phenomena was one and the same. Since 1871 the political autonomy of nations, which had been a reality during the age of agricultural supremacy, had in fact become a myth. By 1914 few nations remained self-contained or self-supporting ; a new civilization had arisen based on steam power, which demanded for its supremacy international interdependence and not national independence. The world, unseen by the politicians, was fast becoming a vast yet single economic unit in which war for national ends was a disruptive and not a creative force. Directly Austria declared war on Serbia the shock vibrated along every economic and financial channel carrying disruption into the most distant extremities of the world, which since 1871 had largely become a European Empire.

If it be granted that the desire of the German people, not necessarily of her Government, was to gain economic dominion over the world (and this, as I have attempted to show, was the case), then to attain this end, her Government, driven on by this popular urge, must first conquer Europe, and secondly, in order to hold her conquests, not necessarily territorial but economic, she must establish a German outlook among the conquered nations. We get here two governing factors, the first is military and the second is moral, or cultural. The second, which would affect and influence all nations, belligerent and neutral, could only be gained by the first, which included two problems—the command of the land and the command of the sea.

Neutral nations, such as the United States and Holland, did not understand this. They could not see that the ultimate aim of Germany was to impose her will on the world, and that her enemies—France, Russia and the British Empire—were in fact protecting them from such a fate. They were so concerned with their economic interests that, until they attained to a more spiritual vision, they passively supported the German ideal. Consequently, from the moral point of view, which is the ultimate point of view, the World War opened with a contest between the Entente Powers and the World, not the Central Powers alone, but the entire civilized world outside France, Russia, the British Empire, Belgium and Serbia.

In nature, this contest was a two-fold one. The Entente had not only physically to conquer the Central Powers, but politically to win over the neutral nations. The Central Powers, on their side, had not only to defeat the Triple Entente, but to maintain the initial outlook of all non-belligerents. The difficulties confronted by both sides were, consequently, complex and involved. They may be examined in turn.

The Entente Powers were a combination of nations without any centralizing political brain. Their immediate objectives did not coincide. Not only had they to win over neutral opinion, but also to establish concord amongst themselves. France (and I am now talking of popular opinion, for it is popular opinion which in democratic countries brings so great an influence to bear on war) was fighting to regain her lost provinces ; England to drive the Germans out of Belgium, and Russia to preserve the integrity of Serbia ; and neutrals, blinded by their economic outlook, were not much concerned about the hardships of these provinces and small countries. The result was that a lack of political objective led to a wasteful use of military means, and even after popular opinion within the Entente began to realize that each ally was fighting for its existence, the military means had been by then so squandered and dispersed that complete unity of effort was never attained. Further, it was not until the Entente Powers, through their statesmen and by their military actions, showed the World that they were fighting for their lives that neutral nations began to side with them.

The political problem of the Entente was how to win over neutral opinion and simultaneously restrict neutral goods finding their way into Germany. Their military problem was how to settle on some one objective which would result in a co-ordination of military force against a vital point. At the beginning of the war these problems were seen but very dimly, and were obscured and complicated by a superstitious fear of popular opinion, by petty statesmanship, international jealousy and puerile political clap-trap. Even as late as 1918, leading politicians in both England and France continued to obscure the main issue of the war by pandering to the supposed sentiments of their respective peoples ; they talked of " the war to end all war " and similar nonsense.

Turning now to the Central Powers ; not only were they so placed as to be able to work strategically on interior lines but, more important still, the dominance of Germany over her allies enabled her to centralize her object. Their initial political mistake, forced on them by strategical necessity, was the violation of Belgian neutrality. Had it been possible to avoid this, the entry of England into the war might have been delayed ; but to have avoided it would have meant that the initial attack would have had to have been made against Russia instead of against France.   The danger of attacking Russia first and France afterwards, was not that Germany might not have been able to have held up a French attack, for this, judging from our present knowledge of fire-power reinforced by trenches and wire, she could have done quite easily. The danger was that had the Central Powers launched such a campaign, the depth of Russia would have secured the Russian Armies against decisive defeat for an indefinite time, as it eventually did.   Meanwhile, England might have come into the war, and the Belgians would certainly have invited England, or France, to hold the Liège gap which would have rendered German decision against France doubtful. The Germans decided, therefore, to risk the shock to neutral nerves which the invasion of Belgium would cause, and to attempt to overwhelm the French Army and any troops England might send over to France in one campaign. Should this prove successful, politics might go to the devil. That was the German point of view.

1914.   THE BREAKDOWN OF THE GERMAN WAR PLAN

The first phase of the war covered the period from the outbreak of hostilities to the end of September, 1914. During this period the war revealed itself, even to the most unobservant of onlookers, as a world struggle.

The first political event of importance was the violation of the Belgian frontier by German troops on August 4. This brought the British Empire into the war and at one blow annulled all Germany's hope of gaining her ultimate object, for her command of the sea was now checkmated.

Politically, the preponderance of the British fleet over the German had a detrimental influence on all neutral countries outside Europe, for now the conflagration appeared to be localized to Europe. The possibility of

Germany winning the war was recognized; but the probability that if she did so it would be but a stepping-stone to another war, mainly a naval one, was too remote to worry public opinion in America. Then, seven days later, the second great political event took place, an event more unlooked for by the Entente than had been the entry of England into the war by Germany. On August 11, the *Goeben* and the *Breslau* steamed up the Dardanelles, and potentially the war was extended to Asia.

I cannot say how far this most decisive and far-reaching naval operation of the entire war influenced neutral opinion at the time, but British public opinion actually looked upon it as a minor Entente victory! Within nine days of this event, the French plan of war having been completely wrecked by the German surprise attack through Belgium, the third great political event took place. On August 20, the day Brussels was occupied by German troops, the first British Order in Council revising the " Declaration of London " [1] was issued, and economically the influence of the war was felt throughout the whole of the civilized world.

On September 10, the Germans were defeated at the battle of the Marne. To the Entente this was a victory of strategical importance, but to Germany it was a political *débâcle*. Her violation of Belgium had shocked Europe, and slightly agitated America. She had recognized its dangers, but had been so sure of effecting a second Cannae within six weeks of the opening of hostilities that she had risked it. In place of Cannae she had met her Marathon, and the world then saw that her army, like the Persian, possessed feet of clay. This defeat on the Marne coupled with the Austrian defeats in Galicia, was slightly mitigated by her superb tactical victories at Tannenberg (August 31), and the Massurian Lakes (September 15). Whilst the Marne had shown her that she had miscalculated the fighting power of France, these two battles in their turn proved that her estimate of Russian generalship was correct.

Germany was now confronted by a dilemma. Should she continue to attempt to gain her original objective, or should she establish a defensive in France and open a determined offensive against Russia ? She decided on the latter course, but before she could open it in strength, the Western front had to be blocked in order to secure this operation.

1914. THE CHANGE IN THE GERMAN OBJECTIVE.

From October 1 to the end of 1914 was a period of transition. On the Western Front mobile operations ceased with the First Battle of Ypres, which began on October 19 and dragged on to November 22. More and more did the Germans and Austrians now concentrate against Russia. In October the battles of Warsaw and Ivangorod were fought ; then followed the battles of Cracow and Lodz, in November and December. Germany was now definitely ranged against Russia, and, to her, the Western Front for the time being became a secondary theatre of war. One reason for this was undoubtedly the general lack of ammunition, especially in the Russian armies, which enabled Germany, who was also running out of shells, to gain greater tactical effect than if she had continued her offensive in France.

During this period the importance of the supply of ammunition came well to the fore, and all sides began to realize that war has its economic as well as its military side.

On October 20 an interesting event took place ; the British merchant vessel S.S. *Glitra* was sunk by a German submarine, and, two days later, the United States issued a circular note to the belligerent governments insisting on the maintenance of the existing rules of international law. This did not, however, deter the issue, on October 29, of a British Order in Council revising contrabands and modifying the " Declaration of London " which was seriously restricting British Naval action.

In November Turkey came into the war ; the British attack on Tanga was repulsed, and a landing of British troops was made at Fao in Mesopotamia. On December 8 Admiral von Spee's squadron was destroyed off the Falklands, and the high seas were virtually rid of German surface craft.

During this period, it is interesting to watch the influence of the change of the German objective on the plans of the Entente Powers. Germany, occupying a central position, could concentrate her forces either against France or against Russia ; the Entente, possessing command of the sea, could land forces almost anywhere. Germany's strategy was based on the locomotive, British on the steamship. Whilst the Germans used their railways to concentrate their troops, the English used their ships to disperse theirs. A stalemate had been established on the Western Front, and Great Britain should have rejoiced in a situation that enabled her to gain time wherein to develop her resources and raise new armies. But it was looked upon as an evil, and pushful Ministers in London started a variety of minor expeditions. Because Germany had abandoned the Western Front as the decisive theatre of operations, the Entente Powers did likewise, and started searching for other theatres, whilst to the strategist the decisive theatre was obviously North Eastern France.

1915. THE YEAR OF POLITICAL BLUNDERS.

The year 1915 constituted a period of political blunders originating from a faulty use of sea-power, not only on the part of the Entente but on that of the Central Powers as well.

The tightening of the blockade was being seriously felt by Germany, and in spite of Dutch and American opposition to it, there appeared to be little likelihood of it being relented ; consequently, Germany determined, on February 18, to establish a submarine blockade of the British Isles. Her argument in support of this action was that if it were right for the Entente Powers to starve Germany into surrender, Germany was justified in using her submarines to starve Great Britain.

There was, however, a serious flaw in this argument, due to German lack of psychological insight. It was not a question of what was logically right or wrong but of what was wise in the circumstances. Germany, by abandoning her offensive against France and turning upon Russia, had changed her military objective, and now, by proclaiming a submarine blockade of Great Britain, she began to change her political objective. Up to the present Great Britain had occasioned considerable neutral hostility on account of her persistent attempts to shake off the "Declaration of London." Now Germany not only risked doing likewise, but must inevitably embroil herself with every neutral country trading with the British Isles, for these were rapidly becoming the Allied war arsenal and, consequently, the focal point of neutral commerce.

On the day following the declaration of this blockade a Norwegian ship was torpedoed without warning, then a Swedish vessel was sunk; yet the Dutch still protested against the blockade policy of the Entente, until, on May 1, the inevitable happened : S.S. *Gulflight*, a U.S.A. merchantman, was torpedoed without warning. If this were not bad enough, on May 7 Germany perpetrated one of those mad acts which showed how completely she was out of touch with world opinion : the *Lusitania* was sunk off Queenstown, and American sentiment began to veer definitely towards the Entente. This, to the foreseeing, was the beginning of the end, for it was a moral and political German defeat of the first order.

Not only was this use of the submarine a political blunder, but also a naval one, for the simple reason that Germany did not possess sufficient submarines to gain decisive results, and once this campaign was launched, complete surprise was at an end.

Whilst Germany thus aimed at obtaining an economic decision by underwater attack on her enemies' commerce, England and France, possessing as they did surface command of the sea, extended their blockade policy by changing their military object.

On December 30, 1914, the Grand Duke Nicholas, Commander-in Chief of the Russian Armies, had suggested to the British Government an expedition against the Turks in order to ease the Russian situation in the Caucasus, which had been brought about by Turkey entering the war (October 29, 1914). The upshot of this was that, on January 13, the British War Council considered a naval attack on the Dardanelles, and, on the 28th, the British Government decided in its favour. A naval bombardment was opened on February 19, repeated on March 18, and the Entente forces landed on April 25 and 26. Concurrently with these events, the army in Mesopotamia was re-inforced, and the Battle of Shaiba took place on April 12 to 14.

In these operations we see the beginnings of that encircling policy by which, by laying siege to the Central Powers and Turkey, it was hoped to reduce them to surrender through starvation instead of by direct attack. They were destined to fail, because they were strategically, tactically and politically unsound ; because the steamship working on exterior lines cannot compete with the railway working on interior lines ; because the submarine was restricting more and more the use of surface craft ; because the Entente Powers did not possess sufficient man-power or resources for this colossal siege, and to attempt to undertake it with insufficient forces must lead to a violation of concentration of force. Politically it must inevitably lead to friction.

No sooner was the Dardanelles campaign launched than Italy denounced the Triple Alliance (May 4) and declared war on Austria (May 23). This was the result of a secret agreement signed in London between the Italian Government and the Entente on April 26. Already, earlier in the year, the British Government had suggested to Greece and Roumania to enter the war and assist Serbia, but with no results.

During this period we see strategy completely over-ruled by diplomacy which, more and more, aimed at encircling the Central Powers in place of concentrating against some one vital point. On February 23, the island of Lemnos was occupied by British Marines; the Greeks objected to this occupation, but the British Government pleaded military necessity, the same plea put forward by the Germans when they entered Belgium. This wrangle with Greece and the Balkans led not only to a diplomatic but to a military fiasco. In October Bulgaria entered the war against the Entente; Entente troops were sent to Salonika, in spite of Greek protests, and in December the evacuation of Gallipoli was begun and was completed by January 8, 1916.

From all points of view 1915 was a year of grotesque failure, traceable mainly to the change of military and political objectives. The Germans pushed on to Vilna and Pinsk, and yet Russia remained undefeated. On September 1 Germany acknowledged her submarine error by accepting the limitations of submarine activity laid down by the United States. The Entente Powers carried out a series of disjointed attacks all over the world. On the Western Front were fought the First Battle of Champagne (December 20-March 17); the Battle of Soissons (January 8-14); the Battle of Neuve Chapelle (March 10-13); the Battle of Festubert (May 15-25); the Second Battle of Artois (May 9-June 18); the Battle of Loos (September 25-October 8); the Third Battle of Artois (September 25-October 15), and the Second Battle of Champagne (September 25-November 6), and, except for the last three, there was little attempt at co-ordination. Italy engaged in a war of her own on the Isonzo; the Serbians were driven out of their country; the Dardanelles campaign was closed down; the Battle of Ctesiphon was won (November 22), but General Townshend was forced to retire to Kut-al-Amara, where the Turks besieged him, on December 7. In fact this year was a year of disasters, because the Entente possessed no definite

object and, consequently, no strategy. The only
shadowy attempts at co-ordination were the formation
of the Coalition Ministry in Great Britain on May 25,
followed, on June 5, by a conference at Calais between
British and French Ministers to co-ordinate war policy
and strategy, the one thing wanted to win the war.

1916. THE YEAR OF PHYSICAL ATTRITION.

The strategical chaos, established during 1915, was
straightened out a little during the following year, and
though the main idea of both the Entente and the
Central Powers still remained the economic attack on
each other's resources, extensive field operations took
place.

The Allied campaign of September 1915, which had
shown some idea of strategical co-operation, came as a
shock to the German Supreme Command.   The operations in Russia were progressing slowly, too slow to
warrant their completion before another Allied offensive
took place in the West.   Germany determined, therefore, to pause in Russia and to hit at France before
Great Britain was ready to co-operate in the attack,
and, simultaneously, strike at England by a renewal of
the submarine campaign.   The first step in this temporary change of policy was the Battle of Verdun which
opened on February 21, and dragged on to August 31,
costing Germany about 500,000 casualties.   An extended
submarine campaign was opened on March 1, and was
followed by expostulations on the part of America.   Its
economic effect was startling, and at first it looked as if
Germany had at last discovered the weapon which
would enable her, if not to win the war, at least to
induce the Entente Powers to consider terms of peace.

Though the attack on Verdun had upset the French
and British spring offensives, a combined operation
was decided on between Russia, France and Great
Britain.   This opened with Brusilov's attack, on June 4,
which came as welcome news to England after her naval

N

fiasco at Jutland. Brusilov's offensive lasted until August 17, and during these eleven weeks his losses amounted to nearly a million men ; the Russian Army was in fact bled white.

Meanwhile, France and Great Britain followed in his footsteps. The Battle of the Somme opened on July 1 and dragged on to November 18, by which time the British casualties alone amounted to 475,000.

In the Balkans, the Roumanian Government had entered upon negotiations with the Russian Government as early as January 22, but it was not until August 17, the day Brusilov's offensive *ended*, and the failure of the Somme battle had become patent to all men, that Roumania concluded an agreement with the Entente Powers, and, on the 27th, declared war on Austria-Hungary. On December 6 Bukharest capitulated to the Germans.

The lack of unity of effort between Roumania and the Entente Powers was only exceeded in the case of Greece. Greece was openly pro-German and did not want to have anything to do with the Entente, which nevertheless bullied her into the war by a series of measures which would undoubtedly have brought down the wrath of the neutral world had not the German submarine campaign forced all neutral States to side with her enemies. So great was this change of feeling that the British Government issued on July 7 an Order in Council rescinding the " Declaration of London." This was met by formal objections only on the part of the United States.

As regards British relationship with Greece, the following facts are of interest, as they show that immorality in war is only justifiable after neutral opinion has been won over. On January 11, the French occupied Corfu, the Greeks strongly objecting ; between June 6 and 22, Greece was blockaded by the Entente Powers; on September 9, Macedonia was blockaded ; on October 11, the Greeks were compelled to surrender their fleet; eventually, in November, a Provisional Government,

under M. Venizelos, was forced upon Greece ; troops
were landed in the Piræus and, on December 14, the
Greeks were compelled by ultimatum to withdraw their
entire forces from Thessaly. These actions, which were
anything but honourable, show the growing strength of
the Entente. From now onwards, the Central Powers
are ranged against the Entente and the world. This is
realized by Germany and her Allies, for, on December 12,
they each separately presented notes to the United
States Ambassadors in their respective countries request-
ing them to inform the Governments of the Entente
Powers that they were ready to negotiate for peace.
On December 30, the Entente Powers rejected these
proposals.

During this year we see developing the physical
attrition of both sides ; but, added to this, the Central
Powers are also suffering from a moral attrition, and
as they lose neutral support so do their opponents gain it.
The Entente Powers began to attempt some co-ordination of policy and effort. On January 24 the first
Military Service Bill was passed by the House of
Commons, and, before the end of the year, National
Service was established in Great Britain. On March
26-28 an Inter-Allied Conference was assembled at
Paris to enquire into military, economic and diplomatic
affairs, and another was assembled, on November 15,
at which policy and strategy were discussed. Then, on
December 7, the greatest impetus was given for the
continuance of the war : Mr. Lloyd George succeeded
Mr. Asquith as British Premier, and two days later a
War Cabinet was formed in London. The reconstruction of the British Government was immediately followed
by the reorganization of the French, and on the very
day that this took place, namely, December 12, the
Central Powers indented their peace notes to the United
States Ambassadors.

The year ended with a foreboding event ; on
December 31 Rasputin was murdered in Petrograd.

1917.   THE YEAR OF MORAL ATTRITION

Though the physical attrition of 1916 was to continue, the main characteristic of 1917 was the moral attrition of all sides. On the part of the Central Powers this was inevitable. The world having now turned against Germany, its moral support was denied to her, and without it she was henceforth reduced to make demands on the morale of her people without being in any way able to replenish it from outside. On the part of the Entente Powers, the reason for their moral decadence was the opposite. The world was now definitely ranged on their side, and, as we shall see, early in this year America full-heartedly joined their cause. It was not, therefore, outside influence which depressed them, but inside lack of co-ordination. Whilst Germany was able to back her fighting forces by her superb though dwindling patriotism, the Entente Powers had no similar force to unify and stimulate them. The lack of a controlling brain, an organ which could consider one thing at one time, in place of all things at any time, led to intense friction—military and political. Whilst Germany was still controlled by a national spirit, the Entente, as an entity, was obsessed by mob instincts—its members were not only fearful of the common enemy but suspicious of each other. Germany was being morally exhausted through outside pressure, and the Entente Powers through a creeping internal paralysis.

No sooner had the Entente Governments rejected the German peace proposals than the Central Powers made one further attempt to regain world opinion by repudiating any further responsibility for continuing the war, and declaring that, as the war was now forced upon them, they would fight for their hearths and homes to the bitter end. Having thus attempted to place herself in the right, eight days later, on January 11, Germany committed an egregious political blunder. Von Eckhardt, the German Minister in Mexico, was instructed to negotiate an alliance between Mexico and Japan against the United States. Then, not waiting to ascertain the result, on January 31 she announced an unrestricted submarine war in which hospital ships were to be sunk. This campaign opened on February 1.

Her reasons for this drastic measure, which two days later caused the United States to sever diplomatic relations with her, appear to be : first, that she realized that Russian morale was nearing breaking point ; secondly, that the havoc caused by her submarines during 1916, if continued and accentuated, would bring England to her knees ; and thirdly, that these events would be accomplished before America could make her military influence felt. As we know, her reasons were misjudged, mainly because she did not understand British pertinacity and endurance.

Meanwhile the Entente Powers opened the new year with vain attempts to put their house in order and establish some semblance of co-ordination.   On January 5 an Inter-Allied Conference assembled at Rome to discuss co-operation in Macedonia ; on January 17 another was held in Petrograd to establish some form of war policy ; then, on January 24 an Allied Naval Conference took place in London to outline a policy for the Mediterranean, and on February 26 an Anglo-French Conference was assembled at Calais to discuss the co-operation of the British and French Armies, and the co-ordination of operations by the French Commander-in-Chief. Nothing definite came of these conversations, and so the Entente floundered on, not blind-folded and seeing nothing, but many-headed and seeing all things and their shadows at once.

To return to German policy. Ever since the murder of Rasputin things in Russia had gone from bad to worse, till at length, on March 12, the Russian Revolution surged out of the gutters, and three days later Nicholas II abdicated his throne. In England this terrible Entente disaster was acclaimed by the daily Press as a glorious and victory-producing event ! In Germany it was

understood as the beginning of a convulsive end of
Russian military opposition.   So far, German policy was
justified ; then, on April 6, the United States declared
war on Germany, and on May 17 the British Admiralty
at length determined to draw up a plan to convoy
merchantmen, and justification began to grow lean.

To all far-seeing people the Russian Revolution meant
the end of Russia as a military power, for it is manifestly
impossible for a nation to wage successfully a foreign
and a domestic war simultaneously.   To these people
also the entry of the United States on the side of the
Entente Powers meant the ultimate defeat of Germany.
The moral preponderance now brought to bear on the
side of the Entente was enormous.   Though America
was totally unprepared for war her resources were
stupendous.   All that the Entente Powers had henceforth to do was to consolidate the Western Front, cut
down war wastage in order to reduce submarine pressure,
and push the Turks from north of Baghdad towards
Aleppo, Baghdad having been occupied by British
forces on March 11.   Instead, they decided on a decisive
spring offensive, and in doing so they showed, in my
opinion, a complete lack of grand strategical sense.
Apparently it was still considered that Russia could be
supported with profit, and the true meaning of America
entering the war was not appreciated.   What the
Entente Powers lacked was imagination, because they
had no single head which could think clearly.   Further,
the colossal failures of the Verdun and Somme battles,
during 1916, might have suggested to them the un-
likelihood of Germany, even when rid of Russia, being
able to break through the Western Front were it carefully
prepared to meet her onslaught.

This spring offensive, which was to consist in a dual
attack—one from the direction of Arras eastwards, and
one from the direction of Rheims northwards—was
strategically unsound because the prospective battlefields
were too far apart.   It was also tactically unsound in
that the frontage of each battlefield was too restricted.

The Germans smelling out this attack, for lengthy preparation had polluted the air, on February 25 they began to fall back from the river Ancre and by April 5 had completed their retirement to the Hindenburg (Siegfried) line. This strategically threw out of joint the Arras operations; nevertheless the battle of Arras was launched on April 9 and continued until May 4, during which period the British Army lost 155,000 in casualties. On April 16 the French began the Second Battle of the Aisne which ended, four days later, in a complete fiasco. Out of these quite uncalled for operations some good, however, emerged. On May 15 General Nivelle was succeeded by General Pétain as Commander-in-Chief, and General Foch was made Chief of the General Staff of the French Ministry of War. Thus, what many Conferences had been groping after for over a year was eventually attained through disaster. Failure is always the most expensive of masters; and later on we shall again meet with this grim pedagogue.

One factor of importance which became noticeable during the French offensive was the low point to which French morale had fallen. This was largely due to political intrigue, the standing curse of the French Army; also to bad leadership and the terrible casualties suffered in 1916. And yet this lack of morale was made an excuse to continue offensive operations against Germany, and as the French were unable to take a leading part the bulk of the work fell upon the British Army. Thus, I suppose, it was thought that France would, like a phœnix, rise from British ashes. A curious conception.

If the Arras-Aisne operations were unnecessary, those in Flanders, between June 7 (when the Battle of Messines opened) and November 10 (when the Battle of Ypres ended), were doubly so. As regards the former, the excuse could be alleged that it was not possible to see how events would turn out in Russia; but by July 31 (when the Ypres offensive was launched) the Russian summer offensive had petered out and any hope of further Russian support had vanished. In place of Great Britain economizing man-power she squandered it. In Flanders she lost nearly 400,000 men killed, wounded and missing as well as some 200 tanks ; in fact, in these operations, the British Army was bled white, and at a period when it was visible to all that Russia must within a few weeks vanish as an ally and that America could not take her place until the summer of 1918.

The French, having revived, on August 20 opened a strong offensive at Verdun which dragged on to December 15, and tens of thousands more casualties were piled up. The British, failing at Ypres, launched a new offensive at Cambrai on November 20. It opened with a startling success, so startling that no reserves had been assembled to make good the initial penetration. It ended in a startling failure and 75,000 casualties were added to the British total.

Meanwhile, Germany settled with Russia. In July, August and September the Russians were hammered from Galicia to the Baltic. On September 15 the Russian Republic was proclaimed ; on November 8 a Bolshevik *coup d'état* was carried out in Petrograd by Lenin and Trotski ; on December 2 hostilities were suspended between the Russian and German armies, and on the 15th of this month the Armistice of Brest-Litovsk was agreed upon, and Russia went out of the war save for some desultory engagements, peace being finally signed on March 3, 1918.

At length, after three years' incessant fighting on her Eastern front, Germany gained the first half of her military object. Now she was faced by the second half, the conquest of the French and British Armies. In 1914 she had been confronted by 3,000,000 Frenchmen and 120,000 Englishmen, and yet she had failed. Now she was faced by 3,000,000 Frenchmen, 3,000,000 Englishmen, and behind these loomed the United States with an easy 6,000,000 more. In 1914 the world was passively on her side, now it was actively against her. Not only had America declared war on her, but the following countries had done likewise : Honduras, San Domingo, Haiti, Greece, Siam, China, Uruguay, Brazil, Ecuador, Panama and Cuba—nothing very great indeed but dependable as weather-cocks. Her submarine campaign had not brought England to heel, and the spirit of her own navy was low ; for on August 3 a serious mutiny broke out at Wilhelmshaven. Yet the Entente was terrified to meet her ; the Italians had bled themselves white in twelve battles on the Isonzo ; Roumania had ceased hostilities, and the British and French armies had lost between them over a million men. These are, I think, the true reasons, for fear is both the parent and offspring of failure.

If 1915 was a year of diplomatic blunders, 1917 was indeed, on the part of France and Great Britain, a year of military mistakes. Yet all this blundering can be traced to one definite cause, the lack of a thinking head. As the failure of the spring offensive produced Foch, so did the failure of the autumn offensive produce some semblance of unity. On November 7 an Allied Conference was held at Rapallo and a Supreme War Council was agreed upon. On November 27 this Council was appointed, and its four members were : General Sir Henry Wilson, General Foch, General Cadorna and General Bliss. As we shall see, another disaster was necessary before unity was attained.

1918. THE YEAR OF DECISION

We now come to the most interesting year of the war— 1918. In August 1914, all the great belligerent Powers thought they had made up their minds ; before the year was out they tried to make up their minds ; in 1915 they changed their minds before they had made them up ; in 1916 they worked on these suppositional changes ; in 1917 they nearly suffocated themselves in the appalling tangle of substance and shadows, and then, ultimately, in 1918 a decision was arrived at which was undreamt of by all.

Once Russia had turned from her foreign war to fight her domestic enemies, real and imaginary, Germany was left with the solution of a problem which was totally different from the one which confronted her at the end of September 1914. Then, she had two problems: the first, military—the defeat of the Entente Powers; the second, political—the maintenance of world opinion on her side. Now that she had smashed Russia she was left facing not only the Western Front but also the Italian, Macedonian and Mesopotamian fronts; and behind all these fronts stood an angry hostile world in place of neutral nations expecting to grow rich on the turmoil of the war. If the problem of the Western Front had been too hard a nut to crack in 1914, it was many times harder now. In fact there remained but one rational course open to Germany, and that was to hold her Western Front, perhaps to strike at some economic or political objective, but above all to pander to President Wilson's highbrowed idealism *by forcing her enemies to attack her in place of attacking them*, and so show the world that *she was solely fighting for her life*, and not for dominion over others, and that she would accept a just peace even if by it she were slightly crippled.

Was there any inkling that such a policy would have succeeded ? There were at least two: First, the allies had played into her hands during 1917 by exhausting themselves in their irrational attacks ; secondly, on January 8, 1918, President Wilson had delivered his famous message to Congress in which he laid down his " Fourteen Points," and on February 11 he added four more. This was his gospel which, on account of German obtuseness, was destined not only to ruin Germany, but her enemies as well ; had she pandered to it she might have saved her skin at the expense of the Entente.

Instead of attempting to gain her political object, which was peace, and gain it at any decent price, she threw it aside and once again attempted to win her military object which was the decisive defeat of England and France. For two years she had been waging an economic war on Great Britain ; if now she must attack France, she should have selected an economic objective, the capture of ' which would have adversely affected French politics and so have prepared France to consider terms of peace. Such an objective stared her in the face, namely, the Bruay coalfields ; but instead of attacking these, she selected the worst possible strategical point— the junction of the Franco-British armies, a point towards which the total French and British reserves could be rushed from either flank without mutual inter- ference.

The success of this attack was mainly due to the fact that the British Army of 1917 had been bled white in Flanders during the summer and autumn of that year. The causes officially alleged were subsidiary to this paramount cause. The Somme offensive of March and April, 1918, was the coping stone of the work of the British higher command at Ypres, which cost another 90,000 men.

In place of following up the initial tactical success of March 21 with a determined attack on the British Third Army in order to gain the Bruay coalfields which were vital to France, the German Armies followed the line of least resistance, and, through lack of communications and, consequently, of supply, their attack petered out on April 5, a few miles east of Amiens. Then in place of hitting at a *vital* spot, however tough, they committed the deadly tactical sin of looking for a soft spot, and the result was the Battle of the Lys which, beginning on April 9 lasted to April 29, during which the Germans exhausted their reserves and placed themselves in an all but untenable pocket. Then they looked for another soft spot, and on May 27 found it between Soissons and Rheims. The battle fought here, known as the Third Battle of the Aisne, brought the German forces right down to Château Thierry, and another pocket, this time a veritable trap, was formed in which the last of the great German offensives flickered out.

When we examine these battles we see quite clearly that the German tactical gains were the measures of

strategical losses.   In war, a general should aim at a
decisive point ; if this point is also a soft spot so much the
better, but if it is only a soft spot and he still aims at it
he is not a great general.   In 1918 Ludendorff seems to
have lost his mental balance, for by selecting soft spots
he inevitably depleted the German reserves.   This deple-
tion was the most effective step he could have taken to
prepare the inevitable counter-attack of his enemies.

The tactical defeat of the British Army on March 21
was in at least one respect the greatest strategical victory
won by Great Britain and France during the entire
war, for it led to unity of command.   On February 5
the powers of the Supreme War Council had been
increased, and on the following day Sir Henry Wilson
became Chief of the Imperial General Staff in London ;
but it was not until March 26 that the tactical *débâcle* of
the 21st resulted in a decision being arrived at in Doullens
to appoint General Foch Co-ordinator of the French
and British Armies.   Though the next disaster, the German advance on the Lys, promoted him to Commander-
in-Chief of the Allied Armies in France, it was not until
November 5, *six days before the termination of hostilities*,
that he was raised to the position of Generalissimo and
was placed in supreme strategical direction of all forces
operating against Germany on all fronts.

Once the British and French Armies were provided
with a strategical brain, what was the result ?   The
battle front was thinned, soft spots were created and the
men withdrawn from them were concentrated in reserve.
The soft spots became traps and the reserve—the terrier.
On July 18 the Second Battle of the Marne began, and the
French Armies attacked a vital spot as well as a soft one.
On August 8 the British Armies attacked another vital
point, at Amiens, and the end was in sight.   The first of
these battles lasted twenty-one days, the second four.
Battles now followed in rapid succession, and all were of
short duration, not only because the Germans were
falling back but because the Entente Armies were fighting
under a thinking brain, the brain of a pugilist, a man who

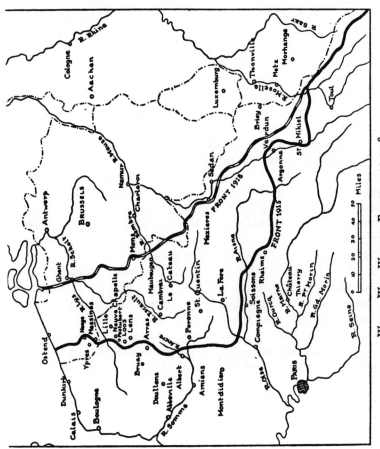

WORLD WAR, WESTERN FRONT, 1914-1918

hits with his left, then with his right, sometimes to the jaw, sometimes on the body, who, in fact, fights like a trained fighter whose brain and fists work together and instantaneously.

The victories in France reverberated through every front. On September 18 the Battle of Monastir-Doiran was fought ; on the 19th that of Megiddo, and on October 24 that of Vittoria-Veneto. The first removed Bulgaria by the Armistice of September 27 ; the second removed Turkey by the Armistice of Mudros, signed on October 30, and the third removed Austria-Hungary by the Armistice of November 3.

Unity of command on the side of the Entente Powers, backed by superiority of man-power and weapon-power and supported by the will of the world, led to final victory. The German armies fought vallantly to the last, but eventually they were overcome, not by the Allied Powers alone but by the flank attacks of their own allies and by the rear attacks of their own people. On October 31 revolution broke out in Vienna and Budapest, and on November 7 Bavaria proclaimed herself a Republic. Already, on November 3, the German crews at Kiel had mutinied ; on the 9th a revolution was proclaimed in Berlin ; on the 10th the Kaiser crossed the Dutch frontier and on the 11th at Rethondes Station in the Forest of Compiègne an armistice was concluded between the Allied and Associated Powers and Germany, and the only belligerent nation who in any way gained her object in the war was England. I will briefly enquire into this remarkable ending.

It has already been mentioned that on January 8 of this year President Wilson outlined his " Fourteen Points," which, as regards the self-determination of nations, closely coincided with the doctrine of Lenin. I have said that if Germany had accepted the " Fourteen Points " at the beginning of 1918 she might well have obtained a peace which would have brought the war to an unpleasant though not a disastrous termination. She waited, however, until October 4, and then sent a note to President Wilson proposing an armistice. President Wilson replied to this note on the 14th, and his reply was accepted by the German Government on the 20th, and on the 23rd was submitted to the Allied and Associated Governments. On November 3 the Allied Governments agreed to Germany's proposal for an armistice, and on the 11th it was signed on French soil; that is the significant point.

There can be no doubt that the German Armies were beaten, that her fleet was beaten, that her allies were beaten, and that her own people were beaten; yet the Allied Powers won only a physical victory and they did not win a moral one. To effect such a victory demanded an unconditional surrender on the part of Germany. Germany never surrendered unconditionally, she surrendered on terms whilst she was still in occupation of French territory. What was the result of this? The handing over of the German fleet removed all threat to the British frontiers; the loss of Alsace and Lorraine did not fully secure the French frontier though it weakened the German. For France the war had resulted in a small gain of security, for Germany in a small loss of it; one of the main causes of the war remained; hence the present trouble in Europe and the probability of another war in which Germany will attempt to re-establish her frontiers of 1871, and France to maintain or enlarge upon her existing one.

CHAPTER XII

THE CHANGING NATURE OF WAR, 1914-1918

The Inner Struggle. Traditional Warfare. Matériel Warfare. Economic Warfare. The Theory of Moral Warfare. The Weapons of the Moral Attack.

THE INNER STRUGGLE

IN this world there is a reason for all things. In every set of circumstances there lurks an uninevitable destiny. In the circumstances which existed before the War, war was a certainty, nothing could have prevented its outbreak except a change in the circumstances themselves. These were : That democracy stood for economic nationalism, whilst commerce, unseen by the men of mercantile mind, stood for economic interdependence ; that democracy gorged itself upon quantity, whilst science sought after quality, not brute force but economy of force, not ever-growing numbers but a deeper and a deeper truth. Science, the urge of Western civilization, which knew no bounds, no national frontiers, which penetrated to the electron and soared beyond the nebulæ, stood as a new symbol of world freedom ; and democracy, which had grown fat on science, ordered itself like a row of village pumps, each drawing its water from the same source, each owner fondly imagining that if he could pump dry his neighbour's well all the water would not only be his but to his benefit.

It was because the Western world was going mad that war was a certainty ; a war which, like a fever, was to debilitate democracy, to undermine its vitality and to shorten its days.

There can be no doubt that the war was an upheaval of democratic nations begotten of democratic policies, and that the spark which detonated it was the maintenance of the liberty of small nations—Belgium and Serbia.

There can be no doubt that its expiring corruscations whirled new nations into the political air, and yet to the thinking there can be no doubt that it was the end of a world order—the death cry of the French Revolutionary epoch. In 1789, " Liberty " became the watchword; in 1914, " Duty " was whispered around the world.

I doubt whether before the war any statesman saw this, even as a dream. I doubt whether any see it now, or seeing it have the courage of George Fox, the founder of the Quakers, who, when the vision came upon him, cried fearfully : " Woe to the bloody city of Lichfield ! "— his symbol of an old and corrupted world.

If statesmen saw nothing, soldiers were utterly blind, for they stumbled into the war like a man over a precipice on a dark night. To them war meant killing, and, consequently, hunting in England was considered the highest form of military training. In 1907 Colonel F. N. Maude, a thinking soldier who had not hypnotized himself on the bayonet point, wrote : " It is Science and Science alone that supplies the power now daily driving us towards a cycle of wars . . . trade-hunger created by inventions is now impelling us towards armed collision."[1] Consequently, if science was driving the world towards war, science would of a certainty drive the world through this war, and therefore to science must the soldier turn in order to win it.

Earlier still, in 1883, General von der Goltz had said : " The day will come when the present aspect of war will dissolve, when forms, customs and opinions will again be altered. Looking forward into the future, we seem to feel the coming of a time when the armed millions of the present will have played out their part. A new Alexander will arise who, with a small body of well-equipped skilled warriors, will drive the impotent hordes before him ; when, in their eagerness to multiply, they shall have overstepped all proper bounds, have lost cohesion, and, like the green-banner army of China, have become transformed into a numberless, but effete, host of Philistines."[2]

o

These words were read by soldiers but, like the seed on the rocky soil, they fell upon petrified minds. Alone in the army of Great Britain was quality rather than quantity aimed at. Musketry had been reduced to an art as high as that of archery during the Hundred Years War. But then there were great generals who understood war as a progressive art. Edward III was no traditionalist, he created a new tactics, whilst the British generals of 1914 copied an old. They, like the French, German, Russian and Austrian, were prepared for war. But what kind of war ? That was the question.

TRADITIONAL WARFARE

The war opened on sound, traditional lines. The armed herds and hordes of men had for over forty years browsed in the lush pastures of pseudo-1866's and 1870's, and were swollen with the wind of the unlimited offensive which involved unlimited slaughter. Two tremendous fallacies underlay this doctrine. The first was that policy is best enforced by destruction, and the second was that tactical strength is founded upon numbers. To the General Staffs of Europe war was an end in itself and not a means to an end. We cannot really blame them for this outlook, for if Clausewitz is right in saying that war is a continuation of national policy, had not the foreign policies of nations since 1871 been in the main destructive of international interdependence in order to foster national independence ? Yet from 1871 onwards a new civilization had arisen in Europe, woven on the enormous growth of railways and the facilities rendered possible by the motor-car and the lorry. Soldiers had studied these means, not in order to mechanize armies, that is to replace muscular power by mechanical power, but to utilize them in such a way that they could submerge their enemy's frontiers under a veritable inundation of flesh. Millions of men would sweep forward and, like immense clouds of locusts, would gain victory by sheer weight of numbers. Such was the cloistered-theory of the generals ; but the private soldiers, the men who fight in the field lands and not in the studies, held another view—an unwritten, even unthought, and, therefore, instinctive doctrine. It was this : The supreme duty of the soldier is to fight and not to die. The military monks, though they swung incense before the moral factors, were so immersed in the scholasticism of dead wars that they forgot that the soldiers who were to fight in the next war were living beings dreading death, yet willing to face battle as long as facing it did not mean wilful suicide.

In August 1914, the German armies, without reserves, were drawn up in phalangial formation from Aachen to Basle. Their right was to wheel through Belgium, round Paris, and then advance eastwards sweeping the armies of France into Germany and Switzerland. This plan was extraordinarily simple, and the railways appeared to render it easy. Tactics had been mechanized in place of weapons, mechanical movement forwards was to replace genius, and the goose-step—intellect.

The French General Staff realized the likelihood of a turning movement through Belgium, but they were in no way perturbed. For long they had been studying the methods of Napoleon, and, presumably, as no railways existed in his day, they overlooked the fact that Paris is the greatest railway centre in France. Instead of holding their frontiers lightly and assembling their reserves there, and then, as the enemy's three hundred mile long phalanx began to twist out of shape as it inevitably must, striking in strength, what did they do ? They concentrated the bulk of their forces on the frontier, with a reserve army close in rear, their intention being to penetrate the phalanx, break it in half, and so dislocate it !

M. Bloch, the Polish banker, now comes in. This carefully planned war was within a few weeks of its declaration smashed to pieces by fire-power ; fire-power so devastating that as armies could no longer live upon the surface of the battlefield there was no choice but to go under the surface ; consequently trenches five hundred miles long were dug, and armies went to earth like foxes.

Then, in order to secure these trenches from surprise attacks, each side turned itself into an immense spider, and spun hundreds of thousands of miles of steel web around its entrenchments. Thus, after a few weeks of *real* warfare, the *offensive à outrance*, that high gospel of the pre-war manuals, was reduced to a wallowing defensive among mud holes and barbed wire. Armies, through their own lack of foresight, were reduced to the position of human cattle. They browsed behind their fences and occasionally snorted and bellowed at each other.

The one problem which now confronted them was, how to re-establish movement ; for until one or both sides could move there was no possibility of a decision by arms —famine alone must become the arbiter.

MATÉRIEL WARFARE

As inundations of men, personnel warfare, had failed beyond hope of redemption, the General Staffs, still obsessed by the quantity complex turned to *matériel,* seeing in shell fire a means of blasting a road to Paris or Berlin. Thus the gun replaced the rifle. War was now to become an artillery duel.

As the entire arsenals of the civilized world could not possibly meet the demand for shells, the General Staffs turned to the industries of their respective nations, and a new contest was begun. Which nation could produce the largest output ? For on this output, so it was thought, would victory depend. Armies now became intoxicated on T.N.T., and strategy and tactics are lost sight of in a storm of shells and roaring high explosives.

For the preliminary bombardments of the Battle of Hooge, in 1915, 18,000 shells were fired ; for those of the First Battle of the Somme, in 1916—2,000,000 were fired ; for those at the Battle of Arras, in 1917—2,000,000, and for those at the Third Battle of Ypres, the same year —4,300,000 ! At this last-mentioned battle the shells fired during the preliminary bombardment, that is before the infantry attack began, weighed 107,000 tons and cost approximately £22,000,000, a figure nearly equal to the total yearly cost of the pre-war British Home Army ! Did this inundation of iron lead to victory ? No ; it could not possibly do so ; for in the process of digging up trenches by shell fire, everything in the neighbourhood of the trenches was dug up. Roads vanished, tracks vanished, railways vanished, and the surface of the ground vanished under the influence of the material earthquake to which all things were subjected. The enemy was slaughtered—true. But though he fled, or was exterminated, an impassable area was created, which in swampy districts, such as Flanders, or when it rained, were turned into a morass of mud. In place of accelerating infantry movement, every shell that fell impeded this all necessary act of winning the war by force of arms. Further still, as these bombardments lasted from seven to twenty-one days, surprise became impossible. The result was colossal slaughter. For example : The battles of the Somme in 1916, and of Ypres in 1917, cost the British Army in killed, wounded and missing over 800,000 men. Yet on the Eastern Front the casualties were still heavier. Before the first year of the war was out the Russian armies had lost 4,000,000 men. In 1917, Brusilov's armies lost 375,000 men in twenty-seven days, and, as I have already mentioned, 1,000,000 men in three months !

" In my own opinion, the monopoly of strategy and tactics by shell bludgeoning prolonged the war in place of shortening it. It dulled the imagination of the higher command, who became obsessed by two ideas : Fill the trenches to hold them, and blow them to pieces to capture them. . . . As the brain-power of the opposing armies grew smaller, for all General Staffs fell victims to the shell-plague, the bodies of these same armies grew bigger and bigger, until the administrative organization for the supply of *matériel* alone absorbed such vast numbers of men that, through shortage of man-power, the fighting troops were nearly strangled by those whose duty it was to administer to their needs—armies had now become pot-bellied and pea-brained." [3]

ECONOMIC WARFARE

The attack by *matériel* failed ignominiously. In the circumstances it could not succeed, because entrenchments could be dug more rapidly than guns could be built, and the defensive zones became so widened out that it was impossible to penetrate them during a single battle. The enormous demands made for all types of munitions of war, however, revealed clearly to the eyes of the General Staffs the economic foundations of the war. So visible did these economic foundations become that it was not long before these Staffs realized that if the food supply of the enemy could be cut off, the foundations of the hostile nation would be undermined and, with the loss of will to endure, its military forces would be paralysed.

Throughout history warfare may be divided under the two general headings of fighting and plundering. In the Middle Ages, when the attack on castles failed armies laid waste the lands of the peasants. In the Thirty Years' War it was much the same, armies learning that to attack the economic foundations of their enemy's military strength is frequently more profitable than attacking him in the field. Thus, in the World War, the *matériel* attack having failed, it at once gave way to plundering operations—attacks on trade in place of the devastation of crops.

To introduce this most barbarous form of war, the first military problem that the Allied Powers had to solve was the circumvallation of the Central Powers ; and the second—their surrender by starvation : That is an attack on the enemy's *civil* stomach, not only on his men but on his women and children, not only on his soldiers but on his sick and his poor. The economic attack is without question the most brutal of all forms of attack, because it does not only kill but cripple, and cripples more than one generation. Turning men, women and children into starving animals, it is a direct blow against what is called civilization.

The encirclement of the Central Powers resulted in the most gigantic siege in history, the lines of circumvallation running from Calais to Kermanshah, and thence through Russia to the Baltic.   The establishment of this immense circle of rifles and guns and entrenchments took time ; but what took longer still for the British Government to realize was, that this siege would prove futile unless the supplies then transported to Germany through neutral countries could be stopped.   The problem was in fact a politico-naval one, and the politician was slow in solving it, not because it was diabolical, but because it might prove detrimental to the pockets of neutrals who, like vampires, were feasting on the blood of the battlefields.

When, however, the blockade began to tighten, Germany, as we have seen, had no intention of committing *felo-de-se* in order to maintain a naval custom or a humanitarian tradition.   She was now fighting for her life ; and, not possessing strength enough to defeat her adversaries on the high seas, she decided to break the blockade by establishing a blockade of her own by means of her submarines. This decision was met by a howl of execration and Germany was outlawed.   But was her action more immoral than that of her enemies ?   " There can be no doubt that, by instituting unrestricted submarine warfare the Germans violated certain laws of war made long before the advent of this weapon ; but also there can be no doubt that, if the slow starvation of German men, women and children by means of investment did not contravene the spirit of international law, then neither did unrestricted submarine warfare contravene it, though it may have infringed the letter of the tradition which this law had created.   If starvation is right in one case it is right in both.   The drowning of non-combatants is but an incident in the operation of killing by starvation, it does not affect the principle underlying this act."[4]

If we examine the basic idea at the bottom of these three phases of the World War—the traditional attack, the *matériel* attack and the economic attack—we find that it was " slaughter," not so much as a means to victory, for by soldiers it was never doubted to be the only means, but as an end in itself. Economically every nation depended on the combined prosperity of all nations, and in the main, being followers of Clausewitz, soldiers and statesmen should have realized that when he declared that war was a continuation of peace policy in another form he did not mean that it was a negation of peace policy. Yet their actions resulted in this negation, because in the days when Clausewitz outlined his doctrine all nations were economically independent, and during the three generations following his death they had become economically interdependent. It was not Clausewitz who was wrong ; they were wrong—still obsessed by the outlook of the Agricultural Age.

THE THEORY OF MORAL WARFARE

If Clausewitz was right in his proposition that war is a continuation of peace policy, what should statesmen and soldiers have done in order to interpret him correctly ? They should have examined the civilization in which they lived. Had they done so they would have seen that though steam-power had physically contracted the world it had also intellectually expanded it. Whereas, in 1750, it took three weeks to travel from Caithness to London, in 1914 Vladivostock could be reached in a similar time. Intellectually what did this mean ? It meant that, as space shrank, intelligence expanded through travel and rapidity of communications.

" This intellectual and moral revolution, which was brought about through a growth in the physical sciences, was not grasped by the military mind. It was not realized that, while only a hundred years ago it took days and weeks and months before a moral blow could be delivered, to-day it only takes minutes and hours. It was not realized that, while in the year 1800 the nervous system of a civilized nation was of a low and ganglionic order, by 1900 it had become highly sensitive and centralized. It was not realized that, as the whole aspect of civilization had changed, so also must the whole aspect of warfare be changed, and, as science had accomplished the civil changes, so also must science accomplish the military ones.

" In 1914, what happened was this : unless the war could be won within a few weeks of its outbreak, armies, as then organized, could not, under probable circumstances, maintain or enforce the peace policies of their respective governments, because these armies, in constitution, belonged to a social epoch which was dead and gone. For over a hundred years civilization had been built upon science and steam-power, yet, in 1914, armies were still organized on muscle-power,[5] the power upon which nations had been constituted prior to the advent of the steam-engine, the dynamo and the petrol-engine, the telegraph and the telephone. As the main target in war—the will of the nation—grew in size through intellectual expansion and sensitiveness, so do we see in order to protect these targets, armies becoming not more intelligent and more scientific, but more brutal, ton upon ton of human flesh being added, until war strengths are reckoned in millions in place of thousands of men." [6]

Yet in spite of this amazing foolishness the soldier remained a human creature controlled by his instinct of self-preservation. The bullet, fired to kill, awoke him from his hallucination and he at once turned to make good his hundred years of scientific neglect.

" Invention was thereupon piled upon invention, but the killing theory still held the field, until towards the close of the war it became apparent to some that science was so powerful that it could even dispense with the age-old custom of killing and could do something far more effective—it could petrify the human mind with fear. It could, in fact, directly dictate the will of one nation to another, and with vastly reduced bloodshed. It could, in fact, enforce policy with far less detriment to the eventual peace than had ever been possible before. The idea of the moral shock, in place of the physical assault, was just beginning to flutter over the blood-soaked battlefields when the Armistice of November 11, 1918, brought hostilities to a close." [7]

I will now turn to the weapons of the moral attack and very briefly examine their powers.

THE WEAPONS OF THE MORAL ATTACK

When kings led their hosts to battle " valour " was the watchword, but when democracies take command it is " cringing fear "; not that the soldiers of to-day are less brave, but that the civil population is more terrified. It always has been so, because the masses lack discipline ; but compared with former times the difference to-day is, that then the common folk were spectators whilst now they are dictators. Their will is behind the will of the Government, even when it exerts its will, which is the exception rather than the rule.

Throughout the history of war treachery has proved itself a powerful weapon, and during the interminable wars of the Middle Ages more castles and walled cities fell through treachery than through starvation—the economic attack, or by force of arms—the military assault. In the World War treachery was attempted through propaganda, the contending newspapers raking dirt out of the gutters of their respective Fleet Streets and squirting it at their country's enemies. All sense of justice was cast aside, the more outrageous the lie the more potent it was supposed to be. In England God sided with the *Daily Mail*, in Germany with the *Berliner Tageblatt* and in Paris with the *Figaro*. Libel, blasphemy, slander and obscenity were mixed up into a nauseating mess and dished out to each nation as its daily food. The behaviour of the English towards unfortunate Germans in England was as disgusting as it was brutal, and the same thing happened in Germany and France, in fact all over the democratic world. Later on in the war, the journalists were drilled into some semblance of order ; yet no Government appeared to realize that the attack by lies besmirched its own future, because the poles of the magnet which must attract all neutrals worth attracting are straight-fighting and straight-speaking.

After all, is it not to the advantage of the world that the "cleanest" nation should win?—That is common sense.

Fortunately, the moral, or immoral, attack did not halt here. The bullet had driven the soldier into his trench, and the shell had failed to dig him out. Then it was that the Germans, adopting Lord Dundonald's idea, replaced steel particles by gas particles, so that an entire battlefield, and all the targets included in it, either above ground or below, might be hit.

The first gas attack took place on April 22, 1915, in which the Germans made two cardinal mistakes : First, they did not use enough to win a decisive battle, and secondly, they used a lethal gas—chlorine—which was unnecessary, because the Hague Convention had not forbidden the use of gases of a non-toxic nature.

The result of this unexpected form of attack was that the traditional soldier was horrified. He pronounced gas warfare to be the invention of the Devil, and forthwith went into partnership with his Satanic Majesty.

The horrors of gas warfare were well advertised, and as usual the anathema pronounced upon it was absurd—in fact public opinion on any vital subject is always wrong, because it generalizes the views of the most ignorant. Here are the true facts :

In the American Army the total casualties were 274,217. Of these 74,779, or 27.3 per cent., were due to gas. Of the gas casualties only 1,400, or 1.87 per cent., resulted in death. Of the remaining 199,438 casualties, resulting from bullets, shell-fire, etc., 46,659, or 23.4 per cent., proved fatal. Out of the 86 men totally blinded during the war only 4 were blinded by gas, and " in the year 1918 there were one and a half times as many cases of tuberculosis per thousand among all American troops in France as there were amongst those gassed." [8]

On July 12, 1917, the Germans made use of mustard gas, a chemical which burnt the skin in place of attacking the blood or the lungs. Few died from its effects, but thousands were incapacitated for months on end. Here, curious to relate, is to be discovered the *true* power of gas as a weapon—*it can incapacitate without killing.* A dead man says nothing, and, when once buried, is no encumbrance to the survivors. A wounded man will spread the wildest of rumours, will exaggerate dangers, foster panic, and requires the attention of others to heal him—until he dies or is cured, he is a military encumbrance and a demoralizing agent. Gas is the weapon of demoralization, it can terrorize without killing. More than any other weapon known it can economically enforce the policy of one nation upon another.

If gas is the weapon of future warfare, as Lord Dundonald believed it to be, the aeroplane is its natural vehicle, because the limiting factor in gas projection is wind; it cannot be propelled against the wind, but it can be dropped from an aeroplane, so that from whatever direction the wind is blowing it can be carried in the desired direction.

Though aeroplanes had been used in Mexico and Tripoli before the outbreak of the World War, it was only during this war that aircraft were first used to bombard industrial centres and cities and so carry the war into the heart of the enemy's country and strike at the very foundations of his military power—the civil will. Here was a means of not only attacking the war makers themselves, but of establishing a condition of treachery which was likely to prove overwhelming.

This method of attack, a method endowed with the power of bringing a war to a rapid termination and thereby vastly reducing the destructive nature of war, was in its turn anathematized. Nations refused to see that if they would continue to practise absolute warfare, that is, if they refused to shake off the democratic idea of " the nation in arms," then to attack the war-workers, whether they were men or women, was as justifiable an act as to attack the fighting-men themselves. In 1918 France had in the field an army of close upon 3,000,000 men, but this army would have proved utterly useless unless the 1,700,000 workers employed in her war industries remained at work. During 1917 the French armies required 225,000 field-gun shells a day. They wanted these shells to kill Germans with. The men and women who made them (and there were 900,000 employed in this work) were as deeply concerned in the problem of killing as the French gunners themselves. If two men go into partnership, one making a knife for the other to cut somebody else's throat with, by the law of every civilized country both will be convicted of murder. In the days of kingly wars it was barbarous to slaughter the civil population, because the people stood outside the quarrel. But in democratic wars the people instigate the quarrel, they are the quarrellers who hire assassins to do the grim work for them. Afraid to commit murder they are afraid of being murdered. The long and the short of the matter is that " a nation in arms " or " a nation in arsenals " is obviously a legitimate war target ; and the oftener a bull's-eye is scored on it the sooner will the war be over.

In the moral attack, as waged under the conditions imposed by democratic warfare, one side of the problem is to hit the civilian in order to terrify him, the other is to stop the soldier from being hit so that he may continue to hit the civilian. Here it is that M. Bolch's theory that the bullet has rendered war impossible breaks down. Considering his amazing foresight and insight into modern warfare, it is astonishing he never saw that the answer to half an ounce of lead was half an inch of steel. Had he seen it, he would have had to rewrite his book from start to finish.

Baron de Jomini saw it vaguely, as I have shown. An armoured traction engine was suggested in the Crimean War ; armoured trains and ships were used in the American Civil War ; armoured wagons in the Franco-Prussian ; armoured traction engines in the South African, and armoured sap-rollers (shields on wheels) in the Russo-Japanese war. Yet, between 1837 and 1914 I know of but one soldier, Colonel C. B. Brackenbury, who was really imbued with what I will call " the tank idea." In July, 1878, he wrote an article for *The Nineteenth*

Century Review entitled *Ironclad Field Artillery*, and the main points contained in it are worth setting out.

In brief his argument was as follows : The leading lesson of the Plevna operations was, " that troops of any kind under cover are practically invincible so long as the enemy is in front of them" ; that the effect of artillery fire " increases as the range diminishes "; " that the destructive power of artillery at close quarters is practically annihilating ;" but that as the power of infantry " has immensely increased," it is not possible to advance the guns to annihilating range. The problem is, how to protect the guns from bullets, and his suggestion is to carry forward " thin iron shields capable of protecting the gunners against infantry fire " in " one or possibly two carriages to each battery," the shields being made in sections. " Then the artillery might calmly await any attack whatever, certain to destroy an enemy long before he could reach the guns. All anxiety as to capture would be extinguished, and we might proceed to build up a system of tactics based upon the supposition that artillery will not need to run away from anything in front of it. . . ." " If two lines of artillery were contending against each other, surely the side which was safe from shrapnel bullets and the infantry fire of the other side ought to overwhelm its antagonists. . . ." " If we can prevent nine-tenths of the loss in killed and wounded, and nearly all risk of capture, we can afford to disregard accidents. . . ." " As surely as ships of war can carry iron plates sufficient for defence against heavy guns, so surely can field artillery carry sufficient protection against the fire of infantry and shrapnel bullets. . . ." " The fire of infantry has become so formidable of late years that defensive measures must inevitably be adopted sooner or later by field artillery. . . " " If . . . we add the use of defensive armour which can be carried by artillery and cannot be carried by cavalry and infantry, a power will be created which must seriously modify the tactics of the battle-field. The development is as sure to come as the day to follow the night. We may hope that England will set the example instead of following other nations."[9]

This idea was realized by the English on September 15, 1916, when tanks advanced over the battlefield of the Somme. Brackenbury saw clearly that " Moral effect is the object aimed at in a battle, for the killed and wounded have no influence on the final retirement."[10] He saw as Frederick the Great had seen " that to advance is to conquer," because of the terrifying moral effect of a *continuous* advance. This was the underlying idea of the " bayonet school " of military thought, an idea pre-eminently sound, but in the circumstanes impossible. The " shell school " of 1914-1917 never grasped this idea ; it could not, or did not, see that the problem was not to reduce the enemy's position to mud and rubble but *to advance the guns* under hostile rifle and machine gun fire ; and that. could such an advance be made, it would prove *not overwhelmingly destructive, but overwhelmingly demoralizing.* This is exactly what the tank—mobile armoured artillery—accomplished and proved.

On the first day (July 1) of the Battle of the Somme, in 1916, a battle fought according to the doctrines of the " shell school," British casualties numbered close upon 60,000. On the first day (August 8) of the Battle of Amiens, in 1918, the most decisive battle of the war, a battle fought according to the doctrines of the " tank school," British casualties were slightly under 1,000 and the Germans captured exceeded the numbers of German killed by thousands.

" During July, August, September, October and November, 1916, the British Army lost approximately 475,000 men, it captured 30,000 prisoners and occupied some 90 square miles of country. During the same months in 1917 the losses were 370,000, the prisoners captured were 25,000, and the ground occupied was about 45 square miles. In July, August, September, October and November, 1918, the losses were 345,000, the prisoners captured 176,000, and the ground occupied was 4,000 square miles. If now we divide these losses by the number of square miles captured, we shall obtain a rough estimate of

casualties per square mile gained. These figures are approximately as follows :

(*a*)   July to November, 1916 :
475,000 ÷ 90 sq. miles = 5,277 casualties per sq. mile.
(*b*)   July to November, 1917 :
370,000 ÷ 45 sq. miles = 8,222 casualties per sq. mile.
(*c*)   July to November, 1918 :

345,000 ÷ 4,000 sq. miles = 86 casualties per sq. mile.
In the third period alone were tanks used efficiently."[11]

The " tank school," the brain of which was the
Tank Corps General Staff, never ceased to think in
terms of the moral attack ; not because they were
kindly disposed to the enemy but because they realized
that this was the most economical and decisive form
of attack. In 1917 they suggested carrying machine
gunners in large tanks *through* the enemy's battle front
and depositing them in rear of it. Why ? Because the
rear is the *morally weakest point* in the enemy's battle
body. In 1918 they again suggested passing high-speed
tanks through the enemy's battle front and attacking the
enemy's command headquarters in rear. Why ? Because
a shot through the brain paralyses the body and leads to a
moral débâcle. This suggestion was accepted by Marshal
Foch as the basic idea of his 1919 plan of campaign.

Then came the armistice and back came the " bayonet
school " into its own. In the 1924 edition of the British
Field Service Regulations we read : " Infantry is the arm
which in the end wins battles. . . . The rifle and the
bayonet are the infantryman's chief weapons. The battle
can be won in the last resort only be means of these
weapons."

CHAPTER XIII

THE INFLUENCE OF THE WAR UPON THE WORLD ORDER, 1914-1932

The Apotheosis of Nationalism.   The Asiatic Revolution.   The Chaos of
Europe.   Disarmament.   War and Civilization.

THE APOTHEOSIS OF NATIONALISM

WAS Europe to become a satrapy of Germany as Asia
and Africa had become satrapies of Europe ? This was
the question in 1914, and the answer, as we have seen,
was " No." In the name of national liberty the war was
declared, and in the name of the self-determination of
nations it was concluded ; for the war ended in the
creation of eight new nations, namely, Hungary, Czecho-
Slovakia, Poland, Lithuania, Latvia, Esthonia, Finland,
and Albania ; whilst Serbia, now Yugo-Slavia, Roumania
and Greece added vastly to their size, and France, Italy,
Denmark and Belgium to a lesser extent to theirs.

Europe, which since 1871 had lain firm on economic
foundations, was in the larger part utterly disrupted.
Not only did the vast Russian Empire split away from
the comity of European Powers but the new nations
were created on ethnographical lines. Further still, the
British Commonwealth of Nations, which after the South
African War had replaced the old Empire, was dissolved,
and became in fact, though not in name, an association
of autonomous communities in no way subordinated to
each other, responsible for their own domestic and external
affairs, and united solely by two emotional links—
allegiance to the Crown and fear of foreign aggression.
In 1921 Ireland became a Dominion with republican
tendencies which in 1932 showed themselves in the
repudiation of the oath of allegiance by the de Valera
Government. In 1931, under the terms of the Statute

of Westminster, Canada, Australia, New Zealand and South Africa became *de jure* as well as *de facto* separate nations.

The British Commonwealth of 1914 had ceased to exist, just as the Europe of 1914 had ceased to exist. A rampant nationalism had swallowed them both, and had digested them into groups of separate nations, fearful of their individual weaknesses and jealous of their neighbours' strength. Each an ethnographic group often without economic foundations ; each striving to create them out of their individual selfishnesses, until ten thousand miles of trade barriers and tariff walls were erected. Then came the economic blizzard which swept over tariff bastions, ravelins and outworks like a gas attack over an entrenched battlefield, penetrating into the financial dug-outs, trade casemates and political headquarters.

As far as the British Empire is concerned, this disruption, bloodless, unseen, and almost unheeded by the masses of the people, whispered in no uncertain terms the words of King Lear :

> " Meantime we shall express our darker purpose,
> Give me the map there,—Know, that we have divided
> In three, [five] our kingdom : and 'tis our fast intent
> To shake all cares and business from our age ;
> Conferring them on younger strengths, while we
> Unburthen'd crawl towards death. . . ." [1]

Is it to be the same for Europe and for Western civilization ? Has the apotheosis of nationalism brought to manhood by the World War sounded the death knell of the white man's supremacy ? In the answer to this question lies much, if not all, of the future of war.

THE ASIATIC REVOLUTION

What was the problem once the World War was finished with ? The reconstruction of a shattered world. An intense and intensified revolution even more potent than the revolutionary storm which swept over Europe

between 1815 and 1848.   It was a cyclone roaring over
the four quarters and the seven seas of the world, and not
merely a gale blowing down the corridors of Europe and
Spanish America.   It was bloodless, or almost so, and this
shows its potency.   Armed risings were few because the
people were already in power ; for 1815-1848 had exalted
them.   The Europe of 1871-1914 disappeared as I have
shown, because the weapon of revolution was not open
revolt but the terror of possible revolt.   It is not so much
the cost of armaments which has ruined Europe as the
cost of the tolls and doles paid to the people, the
proletariat, to keep them from rising.   Armaments and
doles belong to one and the same order ; the first is
supposed to be a security against invasion, the second
against insurrection.   Both in actual fact stand or fall
together.

Whilst Europe was boiling over, throwing the dregs to
the top, Asia was in a state of rapidly increasing fermenta-
tion.   It was here that the greatest revolution was taking
place, a social ripening in this great satrapy of Western
civilization, which one day will assume the proportions
of a volcano.

War has always influenced Asia vastly, because the
Asiatic is a contemplative creature.   Whilst war in the
West is in nature an economic expression, in the East it
assumes a psychological aspect.   In the one it takes the
form of enforced barter—gaining and losing things
material ; in the other of speculation—asking who is
losing, who is gaining power ? What star is in the
ascendant, what star is in the decline ?   For in war the
Asiatic sees the horoscope of future events.

The sorry termination of the Second Afghan War
sent a whisper through Asia, " See the white man
retires ; is it a forced retreat ? " Isandhlwana, Majuba,
Gordon's death at Khartoum, Adowa and the overthrow
of Greece by Turkey in 1897, are speculated upon in the
monasteries of Thibet, the temples of Benares, the
bazaars of Kabul, and in many a village the white man has
seldom seen.   To the Occidental, battles are business

operations, to Orientals—straws of fate pointing which way the storms of power are drifting.

The war between China and Japan in 1894 showed the superiority of European military organization over Asiatic; the war in South Africa showed that even a poorly armed people endowed with the spirit of freedom can become a formidable antagonist. Then came the Japanese victories over Russia, and even in the remotest village of the East, as the *huqqa* was passed round at night time, there went forth a whisper : " The white man's God has feet of clay."

The thunder of the guns at Port Arthur, Liao-Yang, Mukden and Tsushima rolled from Shanghai to Fez and echoed across the Sahara to the Congo and to the shores of Tanganyika. Then came the World War and Europeans were spat upon, and what did the white man do ? Bound hand and foot by his internecine struggle, he offered Egypt freedom and India home rule. China then went up in flames, and the spirit of revolution swept from the Yellow Sea to the Mediterranean. The magic jar had been dredged up by the War, its lid had been removed, the spirit of nationalism had emerged, and no coaxing would induce this terrible jinn to re-enter its bottle.

Outwardly this revolution was against the white man's authority, inwardly it was against the torpor of the East —its sacred myths, strangling customs, archaic economy, in one word—its stagnation. It was not so much a revolt against Western civilization as against its monopoly by Western man. His god was the machine, the East wanted this god as its god, a god who would shower gold on Orientals as he had showered it on Occidentals ; gold, the magic metal, which could turn hovels into palaces and slaves into Califs. The philosopher's stone of the West, that is what Asia desired beyond all things. Politics did not worry her much as long as she had the might of this metal. With it she could conquer the West and make the white man eat dirt, as her peoples had eaten dirt for a hundred years.

What do we see here ? Whilst the West, as will be

shown in the next chapter, was beginning to discover in
nationalism not a reality but a myth, the East set out
along the same road which the West had travelled over
a hundred years before. She was going to form nations,
create industries, educate the proletariat—in one word
achieve Oriental democracy ; and then ?   Internal wars,
coalitions and the Great War with Europe. To those
gifted with prophetic vision, to those who can gaze
knowingly into the crystal of the past, out of the smoke
and the dust and the flames of the World War can be
seen looming forth the form of Ogdai at the head of
his Mongol hordes.

While Asia was gaining strength, dreaming of past
glories and future victory, what do we see in Europe ?
A chaos of littleness. Nothing grand, but everything
small, wormy and miserable. A peace of vengeance ;
a peace dictated at the cannon's mouth ; a peace which
inspired a lasting desire of revenge, and a peace if left
intact must as inevitably as night follows day lead to a
war of rectification.

At Tilsit, in 1807, Napoleon had said : " Within a
hundred years Europe will be Republican or Cossack." [2]
Though his date is wrong, his prevision is immense, for
the Treaty of Versailles attempted to accomplish both.
It humiliated Germany as Napoleon had humiliated
Prussia. In 1807 the French Emperor, in a conversation
with Czar Alexander and the King of Prussia, turned to
the latter and said : " It is part of my system to weaken
Prussia ; I mean that she shall no longer be a power in
the political balance of Europe." [3] This was the
object of the French-inspired peace treaty of 1919.
Germany was not only to be disarmed, cut about and
economically ruined by reparations running into astro-
nomical figures, but she was to be circled round by a
number of new and hostile nations, who, fearing her
possible resurrection, were compelled to prepare for war.
As modern war depends for its sustenance on home

industries, these had to be fostered ; hence the ceaseless rise and strengthening of tariff walls, the strangulation of international trade, fall in prices and financial chaos.

The fashioners of the Treaty of Versailles and the other peace treaties, all bearing French names, looked upon war as an incident and not as a consequence. They could not see that its origins were mainly economic and that unless economic laws were observed all that these treaties could do was to invert Clausewitz's famous saying that " war is a continuation of peace policy " ; that is to reconstruct Europe on the assumption that " peace is the continuation of war policy."

During the war, very naturally and logically, each nation attempted to strangle its enemy's trade. Great Britain blockaded Germany, Germany blockaded Great Britain, and now that the war was at an end Germany was to be blockaded by reparations for an indefinite number of years, if not for ever. To make all the payments demanded of her under the Young Plan of 1929, which drastically modified the original figure, Germany would have had to increase her export trade by fifty per cent. ! This was the only possible way she could pay ; for unlike the alchemists she was unable to transmute lead into gold. The inmates of a lunatic asylum could have foreseen that this was the only answer, and as the statesmen of the Allied Powers were not altogether insane, why did not they foresee it ? They probably did, but were afraid to say so because the truth would have run counter to popular opinion, which is always wrong. So, fearing popular opinion more than they reverenced truth, when Germany offered to pay in goods or in service they answered : " Oh ! no, that would reduce the standard of living of our workers and throw them out of employment. Pay you shall, but not in goods." Then when no payment was made Germany was threatened with punishment for *evading* payment.

Meanwhile the Americans, who had come into the war to make the world safe for democracy, instead of

looking upon the debts the Allied Powers had contracted
with them as subsidies towards the accomplishment of
this end, saw in these debts a political instrument
whereby they might coerce Europe; for the post-war
United States, like pre-war Germany, wanted to make
history as well as gold.

In the ancient days of monarchies kings would at
times pawn their crowns to help their friends; but the
Americans are a democratically minded people; for
over two generations they had been breaking each other
by trade corners and graft; and as they are an ignorant
people it was only natural and logical for them to consider that this was the opportunity to break Europe.
But instead, with the assistance of France, they broke
the back of their own prosperity and then, realizing
that their debts would never be paid to them, because
to receive them in goods would dislocate their own
industries, President Hoover, in June, 1932, with a
gesture of " generosity " seldom equalled in history,
hinted : " If you European nations will disarm I will
forego these debts ! "   What was behind this gesture ?
Japan ! President Hoover knew as well as any man
that the debts were as dead as the dodo but, if an agreement could be reached Japan must be a party to it.
To cripple the naval power of Japan and of Great
Britain was to kill two potentially hostile birds with
one stone.

DISARMAMENT

By the Peace Treaties the defeated Powers were disarmed. Nevertheless, the armament race once again
began, the gesture at Washington in 1921 in no way
checking it, because the Disarmament Conference then
called into being was a normally dishonest political
affair. The United States having embarked upon an
extensive programme of capital ship building, and
finding that these vessels were next to useless, and
fearing public opinion if they were scrapped without
excuse, was prepared to offer them as a sacrifice on the

altar of peace if other nations, Great Britain and Japan in particular, would do the same. It was an astute move as it broke the back of the Anglo-Japanese alliance, and since then the pivot of American foreign policy has been to establish for the benefit of mankind the freedom of the seas, which, more truthfully put, means the hegemony of the oceans for the benefit of the Americans. Thus we see that no sooner was the German High Sea Fleet sunk in the North Sea than the American Fleet rose in its stead, the Panama Canal becoming the Kiel Canal of the West.

Behind this diplomacy stood economic nationalism. No one nation wished to conquer the territories of another, but all nations wanted to conquer each other's markets. From the battlefields of the World War the conflict was carried into the commercial fields of the World Peace. The means were different, but the end was the same. Tariff walls begot entrenchments not built against any one nation but against all nations. The world became a gold rush encampment; each nation, like each gold-digger, carrying a gun on its hip. Why? Not to attack anyone in particular but to defend itself. Defence is now on every man's lips, no one talks of aggression, because the victors wish to hold fast to what they have gained, and the vanquished, as long as they are disarmed, are unable to differ. Fear remains as deep-rooted as ever, and it is the elimination of the causes of fear and not the search after the definition of aggression which is the true problem of disarmament.

Defence is but offence reversed, the difference between these two forms of fighting being simply an attitude of mind which may at any moment be turned upside down by popular emotionalism. It is thought by those of narrow intelligence that fortifications have a permenant defensive value and that they cannot be classed as aggressive in intention. Nothing is more inexact; for the history of war shows again and again that fortifications form excellent bases from which to launch offensive operations. Did not Napoleon say: " The whole art of war consists in a well-reasoned and extremely circumspect defensive, followed by rapid and audacious attack ? "

The problem of disarmament is a problem of causes and not a problem of effects, and until nations see it in this light it will remain a problem unsolved. It is a problem of economics and economic diseases, and also a problem of social psychology and political fear. The peace potential of a nation is its war potential; for a nation which possesses great industries is powerful for war, and a nation which possesses few is incapable even of going to war unless against an equally weak nation, or unless it is allied to an industrial neighbour, or supplied with arms from outside.

As a matter of fact few even of the greatest industrial nations are even from the military point of view self-supporting. For example : " During the last war, the German headquarters was in need of aluminium for the bodies of its Zeppelins and of carburet of cyanamide for its explosives. At the same time the French discovered that the Allied factories could not manufacture magnetos comparable with those of the German factories, which meant inferiority for French aeroplanes. The result was that Switzerland imported magnetos from Germany far beyond its needs and from France quantities of bauxite and cyanamide for which the country itself had no use." [4]

With weak industrial Powers the situation is more astonishing still, for their instruments of national defence lie outside their own control, and because of this the great industrial Powers use these nations as diplomatic weapons. For example : in 1920 British interests demanded that the Turks should be kept away from the Bosphorus, and French interests demanded that the Turks should be propitiated so that French interests in Syria might be consolidated. What happened ? The two Governments turned their backs ; meanwhile the firm of Vickers, on credit, supplied arms and munitions to the Greeks, and the firm of Creusot, on credit, supplied arms and munitions to the Turks. The result was the Græco-Turkish War of 1921-1922 ; a war not only between Greeks and Turks, but also between French and British diplomacy, in spite of the fact that both nations were still bound together by the Entente Cordiale !

Such actions as these are unrealized by the masses of the people, for common man is too simple and indolent to unravel diplomatic tangles. The masses do not notice such " coincidents " as that on the day upon which the American Senate, by ratifying the Pact of Paris, outlawed war, it agreed upon the construction of new cruisers. They are amazed and dazed by emotion-stirring figures. Thus when the Disarmament Conference assembled at Geneva in February, 1932, the people were told that it represented 64 countries, that it was to be attended by 2,400 delegates and experts, 500 journalists and that the two conference rooms had an area of 13,000 square feet. " Assembled here," said Mr. Henderson, " are the chosen spokesmen of seventeen hundred million people. There is no human being, whether his home is in one of the great centres of industry and population, in the deserts of Africa, in the jungles of the East, or amid the ice of the Arctic regions, who has not some one here to speak in his name." [5] Think of that ! The people are enthralled, quantity always " gets " them ; numbers stupefy their imagination with the drug of emotionalism, and the result is that reason vanishes. [6]

What happened at this Conference ? The Russian delegate proposed total disarmament, obviously to foster the proletarian revolution ; the French suggested an international police force under the League of Nations, obviously to control Germany ; the British suggested the abolition of the use of gas, submarines, and bombing from the air, obviously to get back to the insular security of 1914 ; the American suggested the abolition of tanks, heavy mobile guns and gases, obviously because, if granted sufficient time, the United States can build and produce these weapons during war, and, should other nations possess them on the outbreak of war, time wherein to manufacture them will be insufficient;[7] and the Italian agreed as Italy lacks coal and oil, consequently the Italian army dreads mechanization.

It will be seen that each delegate put forward a proposal which would benefit his own country to the detriment of other countries; in fact to prepare for war and not to establish peace. The result was that qualitative disarmament, as it was called, was dragged like a red herring across the main argument which was to disarm. Sir John Simon, the British delegate, considered that the newest arms—tanks, aeroplanes, submarines and gas—being the most recently invented were the easier to scrap, when in fact the reverse is the case. The question as to whether it was morally right to equip an army on obsolete lines, and therefore needlessly sacrifice lives in war, never entered anyone's head. On this point General von der Goltz wrote forty years ago : " Nothing is worse than that the " soldier " should feel himself neglected in this respect, and to believe himself subject without his own fault, to an effect to which he is powerless. Defeat would thus appear excusable, and success cannot have a worse enemy than this feeling." [8]

The likelihood of any solution of the disarmament problem being arrived at in Geneva is remote, because the question is dealt with at the wrong end—the causes of war being left to look after themselves. Until these causes are removed the only factors which will reduce armaments are, economic crisis and lack of money which will force down the military budgets, and the increasing cost in all civilized countries of social reform to prevent social wars. To-day in Great Britain more is being spent on doles to prevent revolution than on the defence forces to safeguard the country in the event of a foreign war. As the cost of the first rises, for lack of money the cost of the second will sink ; yet, as I have said, both stand or fall together, because money in itself can solve neither problem.

WAR AND CIVILIZATION

I have at times drastically criticized the actions of statesmen and politicians, not because they were necessarily dishonest men, but because in their actions may be discovered the nature of the environment in which they were compelled to work. The environment is public opinion, which, as I have shown, has during the last hundred years increasingly influenced politics and through politics war. Between 1914 and 1918 public opinion was the controlling factor, not only in the belligerent countries but in neutral countries also. As the war lengthened out people became more and more credulous and savage, all reason being lost in a primitive animalism, a frantic hysterical striving to end the struggle by every means—fair, foul or damnable.

To-day science is at the disposal of the masses. Not only has science introduced weapons which can strike at the civil will and so terrify it, but it has placed the radio in every house, a mechanical device which can literally electrify terror, hatred and fury. As the whole community will not only physically feel the effects of war, but will mentally live on the battlefields listening in to the thunder of the guns and possibly also to the shrieks of the wounded, since to popular emotionalism there are set no limits; unless the people are highly disciplined or unless the war is short, hysteria will become uncontrollable and animalism rampant. A long war like the last one is likely to end in a catastrophic stroke, not national paralysis only, but also universal chaos. War between nations will almost certainly be followed by war within nations; that is, civil war, in which the sufferings of the people will in most cases be beyond description.

As long as wars continue, and they must continue until their causes are eliminated, the only military solution to this problem is to shorten their length. This means that in military organization quality must replace quantity. To-day nations are obsessed by a neurotic dread of numbers, yet in modern warfare numbers are actually a detriment, for the larger the population, or the mass of troops, the larger the target for the enemy to hit at. It is in the quality of arms and not in the quantity of men that the solution to this problem must be sought. In this light it will at once be seen that qualitative disarmament is its antithesis. To scrap the newer weapons is to prolong wars ; to prolong a war is to commit national suicide whilst temporarily insane— perhaps this is what an all-wise Providence desires. But, as I have already pointed out, the true war potential is the equivalent of the peace potential, because war being a continuation of peace policy in another form, it draws its strength from peace industry. The generating plant for war energy in Europe lies within the area Stockholm, Danzig, Cracow, Budapest, Florence, Barcelona, Bilbao, Glasgow, Bergen and thence to Stockholm; for within this circle lie " all the large coal mines, all the large metallurgical industries, all the large chemical industries, all the large factories of electrical material and railway material, all the big naval dockyards, etc."[9] In Russia the war power-station lies in the Don valley and the Caucasian oil-fields ; and in America in the area Boston-Chicago-St. Louis-Baltimore. These facts are unalterable, for they are acts of God.

Even if it were desirable, how can qualitative disarmament be made a reality ? Bombing aeroplanes are built in the same workshops as commercial aeroplanes ; machinery which turns out typewriters and calculating machines can be adapted to turn out rifles and machine-guns ; railway and tractor works can build tanks and lorry works armoured cars ; chemical works which manufacture pharmaceutical products can readily manufacture high explosives ; dye works can produce tear and mustard gas ; cellulose is used for artificial silk and smokeless powders ; glycerine for soap or dynamite, etc., etc. Thus it comes about that " every great factory in time of peace is a potential arsenal."[10]

Industries are the foundations of war strength, and

industry depends upon power—coal and oil, and to a lesser extent upon water-power. Nations which to-day do not possess power can be disarmed directly the great industrial nations decide to put an end to the arms trade, for a state without industries cannot produce modern weapons. "Without a national carburant there in no national independence," thus writes General Denvignes, and Lord Curzon once said : " Who has the petrol has the Empire" ; a remark which should be remembered each time the United States of America proposes a reduction in naval armaments. The truth would appear to be that though new carburants may be discovered, a time is approaching when no single nation, great or small, will possess within its frontiers all the industries necessary to wage a successful war. Without such industries economic nationalism as understood to-day cannot be guaranteed. This means, that if war cannot be waged by a single state it can only be waged by an alliance of states, and unless this alliance possesses a peace potential capable of fulfilling the demands of scientific warfare, warfare of this nature cannot be waged at all.

Until this climax arises, or until the causes of war are eliminated, wars will and must continue, paradoxically as it may seem, for the advancement of mankind ; for if man will not eliminate the causes of war, which are social and economic diseases, they can only be eliminated by wars which will teach him the deadliness of their nature. What will future warfare then be like ?

It will include many strange contradictions, so strange that unless we have thought them out beforehand we shall be utterly surprised. War will be absolute in the extreme, for whole nations will be besieged ; yet there will be no front of operations, fronts will be everywhere. Again, there will not be one war but two wars, the first waged against the enemy's armies, and the second against his civil population ; the former becoming more and more humane, and the latter more and more brutal, as happened in the Middle Ages.

It is at the moral and industrial centres that the main

blows will be struck, and not so much at military power itself, because military power is founded upon the civil will and upon civil industry, and to attack an army at its foundations is a more certain way of destroying its power than by removing its roof tile by tile. Cities and towns will consequently have to be protected and defended as they were in the Middle Ages, and the people disciplined for war in order to shield themselves against the main weapon of the attacker—their own panic. They must not only be physically disciplined as soldiers are in order to maintain order during a crisis, but mentally disciplined so that they may withstand the corrosive effects of propaganda ; for every human achievement will be distorted by the enemy to further his war ends. Wars will in fact largely become armed propaganda, steel-girt lies, demoralizing shells and stink bombs aimed to shatter the enemy's will, every effort being simultaneously made to render one's own side explosive with fury, scorn, cruelty and hatred for the enemy, his people and his cause—such are the motive forces in democratic wars.

The main military weapon of attack will, I consider, be gas, not because it is so deadly but because it is so terrifying. Yet, possibly, it will be abandoned, for in the minds of a demented and thoroughly animalized people it may be considered too humane. Nevertheless its power to surprise and above all the cheapness of its production should appeal to democracies.

Finally, paradox again, the longer the war the greater will be the improvement in weapons ; armies, instead of deteriorating, as they have done in the past, will progressively grow more efficient, whilst civilians will become more and more demoralized, until terror coagulates into solid panic which the slightest moral shock will detonate into explosion. The final wars of the democratic age, the age of economic nationalism and of nations in arms, will be as unchivalrous as they are scientific ; they will not be pleasant affairs, or profitable ones.

CHAPTER XIV

THE FOUNDATIONS OF INTERNATIONALISM,
1914-1932

War and Internationalism.   The Grouping of the Nations.   World Interdependence and War.   The Spirit of the Age.

WAR AND INTERNATIONALISM

WITHOUT the genius of great men to lead it, Western
civilization is doomed, " For, as I take it," writes Carlyle,
" Universal History, the history of what man has accomplished in this world, is at bottom the History of the Great
Men who have worked here . . . all things that we see
standing accomplished in the world are probably the
outer material result, the practical realisation and embodi-
ment, of Thoughts that dwelt in the Great Men sent
into the world : the soul of the whole world's history,
it may justly be considered, were the history of these."

The World War was doomed through a similar cause—
the lack of genius ; not that war had become impossible,
as Bloch affirmed, but because, as a lethal argument, it
had become inane. Yet this war showed to all who could
see something which had not been seen so clearly before,
namely, an international in contradistinction to a
national spirit. It showed that duty was an equal of
liberty and that national freedom as a thing in itself had
become absurd. For instance, the Allied Powers began
the war as separate nations, but before it ended they
pooled everything, even their higher commands.
Between them free trade was absolute, individual
resources were the common property of all ; they formed
one united, though not always friendly, brotherhood in
arms ; and in spite of their many mistakes, had they not
done so they would have lost the war.

War once was between nations, now it is no longer so, for

it is *within* the civilized world itself. In the Agricultural Age war was isolated ; it was bulk-headed off as it were from all but neighbouring nations, and even these it affected but slightly. In the present Industrial Age it causes a widespread inflammation—moral, economic and financial. It influences not only the belligerents but humanity as a whole, and generates disturbances in population which are almost as strongly marked outside the theatre of war as within it. Professor Hersch writes : " War kills not only directly, on the battle-field or as the result of wounds or diseases contracted by the soldiers in the course of hostilities, but also indirectly by causing an increase of mortality among the civilian population of the belligerent countries and even in many neutral countries." [1]

The reason for this is not far to seek ; it is due to industrial and commercial disturbances. Hersch further writes :

" The fact that war kills not only in the belligerent countries but also in the neutral countries . . . had already been noted during the great wars of the nineteenth century. Thus, during the war year 1866 the increase in the number of deaths was 11,000 in Holland and 29,000 in Belgium. The increase in the number of deaths as a result of the war of 1870-71 was 47,000 in Holland, 55,000 in Belgium and 23,000 in Switzerland. Furthermore, it may be noted that the highest number of deaths was observed in all three of these countries precisely during war years, when all three had remained neutral (except Belgium during the World War). Thus in Holland the number of deaths has only four times exceeded 100,000 and all four correspond to war years, namely, in 1859 (103,067 deaths), in 1866 (101,854), in 1871 (106,978) and in 1918 (with 115,440 deaths). In Switzerland the highest number of deaths (not given for the whole country before 1867) are those of 1870 (72,838 deaths), 1871 (77,998) and 1918 (75,034). Similarly in Belgium the highest figures correspond to the years 1866 (151,116), 1871 (145,746) and 1918 (157,340). At the time of the World War, owing to its extent, the circle of neutrals affected by it was naturally much enlarged. It was observed, for instance, that the maximum of deaths recorded for Sweden for a century and

Q

a half belonged to the year 1918 (104,591). The maximum number of deaths ever observed in Norway also corresponded to the year 1918 (43,603) and in Spain (695,758). . . . The World War . . . claimed nearly 600,000 victims in the neutral countries of Europe alone." [2]

The epidemics which have followed every modern war have been still more devastating. Thus, in 1866 the number of combatants killed or died was about 53,000, yet the cholera epidemic carried off 200,000 civilians. In 1870-71 the Germans lost 41,000 soldiers killed and died and the French about 100,000, yet on account of the small-pox epidemic 270,000 German civilians died and 600,000 French. Finally we come to the influenza epidemic of 1918, which clearly shows how international the effects of war have become. It swept over the entire world killing at least 15,000,000 people. Tuberculosis also swept throughout the world, but more particularly in the blockaded countries. In Germany it rose above its peace level by 61 per cent. and in Austria by 67 per cent. ; yet in Holland it also rose by 50 per cent.

The following is an incomplete balance-sheet of the mortality caused by the War : [3]

Continent	Military	Civilian	Total
Europe ..	12,637,000	12,219,000	24,856,000
America ..	174,000	1,500,000	1,674,000
Asia	69,000	13,700,000	13,769,000
Africa	99,000	900,000	999,000
Oceania ..	76,000	60,000	136,000
	13,055,000	28,379,000	41,434,000

From these figures it will be seen, not only that modern war is universal in its destructive effects, but that the loss in civilian lives is double that of the military losses. This stupendous loss was due almost entirely to the length of the war. Had it been possible to have cut down its

length to a few weeks, or even to a few months, and that
in this shortening of it 1,000,000 civilians had been killed
and disabled by direct attack, the actual saving in life
and reduction of suffering would have been colossal beyond reckoning. However this was not so, and the result
was, that the neurosis of the war was carried into the
peace which followed it.

In 1918-19 the world of 1871-1914 vanished, and
outwardly nationalism seemed to be the only conception
which emerged strengthened by the conflict. Nevertheless this expansion of liberty may be compared to the
growth of a soap bubble : The filament was nationalism,
yet the breath which had caused it to expand was internationalism. We see this clearly not only in the establishment of the League of Nations, but in the ceaseless
assembly of international conferences during the last
fourteen years. Many are forthwith wrecked by the
national spirit ; some lead to definite proposals such as
those which resulted in the signing of the Locarno
treaties and the Pact of Paris ; but the point to note is
that though most end in blind alleys and a few in highways along which no nation dares to travel alone, yet
these conferences continue, and no nation has yet
suggested that any other means of settlement is a practical
one.

A decision which vastly accelerated the decay of nationalism was one which was taken purely to foster it.   In
1932, to rectify her trade balance Great Britain abandoned
her free trade policy, and by doing so put the coping
stone on the ruin of European trade. This accomplished,
it became not only totally impossible for Germany to
pay reparations, for she could only pay them in goods,
but totally impossible for France to continue to believe
that she could pay them. Thus it came about that the
first fruits of British trade protection were not to foster
national prosperity, but to remove a dead weight off the
chest of international prosperity. This happened at the
Lausanne Conference in 1932, when, on July 8, reparations
were finally abolished.

This abolition of reparations, which in a sane world would never have been opposed, was the first step taken since 1918 to throw off the neurosis of the war and get back to sanity ; a step gallic and charmingly confirmed by M. Herriot ; for when he " came down the stairs at the Beau Rivage [Hotel] and was surrounded by a clamorous crowd of journalists . . . perceiving close to him in the front row two girls representing one a French and the other a German newspaper," he said, " ' et maintenant j'embrasserai une française et une allemande,' and acted accordingly, kissing each girl on both cheeks." (4)   The next step is the cancellation of war debts, and the third, and by far the most difficult—a rational revision of international tariffs.

THE GROUPING OF THE NATIONS

Meanwhile other forces, more occult, have been at work ; for in spite of the rise of new nations, and the increasing agitation by fractions of old nations to gain their political liberty however much it might clash with their economic interests, simultaneously with the ending of the war do we see emerging out of nationalism itself the formation of amorphous groups of nations.   In Russia, the revolution of 1917, shattering an empire, theoretically at least created a number of Soviet republics which socially and politically were autonomous ; yet it simultaneously gave birth to the Union of Socialist Soviet Republics, which super-State retains economic autonomy in its own hands.

In America this evolution had been reached after the Civil War, which in its own sphere may be compared to the Russian revolution.   But in 1919, though both these super-States were founded upon economics, the difference between them lay in their economic machinery.   Whilst in the Soviet Union all sources of wealth became State property, in the United States they remained individual property depending upon an intricate banking system. The difference between them was that of S.U. to U.S.

In spite of this fact, S.U. and U.S. were but the heads

and tails of one and the same coin, for both were in spirit international and not merely federal organizations. The Russian aiming at a world revolution which would bring the wealth of the world into the hands of a world super-State, and the American aiming at a world control which similarly would bring the wealth of the world under the government of the central banks dictated to by the international financiers. Both, in their eagerness to gain power over the masses which could no longer control themselves or devise political machinery to control them, sacrificed not only their liberty to autocracy but justice to method. Economically the world was fast becoming a single machine, consequently it was thought, or unconsciously felt, that this machine must be controlled by a single government.

This ideal may or may not be sound; it is as yet impossible to say; but human customs change slowly, and the eagerness of the few, pushed as it was to its uttermost extreme both in Russia and America, soon established such stresses and strains in the old economic and financial world structure that the foundations of Western civilization gave way, bringing the mansion of nationalism tumbling to the ground. In Russia a New Economic Policy had to be resorted to, and then the gigantic Five Year Plan of reconstruction. In America no radical change has as yet been attempted. Meanwhile the world-dominion idea has grown very thin; the Russian ideal being now limited to the hegemony of Asia, and the American to that of economic control of the New World. We thus, to-day, see two great groups of nations forming, one in the East and one in the West, still very inarticulate and amorphous, yet casting shadows which can clearly be analysed.

In between the jaws of this Capitalist-Communist nut-cracker is wedged Europe, the true Europe, that continent which stretches from the Atlantic to the Vistula. As ever, this tract of land is divided between what may be called Latin and Teutonic culture, the dividing line being roughly the Rhine and the Danube.

Behind the economic and political factors which gave birth to the World War stands unseen this cultural urge. The struggle between Rome and the barbarians, between the Papacy and the Holy Roman Empire, between Catholicism and Protestantism and finally between the two cultures begotten of all this struggling. Into this mixture of oil and water were poured by Woodrow Wilson and Lenin the acids of two universal leagues.

For America to become a world power, it was essential that the European war system should be destroyed, for civil wars are incompatible with trading; for Russia to become so, it was essential to destroy the European peace system which was hostile to Communism; yet both overlooked this fact: that the vitality of the cultural struggle in Europe was far deeper rooted than the new-born ideals to which these two great groups of Powers aspired. Two thousand years of conflict have produced an extremely hard shell. Europe is not a nut to be cracked easily; yet the pressure which is being exerted upon her from East and West must in time produce an effect upon her kernel, for if this nut be not altogether hollow, this pressure may so consolidate European fear that it may bring to life the international instinct of self-preservation, which for generations has remained dormant. Then, the nations of this continent may sink their differences and unite in the common cause for European independence. This has happened in the past, in the days of the Crusades; in fact it has always happened when the culture of Europe has been threatened by what we call the barbarism of Asia, whether Persian, Arab, Mongol or Turk.

The League of Nations, established as an American instrument of control, may well prove the focal point of this coalescence. In conception it started as a world league, and though it was an American creation, the United States, not wishing to become entangled in its problems, and wishing to control it by outside pressure, at once refused to enter it; Russia for similar reasons did likewise. It was, therefore, launched as a European League, upon whose keel became attached certain

American and Asiatic barnacles. When this League has rubbed these off on some convenient sand-bank, such as Manchuria, the good ship *Pan-Europa* will move more swiftly through the inter-continental waters. What will the result be ? As the three Leagues trim their sails to the winds of their own salvation, nationalism will begin to lose its all-absorbing interest. Should a league founder, certainly will its crew take again to their national boats ; but should it sail gallantly onwards towards yet another fondly dreamed of garden of the Hesperides, so it seems to me the historians of the future will proclaim that the World War was not fought in vain.

Yet there is one more group which must be considered, namely, the British Empire, or Commonwealth of Nations, which is an inter-continental group, artificial and not geographic—hence its fundamental weakness. Heretofore, fear of foreign invasion, quite as much so as sentiment, has held it together. Further, as at present constituted, its parts are not homogeneous, for it does not only consist of Great Britain and five self-governing Dominions, but it also includes four great non-European sub-empires—India, Malaya, East Africa and the Sudan, and West Africa, as well as many isolated dependencies. What place will this great conglomeration of nations and peoples take in relation to the other three groups ?

The answer to that question lies outside the scope of this book ; but so far as war is concerned, security can be guaranteed only by the establishment of a common policy and a common defence force ; for though fear will draw nations together fear itself will not protect them. The solution to this problem lies in establishing some controlling organ such as an Imperial Council, which, though it may possess no political power, will be able to advise the Empire as a whole on all vital Imperial questions. To-day we possess but one piece of Imperial machinery, an heirloom of the War, namely, the Imperial War Graves Commission, a cynical reminder of the fate which awaits this greatest of the Great Empires unless we also establish an Imperial Commission for the living.

Thus we are finally faced by four possible groups of nations—Russia and Asia, North and South America, Europe, and the British Empire; consequently the question arises what is likely to be the war relationship between them?

WORLD INTERDEPENDENCE AND WAR

There can be little or no doubt that what we call the civilized world is an interdependent unit, and that when the uncivilized portions of it become civilized, then the whole will form one economic unit. But what do we mean by civilization? We really mean " industrialization," and there can be little doubt that industrialization is rapidly gaining hold on Asiatic and African peoples; yet from this it must not be deduced off-hand that when they become industrialized the whole world is going to coalesce; that trade will be liberated from its shackles; that swords will be beaten into ploughshares, and that universal peace will be proclaimed. Rather is the opposite likely; and why?

The answer to this question is to be found in this book itself. It has been shown how it happened that Great Britain became industrialized long before most of the other European nations, and that her industrial supremacy remained unthreatened until 1871, when the rise of the German Empire and of the German tariff system challenged it. Without tariffs Germany could neither have founded her industries nor have entered into competition with Great Britain, and as long as her home markets remained unsaturated her tariffs fostered her prosperity. It was only when once they were satisfied, and she began to dump her goods upon other nations, that her tariffs took on a war-like complexion and had to be supported by armaments. Will not the same evolution take place in Russia and in Asia, and throughout the as yet non-industrialized portions of the world? Look at this question.

Without wishing to be abusive, we can say Asiatic labour is as cheap as dirt; Asiatic resources are almost untouched, and Russia has established a wage system which in Europe proper is considered to be equivalent with slavery. Whether tariffs between European nations are drastically reduced, or whether they vanish, one thing is certain : Europe, in order to safeguard her economic existence, will be compelled to establish formidable tariff walls against what I will call " Russasia." The more the Russian Five-Year Plan prospers the greater will be the conomic pressure brought to bear on Europe, and the greater this pressure becomes the greater will become the inducement for European nations to coalesce politically as well as economically ; for it is outside pressure, and not internal ruin, which will force coalescence, and, consequently, interdependence. Look at the recent advances that Russia has made. Her population is increasing at the rate of 60 millions every twenty years ; her city population has grown 30 per cent. since the war ; school attendance has risen from 8 millions, in 1913, to 20 millions, in 1932 ; in 1930, 842 million copies of 47,000 different books and periodicals in fifteen languages were circulated ; in 1913, 29 million tons of coal were produced, in 1931, 57 million ; in the same period petroleum production has risen from 9 to 23 million tons, and electrical power from 2 to 12 million kilowatt hours. The railways are carrying 50 per cent. more freight than they did before the war, and passenger traffic has increased from 185 millions in 1913, to 709 million in 1931. Finally, in 1913 the post office handled 563 million letters and, in 1931, 1,414 million. [6]

It is true that at the present moment Russian industrialization is incomparably inferior to that of Great Britain, Germany or France ; but when it is remembered how rapidly American industrialization advanced after 1865, and German after 1871, the fact that it is advancing, and rapidly, will soon fill Europe with consternation.

As this consternation grows, if Europe is to survive there can be but one answer ; she must settle her internal quarrels ; establish the freest possible trade

among her now tariff-shackled peoples; erect trade
bastions against " Russasia," and behind them build up
a formidable European army. In place of aiming at
national disarmament as she is doing to-day, the likelihood is that within a generation from now she will be
demanding *compulsory* group, or continental, armaments.
To-day she is paltering with the problem of war, and
under American influence is considering the abolition of
this weapon or that. Her true problem is not to disarm,
but to remain armed and yet prevent civil wars within her
frontiers. To attain this end there is but one course to
take, namely, to eliminate the causes of European quarrels,
and, as this will take time, meanwhile to deprive the
victor in a civil war, such as the World War, of legal
rights to his gains. That is to say, that he is entitled to
no tribute, territory or reparation arising out of the
War, and that all non-belligerent nations which desire
to assist a belligerent may do so by direct subsidies and
not by credit or by loans. Though agreements may not
be kept, it seems to me wiser, especially when the future
is borne in mind, to restrict the profit side of war instead
of the preparative side. Let nations fight if they will,
and if they are determined to fight nothing will stop
them; but if they do fight, then render illegal their
profits; for even if they refuse to surrender them, as
long as they hold them they will remain outlawed in
the eyes of all other nations. To outlaw the victor is
sense, because there can be no question who the victor
is; but to outlaw the aggressor is nonsense, for who is
the aggressor?

To turn back to the main problem. In a European
army there will be no national armies, such as a purely
British, French, or German army; but in place one
continental army. Not a horde of national contingents,
as gathered together in the army of Darius, but a
scientifically organized force which is likely to be centred
at the very place which to-day most nations are determined that no army of any size shall be centred, namely,
Berlin. It is from the East that Europe will once again

be threatened; and was it not at Liegnitz, in April, 1241,
that Henry of Silesia and good King Wenceslaus of
Bohemia, girt in their armour, drove back the Mongol
hordes ? In such an army it is more than likely that
a camp language will spring up as happened in Akbar's
polygot army at Delhi, and should this prove the case,
then not the least of its blessings will be to give back
to Europe a *lingua franca*.

THE SPIRIT OF THE AGE

This book draws to its end. Not alone the end that
I have set to it ; but, for lack of wisdom in man, the
end which Destiny has agreed upon. It opened in
chaos and it ends in chaos, and within these two dismal
covers lies its text—the emanation of nationalism. We
have watched it grow from a distant hope into a reality,
and now before us glimmers a distant and yet greater
hope.

War has been the instrument, the surgical instrument
as it were, which has cut the living flesh free from the
dead flesh. Without war a putrefaction would have set
in and with it a creeping paralysis embracing in its
chilly arms not only society and politics, but science
and industry ; for all the activities of mankind are
correlated, at bottom they are but the expressions of
one activity—life.

This book opened with nationalism as an ideal, and
it ends with yet another ideal—continental coalescence,
or group nationalism ; and because this ideal is upon us,
it does not follow, as it may be thought, that we are
about to sink our individualities in one common herd.
We shall do the very opposite ; for free contact between
nations enhances and does not obliterate their essential
differences. Men do not go to war because they are
artists, scientists or musicians. It is their similarities
which engender wars, eating, drinking and wiving—the
animal side of their nature.

In Europe, so it seems to me—and it is with Europe
that this book has mainly been concerned—once the

animal, that is the economic, necessities are placed on a rational footing, the present war age will pass and we shall enter another age of war ; not wars between nations but wars between continents.

The unseen changes which will produce this change coalesce in the Spirit of the Age. If, in 1832, the world could have seen clearly the progress between that date and 1932, all wars could have been avoided. But such seership is not given to man ; yet if we can but grasp the skirts of the Spirit of the Age, we may avoid many blunders and in avoiding them not a few wars.

To-day the Western world is still shell-shocked, and its outlook upon war is blurred by hysteria. Should this book in any way help to rectify our vision, then its purpose will have been achieved. Be it remembered, however, that war is an activity which cannot be charmed away. There are reasons for war, and as long as these reasons endure wars will continue. War is a God-appointed instrument to teach wisdom to the foolish and righteousness to the evil-minded. So it happens, as Donoso Cortes says :[6]

" When a nation shows a civilized horror of war, it receives directly the punishment of its mistake. God changes its sex, despoils it of its common mark of virility, changes it into a feminine nation and sends conquerors to ravish it of its honour."

FINIS

APPENDIX

CHRONOLOGY OF WARS
1832—1932

1832	Don Pedro invades Portugal.
	The French lay siege to Antwerp.
	French troops land in Ancona.
1832—1841	Turko-Egyptian War.
1833	Napier destroys Dom Miguel's fleet off Cape St. Vincent.
1834	Carlist outbreak in Spain.
1834—1835	Sixth Kaffir War.
1835—1839	French campaigns in Algeria.
1836	Insurrection in Texas.
1836—1840	First Carlist War.
1837	French capture Constantine in Algeria.
	Papineau's rebellion in Canada.
1838	Boer-Zulu War.
1838—1842	First Afghan war.
1839	Aden occupied by the British.
1840	Operations in Scinde, India.
1840—1842	Opium war in China.
1842	Russian conquest of Amur Darya.
	War between England and the Natal Boers.
1842—1843	Conquest of Scinde.
1843	Gwalior war, India.
1844	French victory of Isly, Algeria.
1845—1846	First Sikh war.
1846—1848	American Mexican war.
1847	End of civil war in Portugal.
	Civil war in Switzerland.
1848	Sir Harry Smith defeats Boers at Bloomplatz.
1848—1849	Italian war of liberation.
1848—1849	Austro-Hungarian war.
1848—1849	Second Sikh war.
1848—1850	First Schleswig-Holstein war.
1850—1864	Taiping rebellion in China.
1850—1854	Kaffir war.
1851—1858	Russian campaign in the Amur district.
1852	Second Burmese war.
1853	Russo-Turkish war begins.

1854	Operations of the Eureka Stockade, Australia.
1854—1856	Crimean war.
1855	Sardinia joins in the Crimean war.
1856—1857	Anglo-Persian war.
1857—1860	Franco-British Chinese war.
1857—1859	Indian Mutiny.
1859	Austro-French-Italian war.
1859—1860	Spanish campaign in Morocco.
1860	Liberation of Sicily and invasion of Naples.
1861—1865	American Civil War.
1862	Garibaldi defeated at Aspromonte.
1862—1867	French invasion of Mexico.
1863	Revolution in Poland, battle of Brody.
	Umbeyla campaign, India.
	Prussia and Austria invade Denmark.
1863—1864	Maori wars.
1863—1864	Major Gordon's campaign against the Taiping rebels.
1864	Second Schleswig-Holstein war.
1864—1870	Brazilian war.
1865	French occupation of Saigon.
1866	Austro-Prussian war.
	Spanish war with Peru and Chili.
1866—1867	Italian war of liberation.
1866—1868	Insurrection in Crete.
1867	Garibaldi defeated at Mentana.
1867—1868	British invade Abyssinia.
1868	Civil war in Spain and Cuba.
	Russia occupies Samarcand.
	Red Indian war.
1868—1871	Civil war in Japan.
1868—1878	Rebellions in Canada.
1870	Red River rebellion, Canada.
1870—1871	Franco-Prussian war.
1870—1871	Italian unity accomplished.
1871	Civil war of the Commune in France.
	Maori wars end.
1872	Philippine Islands rebel against Spain.
1872—1874	Carlist war in Spain.
1873	Russian Khiva campaign.
	Dutch war in Achin.
1873—1874	British Ashanti war.
1875	Herzegovina insurrection.

1875—1876	Russians invade Khokand.
1876	Serbo-Turkish war.
	Red Indian war.
1877—1878	Russo-Turkish war.
1878—1880	Second Afghan war.
1879	Zulu war.
1879—1881	Chili-Peruvian war.
1880—1881	Boer war in Transvaal.
1881	French expedition to Tunis.
	Rising of the Mahdists in the Sudan.
	Chili and Argentine war.
	Russian campaign of Geok Tepe.
1882—1883	Egyptian War.
1883—1885	Mahdist war, Egypt.
1884—1885	Franco-Chinese war.
1885	Third Burmese war.
	Riel's revolt in Canada.
	Serbo-Bulgarian war.
1885—1886	Penjheh incident, Afghanistan.
1887—1889	Italo-Abyssinian war.
1888—1891	British campaigns against the Mahdi.
1890	British East African operations.
1891	Chilian civil war ends.
	Storming of the Nilt forts, India.
1892	French Dahomy war.
	British Ashanti war.
	Italo-Mahdist operations.
1893	Matabele war in South Africa.
	Italian Sudan campaign.
	French occupation of Timbuctoo.
	French expedition to Siam.
1894—1895	Chino-Japanese war.
1895	British Chitral campaign.
	British Ashanti campaign.
	French invade Madagascar.
	Brazilian civil war ends.
1895—1896	Jameson raid in Transvaal.
1895—1896	Italo-Abyssinian war, battle of Adowa.
1896—1898	British Sudan war.
1897	Græco-Turkish war.
	Insurrection in Crete.
1897—1898	North-West-Frontier campaign, India.
1897—1898	Spanish American War.

1898—1900	Boxer rebellion in China.
1899—1902	South African war.
1901	International forces occupy Pekin.
1903	British campaign in Somaliland.
1904	British Thibet operations.
1904—1905	Russo-Japanese war.
1904—1908	German operations in West Africa.
1908—1909	Revolution in Turkey.
1911	Italo-Turkish war.
1912	Albanian revolt
1912—1913	First Balkan war.
1913	Second Balkan war.
1914—1918	World War.
1915	Italy declares war on Austria.
	Bulgaria declares war on Serbia.
1916	Arab revolt under Sherif of Hejaz.
	Roumania enters World War.
1917	U.S.A. declares war on Germany.
	Revolution in Russia begins.
1918—1919	War with Soviet Russia.
1919	Communist revolution in Hungary.
	D'Annunzio occupies Fiume.
	Rebellion in India.
	Third Afghan war.
1920	French troops occupy Frankfort and Darmstadt.
	Greece attacks Turkey in Asia Minor.
1920—1921	War between Soviet Russia and Poland.
1921—1922	Rebellion in Ireland.
	Græco-Turkish war.
1923—1924	French occupation of the Ruhr.
1925	Collision between Greek and Bulgarian forces.
	Civil war in China takes acute anti-foreign form.
1926	French operations in Morocco.
	French operations in Syria.
1927	International intervention at Shanghai.
1928	Revolution in Afghanistan.
1930—1931	Evacuation of the Rhineland.
1931	Revolution in Spain.
1931—1932	Japanese operations in Manchuria.
1932	Japanese bombard Shanghai.
	Revolution in South America.
	Revolution in Siam.
	Bolivia-Paraguay Conflict.

REFERENCES

INTRODUCTION

(1) *Œuvres Militaires de Guibert*, Guibert, vol. iv. p. 74 (1803). See also Plutarch's *Counsels for Political Life*.

(2) *Lectures on Heroes*, Thomas Carlyle, Lecture VI.

(3) *Encyclopædia Britannica* (Eleventh edition), vol. ix, p. 934 (1911).

(4) Quoted from *The Nation in Arms*, Baron Colmar von der Goltz (English edition), p. 137 (1906).

(5) *The Cambridge Modern History*, vol. x, p. 2 (1907).

(6) *A History of Modern Europe*, C. A. Fyffe, vol. ii, p. 72 (1886).

(7) *A History of the British Army*, The Hon. J. W. Fortescue, vol. xi, p. 2 (1923).

(8) *The Cambridge Modern History*, vol. x, p. 2 (1907).

(9) *Ibid*, vol. x, p. 1.

(10) *A History of Modern Europe*, C. A. Fyffe, vol. ii, p. 169 (1886).

(11) *Ibid*, vol. ii, p. 171.

(12) *The Autobiography of a Seaman*, Thomas, Tenth Earl of Dundonald, p. 450 (1890).

(13) *Ibid*, p. 538.

(14) *The Nation in Arms*, Baron Colmar von der Goltz (English Edition), pp. 9, 11 (1906).

(15) *Problems of Power*, Wm. Morton Fullerton, p. 177 (1913).

(16) *Encyclopædia Britannica* (Eleventh Edition), vol. xii, p. 684 (1911).

(17) *Summary of the Art of War*, Baron de Jomini (American edition), p. 65 (1854).

(18) *War and the World's Life*, Colonel F. N. Maude, p. 7 (1907).

(19) *Jane Austen's Sailor Brothers*, Austen and Edith Hubback, p. 39 (1906).

(20) *Revue des Deux Mondes*, June 1, 1912, pp. 619, 620.

(21) *Decisive Battles since Waterloo*, Thomas W. Knox, p. 85 (1887).

(22) *Le Maréchal Berthier*, V. B. Derrécagaix, vol. i, p. 399 (1905).

(23) *Correspondance de Napoléon I*, October 30, 1811.

(24) Quoted from *The Influence of Firearms upon Tactics* (English edition), p. 83 (1876).

(25) *Ibid*, p. 32.

(26) *Correspondance de Napoléon I*, vol. xxi, p. 328 (1869).

(27) *Ibid*, vol. xxxii, p. 27.

(28) *Ibid*, vol. xxx, p. 447.

(29) *L'armée française en 1867*, Général L. J. Trochu, p. 210 (1867).

(30) *Histoire de la tactique de l'infanterie française, 1791-1905*, Commandant Thiery, p. 10 (1905).

(31) *Précis de l'art de la guerre*, Général Jomini, vol. ii, p. 226 (1838).

(32) *Correspondance de Napoléon I*, October 3, 1813 (1869).

(33) *A Review of the History of Infantry*, Colonel E. M. Lloyd, p. 232 (1908).

(34) *A History of the British Army*, The Hon. J. W. Fortescue, vol. xi, p. 47 (1923).

(35) *Ibid*, p. 51.

(36) *The Soldiers' Pocket Book*, Sir Garnet Wolseley, p. 273 (1874).

(37) *A History of the British Army*, The Hon. J. W. Fortescue, vol. xi, p. 92 (1923).

(38) *Hansard*, vol. xvi, p. 559.

CHAPTER I

(1) *Journal of the Royal United Service Institution*, vol. lxxvi, No. 502, p. 258 (1931).

(2) *Ibid*, p. 270.

(3) *The Autobiography of a Seaman*, Thomas, Tenth Earl of Dundonald, p. 539 (1890).

(4) *Ibid*, p. 546.

(5) *New Principles of Gunnery*, Benjamin Robins, p. 341. First printed in 1742 (1805).

(6) *War and the World's Life*, Colonel F. N. Maude, p. 90 (1907).

(7) *The Cambridge Modern History*, vol. xi, p. 1 (1909).

(8) For these ages see : *The Staff and the Staff College*, Major A. R. Godwin-Austen, p. 86 (1927) and *Journal of the Royal United Service Institution*, vol. lxxvi, No. 502, pp. 255-256.

(9) *A History of the British Army*, The Hon. J. W. Fortescue, vol. xi, pp. 10-30 (1923). The conditions in the Navy were

equally bad. "Prior to 1837 certain women had been allowed in ships and they were definitely borne on the strength for rations and had certain duties allotted to them, one of which was to care for the sick."—*Journal of the Royal United Service Institution*, vol. lxxvi, No. 502, pp. 263-268.

(10) *Ibid*, vol. xi, p. 492 (1923).

(11) *The Cambridge Modern History*, vol. x, p. 617 (1907).

(12) *A History of the British Army*, The Hon. J. W. Fortescue, vol. xii, p. 43 (1927)

(13) *On War*, General Carl von Clausewitz (English edition, 1908). The following quotations in order will be found in: vol. i, p. 33 ; vol. i, p. 23 ; vol. iii, p. 121 ; vol. iii, p. 122 ; vol. iii, p. 123 ; vol. i, p. 1 ; vol. ii, p. 288 ; vol. i, p. 4 ; vol. i, p. 42 ; vol. i, p. 253 ; vol. i, p. 16 ; vol. i, p. 40 ; vol. i, p. 207 ; vol. i, p. 231 ; vol. ii, p. 341 ; vol. i, pp. 20-21 ; vol. i, p. 179 ; vol. i, p. 187 ; vol. ii, p. 9 ; vol. ii, p. 135 ; vol. iii, p. 254 ; vol. i, p. 285 ; vol. i, p. 93 ; vol. i, p. 77 and vol. i, p. 121.

(14) *The Military Opinions of General Sir John Fox Burgoyne*, Captain the Hon. George Wrottesley, vol. i, pp. 453-455 (1859).

CHAPTER II

(1) *The Cambridge Modern History*, vol. xi, p. 262 (1909).

(2) *A History of Modern Europe*, C. A. Fyffe, vol. iii, p. 40 (1889).

(3) *Ibid*, vol. iii, p. 34.

(4) *Recueil des Traites d'Alliance et de Paix*, G. F. von Martens (continued by F. Murhard), vol. xii, p. 248 (1802-1875).

(5) Even in the army, judging from the following Mess Bill of May, 1850 :

	£	s	d
Share of Mess Guests			2½
To ale			4
2 Cigars			10
Luncheon		2	0
Share of H.R.H. Prince George's Luncheon			6½
3 Breakfasts		3	9
1 Cigar			5
2 Cigars			10
Luncheon and Soda Water		1	11
19 Dinners	1	18	0
	£2	8	10

Recollections of a Military Life, General Sir John Adye, pp. 8-9 (1895).

(6) *A History of Modern Europe*, C. A. Fyffe, vol. iii, p. 62 (1889).

(7) *Encyclopædia Britannica* (Eleventh edition), vol. xix, p. 213 (1911).

(8) *Ibid*, vol. xix, p. 213.

(9) *A History of Modern Europe*, C. A. Fyffe, vol. iii, p. 179 (1889).

(10) *The Cambridge Modern History*, vol. xi, p. 286 (1909).

(11) *A History of Modern Europe*, C. A. Fyffe, vol. iii, p. 178 (1889).

(12) *Ibid*, vol. iii, p. 180.

(13) *A History of the British Army*, The Hon. J. W. Fortescue, vol. xii, p. 560 (1927).

(14) *British Light Infantry in the Eighteenth Century*, Colonel J. F. C. Fuller, p. 173 (1925).

CHAPTER III

(1) *The Military Opinions of General Sir John Fox Burgoyne*, Edited by Captain the Hon. George Wrottesley, pp. 453-456 (1859).

(2) *Recollections of a Military Life*, General Sir John Adye, p. 13 (1895).

(3) *A History of the British Army*, The Hon. J. W. Fortescue, vol. xiii, pp. 138-139 (1930).

(4) *Ibid*, p. 204.

(5) See: *The War in the Crimea*, General Sir E. Hamley, p. 56 (1891).

(6) *Summary of the Art of War*, Baron de Jomini (American edition), p. 60 (1854).

(7) *The Ancestors of the Tank*, Colonel J. F. C. Fuller, *The Cavalry Journal*, April, 1928, p. 244.

(8) *The Autobiography of a Seaman*, Thomas, Tenth Earl of Dundonald, p. 340 (1890).

(9) *Ibid*, p. 552.

(10) *Ibid*, p. 545.

(11) *The Romance of the Submarine*, G. Gibbard Jackson, p. 22 (no date).

(12) *Ibid*, p. 29.

(13) *Essays*, by Sir Henry Lawrence (1859). Quoted from *Recollections of a Military Life*, General Sir John Adye, p. 153 (1895).

(14) *A Hundred Years of Conflict*, Colonel Arthur Doyle, p. 154 (1911).

(15) *Recollections of a Military Life*, General Sir John Adye, pp. 125, 127 (1895).

(16) *A History of the British Army*, The Hon. J. W. Fortescue, vol. xiii, p. 305 (1930).

(17) *Ibid*, p. 388.

(18) Quoted by Fortescue. *Ibid*, p. 393.

(19) *Recollections of a Military Life*, General Sir John Adye, p. 143 (1895).

(20) *A History of Modern Europe*, C. A. Fyffe, vol. iii, p. 249 (1889).

(21) *Die französische armee auf dem exercirplatze und im felde*, Olberg, p. 195 (1861).

(22) *La guerre d'Italie, 1859*, A. Duquet, p. 288 (1882).

(23) Colonel Chesney in *The Edinburgh Review*, January, 1866.

(24) *Campagne d'Italie en 1859*, Graf H. von Moltke (French edition), p. 50 (1862).

(25) *The Influence of Firearms upon Tactics*, by an Officer of Superior Rank, p. 92 (1876).

(26) *Ibid*, p. 95.

CHAPTER IV

(1) *John Brown's Body*, Stephen Vincent Bénet, p. 375 (1928).

(2) *The Life and Campaigns of General Lee*, Edward Lee Childe, p. 5 (1875).

(3) *The Cambridge Modern History*, vol. vii, p. 143 (1903).

(4) For a fuller account of the origins and nature of this war, see : *The Generalship of Ulysses S. Grant*, Colonel J. F. C. Fuller, Part I (1929).

(5) *The Story of the Civil War*, Colonel W. R. Livermore, Part III, Book I, p. 98 (1913).

(6) *Meade's Headquarters, 1863-1865*, Colonel Theodore Lyman, p. 224 (1922).

(7) *The Soldier in Battle, or Life in the Ranks of the Army of the Potomac*, Frank Wilkeson, p. 89 (1896).

(8) *Meade's Headquarters, 1863-1865*, Colonel Theodore Lyman, p. 101 (1922).

(9) *The Crisis of the Confederacy*, Captain C. Battine, p. 410 (1905).

(10) *The Science of War*, Colonel G. F. R. Henderson, p. 263 (1905).

(11) *Papers of the Military Historical Society of Massachusetts*, vol. iv, pp. 365, 405 (1895-1918).

(12) " Without the cotton gin, there can be hardly a doubt that the Civil War would not have happened."—*Meet General Grant*, W. E. Woodward, p. 65 (1928).

(13) *Battles and Leaders of the Civil War*, vol. ii, p. 513 (1884-1888).

(14) *The War of the Rebellion* (Official Records), vol. lxix, pp. 888-889 (1880-1900).

(15) *Papers of the Military Historical Society of Massachusetts*, vol. xiv, pp. 450-453 (1895-1918).

(16) *Meade's Headquarters, 1863-1865*, Colonel Theodore Lyman, p. 284 (1922).

(17) *Southern Generals, Who they are, and What they have done*, W. Parker Snow, p. 105 (1865).

(18) *The Soldier in Battle, or Life in the Ranks of the Army of the Potomac*, Frank Wilkeson, p. 80 (1896).

(19) *Ibid*, p. 72. One of the minor benefits of this war was the impetus given to canning food stuffs. Napoleon I offered a large prize to anyone who discovered a practical way of preserving field rations. " It was won by Nicholas Appert, who, though he used glass containers, may justly be said to have been the father of the canning industry. It was Bonaparte, however, who provided the inspiration."—*First Canned Rations*, W. B. Chivers, *British Canning Industry Number, The Times*, November 17, 1931.

(20) *Militair Wochenblatt*, July 8, 1865.

(21) *Three Main Military Questions of the Day*, Sir Henry M. Havelock, bart., p. 27 (1867).

(22) *Recollections of a Military Life*, General Sir John Adye, p. 253 (1895).

CHAPTER V

(1) *A Short History of the Chief Campaigns in Europe since 1792*, General A. von Horsetzky (English edition), p. 14 (1909).

(2) *Encyclopædia Britannica* (Eleventh edition), vol. xi, p. 873 (1911).

(3) *Military Reports*, Stoffel (English edition), p. 64 (1872).

(4) *A Short History of the Chief Campaigns in Europe since 1792*, General A. von Horsetzky (English edition), p. 369 (1909).

(5) *The Influence of Firearms upon Tactics*, by an Officer of Superior Rank (English edition), p. 102 (1876).

(6) *War and the World's Life*, Colonel F. N. Maude, p. 48 (1907).

(7) *Three Main Military Questions of the Day*, Sir Henry M. Havelock, Bart., p. 34 (1867).

(8) *Ibid*, p. 54.

(9) Quoted from *Recollections of a Military Life*, General Sir John Adye, p. 256 (1895).

10) *Ibid*, p. 290.

(11) Quoted from *The Development of Strategical Science during the 19th Century*, Lieut.-General von Caemmerer (English edition), p. 214 (1905).

(12) *The Transformations of War*, Commandant J. Colin (English edition), p. 30 (1912).

(13) *Tactical Deductions from the War of 1870-71*, A. v. Boguslawski (English edition), p. 7 (1872).

CHAPTER VI

(1) *A History of Modern Europe*, C. A. Fyffe, vol. iii, p. 421 (1889).

(2) *Ibid*, p. 430.

(3) *Experiences of the War between France and Germany*, Archibald Forbes, p. 89 (1871).

(4) Quoted in *The Battle of Wörth*, Colonel G. F. R. Henderson, p. 75 (1899).

(5) *The Cambridge Modern History*, vol. xi, p. 596 (1909).

(6) *Personal Memoirs*, General P. H. Sheridan, vol. ii, p. 375 (1888).

(7) Quoted from *The Cambridge Modern History*, vol. xi, p. 498 (1909).

(8) *Tactical Deductions from the War of 1870-71*, A. von Boguslawski (English edition), p. 70 (1872).

(9) *Experiences of the War between France and Germany*, Archibald Forbes, vol. ii, p. 18 (1871).

(10) *The Influence of Firearms upon Tactics*, by an Officer of Superior Rank (English edition), p. 130 (1876).

(11) *The Transformations of War*, Commandant J. Colin (English edition), p. 41 (1912).

(12) *Tactical Deductions from the War of 1870-71*, A. von Boguslawski (English edition), p. 64 (1872).

(13) *Letters on Infantry*, Prince Kraft zu Hohenlohe-Ingelfingen (English edition), p. 1 (1889).

(14) *A Summer Night's Dream*, Meckel (English edition), *United Service Magazine*, June, 1890.

(15) *Tactical Deductions from the War of 1870-71*, A. von Boguslawski (English edition), pp. 79-81 (1872).

(16) *Decisive Battles since Waterloo, 1815-1887*, Thomas W. Knox, p. 358 (1887).

(17) *My Experiences of the War between France and Germany*, Archibald Forbes, vol. i, p. 236 (1871).

(18) *Prussian Official History of 1870-71* (English edition), vol. 1, p. 50.

(19) *The Cambridge Modern History*, vol. xii, p. 213 (1910).

(20) *My Experiences of the War between France and Germany*, Archibald Forbes, vol. i, p. 219 (1871).

(21) *Ibid*, vol. ii, p. 464.

(22) *The Cambridge Modern History*, vol. xii, pp. 135-136 (1910).

(23) *Ibid*, p. 136.

CHAPTER VII

(1) *Problems of Power*, Wm. Morton Fullerton, p. 214 (1913).

(2) *History of Modern Europe, 1878-1919*, G. P. Gooch, p. 227 (1923).

(3) *Ibid*, p. 79.

(4) *The Cambridge Modern History*, vol. xii, p. 167 (1910).

(5) *History of Modern Europe, 1878-1919*, G. P. Gooch, p. 261 (1923).

(6) *Ibid*, p. 228.

(7) *Spinoza, Opera Posthuma*, pp. 269-270 (1667).

(8) *Encyclopædia Britannica* (Eleventh edition), vol. xxi, p. 17.

(9) *The Cambridge Modern History*, vol. xii, p. 15 (1910).

(10) Quoted from *A Review of the History of Infantry*, Colonel E. M. Lloyd, p. 270 (1908).

(11) *Journal of the Royal United Service Institution*, vol. xxxii, p. 985.

(12) *The Defence of Plevna*, W. von Herbert, p. 126 (1895).

CHAPTER VIII

(1) Quoted from *Battle Studies*, Colonel Ardant du Picq (American edition), p. 10 (1921).

(2) Quoted from *A Précis of Modern Tactics*, Colonel Robert Home, p. 42 (1896).

(3) *The New Tactics of Infantry*, Major W. von Scherff (English edition), p. 169 (1873).

(4) *War and the World's Life*, Colonel F. N. Maude, p. 214 (1907).

(5) *The New Tactics of Infantry*, Major W. von Scherff (English edition), pp. 23-24 (1873).

(6) *The Defence of Plevna*, W. von Herbert (English edition), p. 198 (1895).

(7) Quoted from *A Précis of Modern Tactics*, Colonel Robert Home, p. 43 (1896).

(8) *The Transformation of War*, Commandant J. Colin, p. 44 (1912).

(9) Quoted from *A Précis of Modern Tactics*, Colonel Robert Home, p. 43 (1896).

(10) Extracted from the American edition *Battle Studies*, Colonel Ardant du Picq (1921).

(11) *Aperçu sur quelques détails de la Guerre*, Thomas Robert Bugeaud de la Piconnerie (1832).

(12) *Cavalry in Modern Warfare*, Revue des Deux Mondes (1890).

(13) Quoted from the English edition, *The Principles of War*, Marshal Foch (1918).

(14) It would appear that before writing this Foch must have remembered Luke xiv, 31.

(15) A study of the Matabele Campaign of 1893 might have prevented Foch propounding this absurdity.

(16) *The Principles of War* (English edition), Marshal Foch, pp. 35-37 (1918).

(17) *Is War Now Impossible?* I. S. Bloch (1899).

CHAPTER IX

(1) *The Military Life of H.R.H. George Duke of Cambridge*, Colonel Willoughby Verner, vol. ii, p. 421 (1905).

(2) *Life of Sir George Pomeroy-Colley*, Lieut.-General Sir W. F. Butler, p. 318 (1899).

(3) *The War in South Africa*, German Official Account (English Translation), vol. i, p. 71 (1904).

(4) *Ibid*, vol. ii, p. 116.

(5) *Ibid*, vol. ii, p. 328.

(6) *The Mechanism of War*, "Linesman," p. 36 (1902).

(7) *A Staff-Officer's Scrap-Book*, Lieut.-General Sir Ian Hamilton, vol. i, p. 5 (1905-06).

(8) *The War in South Africa*, German Official Account (English edition), vol. ii, p. 336 (1906).

(9) *Kriegsgeschichtlichen Einzelschriften*, Nos. 34-35, p. 171.

(10) *The War in South Africa*, German Official Account (English edition), vol. ii, p. 344 (1906).

(11) *The Russo-Japanese War, Reports from British Officers*, vol. iii, p. 202 (1908).

(12) *Ibid*, vol. iii, p. 227.

(13) *Ibid*, vol. iii, p. 117.

(14) *Ibid*, vol. iii, pp. 209-210.

CHAPTER X

(1) Quoted from *History of Modern Europe, 1878-1919*, G. P. Gooch, p. 447 (1923).

(2) *Memories*, Lord Fisher, p. 64 (1919).

(3) *History of Modern Europe, 1878-1919*, G. P. Gooch, p. 385 (1923).

(4) *Ibid*, p. 397.

(5) Quoted from *A Critical Study of German Tactics*, Major de Pardieu (American Translation), p. 116 (1912).

(6) *Ibid*, p. 48.

(7) *Ibid*, p. 117.

(8) *L'Artillerie*, Général Herr, pp. 4-5 (1923).

(9) *Problems of Power*, Wm. Morton Fullerton, p. 227 (1913).

(10) *Ibid*, p. 215.

(11) *Ibid*, p. 225.

(12) *Encyclopædia Britannica* (Twelfth edition), vol. xxxi, p. 22.

(13) *History of Modern Europe, 1878-1919*, G. P. Gooch, p. 514 (1923).

(14) *Ibid*, p. 514.

CHAPTER XI

(1) According to Grotius, *De Jure Belli et Pacis*, lib. III, chap. i, sec. 5, articles of commerce are divided into two groups : those which " are of use only in war," and those which " serve only for pleasure " ; as regards those which are useful in war and peace he bases any restriction of them during war time on the vague factor of " justice." Under the " Declaration of London," agreed upon on February 26, 1909, but never ratified, articles were divided under three headings : (1) warlike goods ; (2) goods exclusively used for peaceful purposes, and (3) goods which may be used for peace or war. Directly war was declared it was found that practically all goods could be used for peace and war and the result was constant friction.

CHAPTER XII

(1) *War and the World's Life*, Colonel F. N. Maude, p. 15 (1907).

(2) *The Nation in Arms*, Baron Colmar von der Goltz (English edition), p. 5 (1906).

(3) *The Reformation of War*, Colonel J. F. C. Fuller, pp. 88-89 (1923).

(4) *Ibid*, pp. 97-98.

(5) In the British Army the ban on the use of petrol was only raised in 1912. Up to that date it was considered too dangerous a fluid to entrust to soldiers !

(6) *The Reformation of War*, Colonel J. F. C. Fuller, pp. 102-103 (1923).

(7) *Ibid*, pp. 103-104.

(8) *The Report of the Surgeon-General U.S.A. Army* (1920).

(9) *The Nineteenth Century*, vol. iv, July, 1878, pp. 40-50.

(10) *Ibid*, p. 49.

(11) *The Reformation of War*, Colonel J. F. C. Fuller, p. 116 (1923).

CHAPTER XIII

(1) *King Lear*, Act I, Scene 1.

(2) Quoted from *Problems of Power*, Wm. Morton Fullerton, p. viii, (1913).

(3) *Quarante-Cinq Années de ma Vie: 1770-1815*, Princess Radziwill, quoted from *Problems of Power*, Wm. Morton Fullerton, p. vii (1913).

(4) *The Importance of a War Industry for a Particular Country. International Ramifications of War Industry*, Francis Delaisi, in *What would be the Character of a New War?* pp. 199-200 (1931).

(5) *The Times*, February 3, 1932.

(6) In respect to the influence of numbers and bulk-weight, etc., on democracies it is interesting to note that Mr. Baldwin in his broadcast on the War Loan Conversion scheme said : " The Chancellor said last night, in order to show that we meant business, and that we want to do business on super-business lines, that he would print 15,000,000 forms and send them out to 3,000,000 holders in 3,000,000 envelopes within 24 hours." (*The Times*, July 2, 1932.)

(7) During the World War " four cannons only among all those manufactured by the United States during the war arrived at the front before the end of hostilities, nineteen months after the declaration of war," and not a single tank.

(8) *The Nation in Arms*, Baron Colmar von der Goltz (English edition), p. 147 (1906).

(9) *What would be the Character of a New War?* p. 188 (1931).

(10) *Ibid*, pp. 186-187.

CHAPTER XIV

(1) *La mortalité causée par la guerre mondiale*, L. Hersch, p. 3 (1927).

(2) *Demographic Effects of Modern Warfare*, Professor L. Hersch, *What would be the Character of a New War?* pp. 289-290 (1931).

(3) *Ibid*, p. 291.

(4) *The Times*, July 9, 1932.

(5) *The Living Age* (U.S.A.), July, 1932, p. 384.

(6) Quoted from *Battle Studies*, Colonel Ardant du Picq (American edition), p. 24 (1921).

INDEX